CW01455256

TE MURA O TE AHI

Wira Gardiner (Ngati Awa, Ngati Pikiao, Whakatohea, Te Whanau-A-Apanui) is Chief Executive of Te Puni Kokiri (The Ministry of Maori Development). He joined the Army in 1963 and saw active service in Vietnam, later completing his education at Massey and Canterbury Universities and King's College, London. In 1981, on his appointment as Director of Defence HQ, he was made a Lieutenant-Colonel. From 1983 to 1985 he was National Director of Civil Defence, and later he became Director of the Waitangi Tribunal and Chief Executive of the Iwi Transition Agency. He lives in Wellington.

TE MURA O TE AHI

The Story of

THE MAORI BATTALION

Wira Gardiner

REED

First published 1992 by Reed Books, a division of Reed Publishing (NZ) Ltd, 39 Rawene Road, Birkenhead, Auckland. Associated companies, branches, and representatives throughout the world.

First published in paperback 1995
Reprinted 1997, 2000, 2002

Copyright © Wira Gardiner 1992

This book is copyright. Except for purpose of fair reviewing, no part of this publication may be reproduced or transmitted in any form or by any means, electronic or mechanical, including photocopying, recording, or any information storage and retrieval systems, without permission in writing from the publisher. Infringers of copyright render themselves liable to prosecution.

National Library of New Zealand
Cataloguing-in-Publication data

Gardiner, Wira, 1943-
    Te mura o te ahi: the story of the Maori Battalion / Wira
Gardiner. Auckland. [N.Z.]: Reed, 1992.
    1v.
    Includes bibliographical references and index
    ISBN 0-7900-0394-5
    1. New Zealand. Army. New Zealand Expeditionary Force, 2nd.
Battalion, 28.
    2. World War, 1939-45 — Participation, Maori.
    I. Title.
    940.541293

Printed in New Zealand

CONTENTS

PREFACE

An ancient Maori proverb declares 'Ka tuwhera te tawaha o te riri, kaore e titiro ki te ao marama' (When the gates of war have been flung open man no longer takes notice of light and reason). From the time our first forebear grasped a lump of rock or a piece of wood and dashed out the brains of his antagonist or victim, we have pursued inexorably the path of war to achieve our aims and aspirations.

This book is about war and the Maori soldier. It is written from the perspective of an amateur historian and professional soldier and sets out to portray how Maori soldiers coped with the pressures on and off the battlefield during the Second World War.

Warfare is a vast canvas and the lives, tragedies, humour, savagery and outstanding bravery of the Maori soldier can only be depicted as splashes of paint on that broad surface. Nevertheless this personal and sometimes fleeting view of some of the men and incidents of the 28 (Maori) Battalion gives an insight into one of the finest fighting units of the Second New Zealand Expeditionary Force.

Chapter 1

MAORI MILITARY HERITAGE

Every society has a war memory. For Maori that memory spans over 1000 years since the arrival of their ancestors to this land. In that war memory are manifested the characteristics which distinguish Maori soldiers from soldiers of other races including their Pakeha comrades-in-arms.

As we are a product of our past, it is important that we look to our heritage to identify trends and behaviour patterns which might explain the way in which Maori soldiers reacted to certain situations and events.

In pre-European New Zealand, warfare was often the consequence of some slight or unavenged injury. The powerful influence of utu, or vengeance, was, as Elsdon Best has pointed out, 'the cause of innumerable wars'. He added that the 'spirit of revenge was very strong in the native character and this, combined with the fact that they were very prone to take offence, meant that fighting between tribes, and even different divisions of the same tribe, might break out at any time. To avenge a wrong was held to be a sacred duty.' [1]

R.S. Oppenheimer noted that the relationships between groups of Maori were profoundly affected by the ideas of revenge which were current in Maori society. 'These were embodied in the word utu (payment), the redress either in blood or plunder, which had to be exacted for any wrong.' [2]

Professor A.K. Vayda agreed. 'The memory of unavenged injuries was handed down as an heirloom, and the necessity for revenge is said to have been one of the first lessons taught to Maori children.' [3] On numerous occasions during the wars of contact with European soldiers in the nineteenth century and in the First and Second World Wars, Maori soldiers sought revenge for the loss of a relative or kinsman. In this respect they were living out the ways of their ancestors.

The concept of utu was multi-faceted. In an extraordinarily perceptive article on utu written by F.A. Hanson and L. Hanson, 'Counterpoints in Maori Culture', these facets were discussed. [4] They argued that 'Maori vengeance was not just to punish the author of an affront.' Moreover, they continue, given that 'a prime index of the Maori's success and vitality was his strength and control over what happened in his life, any deleterious external influence that penetrated his range of control signified mate, or weakness, on his part.'

Therefore when he had been wronged, 'this brought on the psychological state of melancholy in which the offended one brooded and despaired, over the threat to his strength and honour.' In other words, the violent act of retribution enabled the offended to regain control over his morbid state. 'Revenge restored his soul – his self-esteem and social standing.'

Maori soldiers were also driven by the imperative of their tribal heritage and the need to maintain intact the prestige, or mana, of the tribe. In 1943, Sir Apirana Ngata wrote in his essay on 'The Price of Citzenship' that Maori soldiers on the battlefields of the Second World War had acquitted themselves well, like their ancestors.

'In those olden days,' he wrote, 'there were no decorations for prowess in war. But brave deeds were commemorated in song, and the fame of warriors was on the lips of men and excited the passions of devoted women.'[5]

Many of the men of 28 (Maori) Battalion were familiar with the feint and parry of the ancient Maori hand-held weaponry and ancient tactics such as the 'kawau maro, the swift advance of the stiff- necked, headlong shag. They charged in the massed irresistible whana tukutahi, the precursor of the bayonet charge.'[6]

Leadership was also a critical element in the development of a Maori military style. The hereditary and natural leaders of Maori communities led by example rather than by command. Even in peacetime activities such as cultivating, the chiefs 'set an example by labour'. Therefore in war, warriors were led by chiefs who understood that example was often more important than counsel.

The lack of formal hierarchical rank meant that chiefs had to persuade and motivate rather than command. Discipline was thus a matter to be won by respect and certainly not by authority. Vayda noted that 'in general, Maoris' tactics in fighting were such that they could be executed by a relatively small unit under the personal leadership of a chief.'[7]

There were obvious weaknesses in such an approach, as Best noted. 'A chief did not arbitrarily order the people to adopt any course of action . . . he could call on no force, military or civil, to carry out harsh decrees affecting the people. The military force was a volunteer one . . . if it did not approve of a proposed campaign, it simply declined to march.'

The absence of clear leadership or hierarchical command systems had a significant impact upon the military discipline of the warriors. In the 'general absence of military discipline among the Maoris and the importance of the mere presence of the chiefs, although not as a commander or disciplinarian, is brought out by the fact that it was common, perhaps very common, for Maori fighting men to flee if the chiefs leading them were slain.'[8]

The repetition of tribal history focusing on famous chiefs and their battles, and the recitation of whakapapa, or genealogical relationships, reminded the Maori of their military heritage. The mana, or prestige, of the tribe rested on the deeds of its ancestors.

Mana could be inherited or achieved by deeds. Inherited mana, however, did not automatically guarantee privileged status. Rather it was a 'silver spoon', which had to be retained by a continued demonstration of worthiness. Mana could also be achieved by a commoner through success in war. Oppenheimer noted that, within a group of chiefs, closely related distinctions of inherited mana could be offset by achieved mana.[9]

The exploitation of this concept of achieved mana allowed Maori soldiers in both world wars to attain status which they might not have attained in a tribal environment in times of peace.

The spiritual dimension of Maori warfare was significant. The concept of tapu placed tight strictures on the everyday behaviour of Maori. Tapu, in Oppenheimer's view, described 'a special kind of relationship between people . . . which arose from the belief that the persons or things in that relationship were so because of their contact with the supernatural.'[10] In a sense, the tapu concept placed a more stringent discipline on individuals and groups than any authoritarian system.

War parties before setting off for war were made sacred to their mission by tribal tohunga. They remained under this tapu umbrella until it was lifted on their return from their mission. Best described the ritual of tohi, 'which was performed over fighting-men about to raise the war-trail. It included a form of baptism, and it brought those men under the tapu of the war-god. Another, known as tira ora, was a form of absolution. This purified the men from the effects of any offences, however slight, committed against the gods, and so saved them from any disabilities the gods might have inflicted on them.'[11]

Pre-European warfare, therefore, was characterised by a cooperative rather than coercive approach as chiefs set out to persuade their followers rather than command them through a formal military command and control system. Issues of personal and tribal mana, the religious ceremonies and rituals associated with war parties and the powerful bonds of kinship ties, all contributed to the way in which Maori approached the business of war.

The all-pervading influence of utu was perhaps the most powerful motivation for Maori to raise the war-trail. In the name of utu, war parties had ranged up and down the coastline of New Zealand to avenge past grievances, and tribal settlement patterns and the landscape of some tribal entities were severely disrupted or destroyed.

The settlement of New Zealand by explorers and colonists in the eighteenth and nineteenth centuries did not change the underlying nature of Maori warfare much. While at a tactical level Maori adapted to the arrival of new technology in the form of guns and imperial military doctrine, they nevertheless retained and continued to apply much of their war heritage.

James Belich in his brilliant book on the New Zealand Wars, noted that the wars during the 1840s in the north were notable as much for exemplifying the dual nature of the Maori's thinking as for demonstrating his ability to adapt brilliantly to the British tactics. In this latter respect the battles of Kororareka, Puketutu, Ohaewai, and Ruapekapeka saw the Maori deliberately avoid tackling the British in the open. In adapting his pa sites to cope with British naval, artillery and small-arms gunfire, the Maori, under the wily northern generals Hone Heke and Kawiti, developed the gunfighter pa, which much frustrated the British in their efforts to try and defeat the Maori.

Later, in the 1860s, during the battles of Taranaki, Waikato and the Bay of Plenty, Maori further demonstrated their ability to withstand for a prolonged period the might of the British Empire with its attendant technology and logistic support.

It was during these battles that the Maori leaders and soldiers demonstrated quixotic characteristics which the British found hard to understand. An anecdotal incident which occurred in 1864, during the British advance south from Auckland along the axis of the Waikato River, illustrates this point.

A young Waikato chief was wounded and captured in battle. The British surgeons found it necessary to amputate one of his legs below the knee. As a gesture to their enemy, the British commanders returned the young chief to his tribe. In response the tribe sent back to the British a canoe-load of food and supplies and a letter. In the letter the Waikato thanked the British for the return of their son. They also added that in future they would treat British prisoners in a similar manner, ie they would return British prisoners less one leg!

This attitude was illustrative of one level of the notion of utu – an eye for an eye and a tooth for a tooth. It is also illustrative of a wicked sense of humour which Maori soldiers have indulged in ever since.

In 1864, when Lieutenant-General Cameron moved his army to Tauranga to quell the local tribes he camped on the beach. Meanwhile his antagonists were camped some miles inland on ground of their own choosing. When the British failed to move against them, the local Maori offered to build a road from the beach to their stronghold. When this offer was ignored they moved closer to the British so that fighting could commence.

This was an example of Maori impatience to engage with the enemy rather than to outwit him by remaining on the ground of Maori's own choosing. From one point of view it could have been viewed as tactical lunacy. However, from another viewpoint it could also be viewed as the application of unorthodox tactics: don't do what the enemy expect you to do.

Throughout the history of Maori warfare the element of unorthodoxy has played a key role. Against a modern army its utility was limited. However, on occasions, as was demonstrated by the 28 (Maori) Battalion in the desert during the Second World War, its application could produce brilliant and spectacular results.

By the turn of the twentieth century, Maori had already experienced over a century of contact and conflict with European explorers and settlers. The military heritage from pre-European times and the experiences gained during the wars of the nineteenth century had led to the accumulation of a tradition of warfare which tribes recounted and relived on the numerous occasions they gathered on their marae.

However, no matter how large these experiences may have appeared in the context of the Maori horizon of the time, they were merely small-scale when compared to the vast scope and sustained violence of the First World War, which burst upon the world in August 1914.

Chapter 2

BAPTISM OF FIRE: MAORI IN THE FIRST WORLD WAR

On the evening of the 6 August 1915, the battle cries of the sons and warriors of Tumatauenga were for the first time heard on foreign soil.

The 1st Maori Contingent, comprising some 500 Maori soldiers, was taking part with the rest of the New Zealanders in a night attack in the Gallipoli campaign. They were part of a concerted Allied effort to capture from the Turkish Army the imposing heights of Chunuk Bair. The capture of these heights would allow the British to observe the straits of the Dardanelles, and help open the narrows to the British Fleet. The captured ground would allow British troops to interfere with the flow of Turkish reinforcements into the area.

The New Zealand troops were given the task of attacking and capturing the Sari Bair ridge.[1] Te Rangi Hiroa, who had resigned his seat in Parliament to accept an appointment as Medical Officer to the 1st Maori Contingent, recorded for posterity part of the attack: 'I knew that a Turkish trench had been captured in the darkness at the point of the bayonet. But more wonderful to me was that the night air was broken vigorously by the Maori war cry of "Ka mate, ka mate! Ka ora, ka ora!" ("Tis death, tis death, tis life, tis life!").'

He knew from the sounds that a platoon of Maori had helped to capture the trenches. Hardly had the sound died down than another burst of rapid fire occurred on another ridge with the same impressive sequence and 'my heart thrilled,' he wrote, 'at the sound of my mother tongue resounding up the slopes of Sari Bair.'[2] The Maori soldiers had passed into te mura o te ahi (the fires of hell). They had confronted their baptism of fire. The price was, however, high. The dead and wounded numbered over 100 and serious questions were asked about the behaviour and performance of a handful of Maori officers during the course of the battle.

Just less than one year earlier, much effort and a great deal of frustration had accompanied the raising and training of the first formed Maori unit to leave New Zealand for active service overseas. The raising of a native contingent to serve in the First World War had its genesis in the tentative efforts made on a number of occasions during Queen Victoria's reign to deploy Maori on overseas service. The last of these attempts had occurred during the Boer War when a suggestion was made that a native contingent be raised to serve in South Africa. This attempt was stifled by Imperial policy on the grounds that it was a 'white man's' war and there was certainly no place in such a war for native troops.

This policy of general exclusion did not, however, prevent Maori and part-Maori soldiers from volunteering as individuals, as a number did, for service in the various contingents.

When war against Germany and her allies was proclaimed in August 1914, there was an immediate response from tribal groups throughout the country. The first responses came from the Te Arawa tribe of the Bay of Plenty, who had played a major role in fighting on the side of the British and the New Zealand colonists during the latter stages of the New Zealand wars of the 1860s, and Ngati Kahungunu of the Hawke Bay area. Their offers of help were quickly followed by offers from Ngati Porou of the East Coast of the North Island and the North Auckland tribes.[3]

The Imperial Government's response to these offers was consistent with its previous policy of not allowing native troops to participate in wars between Europeans.

This time, however, there was a determination by the four Maori members of Parliament, Te Rangi Hiroa (Dr Peter Buck), Northern Maori; A.T. Ngata, Eastern Maori; Maui Pomare, Western Maori; and Taare Parata, Southern Maori to recruit and train a Maori contingent for overseas service with the Expeditionary Force raised by New Zealand as its contribution to the British war effort.

Their persistence and determination is hardly surprising when viewed against the background of a resurgence in Maori life in the last decade of the nineteenth century and the first decade of the twentieth century. During the last years of Queen Victoria's reign, the Maori race had undergone a disastrous decline. The spread of disease and the drastic drop in living standards among Maori had led medical experts to predict their imminent demise.

However, during the first decade of the new century, a younger and more dynamic group of leaders, articulate in the ways of the Pakeha and dedicated to the eradication of Maori health problems, the raising of education levels, and the attainment of equal status, led the battle. Ngata, Te Rangi Hiroa and Pomare, the latter two initially in their role as trained doctors and later as members of Parliament, were in the vanguard of the new Maori movement. They, together with Sir James Carroll, another distinguished Maori leader, were the founding members of the Native Contingent Committee set up by the Government to organise and supervise the recruitment of Maori soldiers for the first contingent.

Ngata, perhaps the most vociferous and certainly the most hard-line member of the committee, and his colleagues saw the First World War as an opportunity to raise the profile of the Maori and to prove that he was the equal of his Pakeha comrades. What better way to attain these goals than on the field of battle? Ironically, a generation of young Maori without first-hand knowledge of war and untested in the skills of the warrior would be required to win recognition by emulating the deeds of their ancestors.

Older New Zealanders who had fought in the wars of the 1860s thought that, given the heritage that they possessed, it would not be difficult for them to do well. The members of the Native Contingent Committee had a similar confidence.

Any further objection to Maori serving overseas as a formed body disappeared when news was received that Indian troops were to be deployed as security troops to protect the Suez Canal. On 3 September 1914, the New Zealand Government cable-grammed, via the Governor-General, a message to the Secretary of State, formally requesting the establishment of a Maori contingent.

Three days later the Army Council in Britain agreed to the request and authorised the raising of a 200-strong contingent. Less than a week later, the New Zealand Government sought a further increase in the strength of the contingent to allow for the relief of combat soldiers serving in Samoa so that they could be redeployed to Egypt with the rest of the Expeditionary Force. No objections were raised by the British and the strength of the contingent was raised to 500.[4]

From the outset, Major-General Sir Alexander Godley, who was to command the New Zealand Expeditionary Force throughout the war, did not intend using Maori as combat troops. Rather, he saw them as being suitable for garrison protection duty. For these reasons, he set the training period of the contingent at four weeks so that it could be ready in time to deploy from New Zealand with the first reinforcements for the Expeditionary Force.[5]

Godley also had firm ideas about the recruitment and nomination for all but the key officer appointments. He believed that these matters should be left to the Maori to decide, as he did not want the Army to 'get mixed up in their tribal jealousies, degrees of rank, etc'. The two senior appointments of the contingent were, however, to be Pakeha. Neither of the two original Pakeha officers chosen for Officer Commanding the contingent and the Adjutant were able to pass the medical board's tests and a Captain Peacock (later promoted to Major) was chosen to lead the contingent.

His subsequent illness from typhoid contracted from the Maori led to the appointment of another officer, Major A.H. Herbert, to command the group. The friction between Herbert and the Maori was to lead to major difficulties within the contingent before, and during, the contingent's first action on Gallipoli.

Clearly, Godley's abrogation of the traditional method of officer selection was bound to lead to difficulties. In essence, a small group of highly motivated Maori civilians, who were also the political leaders of Maoridom, were left with the task of selecting the officers and non-commissioned officers for service within a military environment. Accordingly, the selection criteria for the Maori officers did not necessarily accord with the needs of military effectiveness, being based as they were on tribal leadership patterns.

Accompanying the 224 soldiers from the East Coast were eight separately appointed elders, each charged with the responsibility of ensuring that the mana and kawa (customs) of the tribe were maintained.[6] Clearly, if these men had at the same time been given formal rank the potential for the frustration of military orders would not have been an issue. However, not all were given formal rank within the contingent and therefore there were bound to be difficulties. The problems for Pakeha officers – particularly those unaware of Maori customs and behaviour – were almost insurmountable.

Herbert, in ignoring the ethnic dimension, paid the price of personal attack and ridicule from the Maori for his insensitivity to such matters and his mishandling of Maori officers and soldiers.

While the Maori elders were keen to see their kinsmen volunteer and train for active service overseas, others protested strongly against the recruitment of Maori soldiers. The Auckland Medical Officer of Health thought that it was impossible for Maori to be taught sanitary precautions. Furthermore, in a letter to his superiors, he wrote that if the Defence Department were foolish enough to proceed with the scheme, then the least they could do was to ensure that the Maori soldiers should not be allowed to camp next to European troops. Finally, he added that if Maori troops were to be deployed overseas, then it was advisable to ensure that they travelled on separate troop ships so that they did not pass on their diseases to the European troops.[7]

It could be argued that the Medical Officer's viewpoint had a basis in fact in that many of the Maori soldiers had typhoid. Indeed the contingent's first Officer Commanding, Major Peacock, caught the disease from his troops and had to be evacuated from Australia while the contingent was on the way to Egypt. While the Medical Officer's department did not share his extreme views (at least publicly), it did agree that a major medical problem had to be resolved. The solution was simple – all recruits were inoculated against typhoid.

The initial decision to deploy part of the contingent to Samoa and the remainder to Egypt drew sharp reactions from two unlikely allies, the Administrator in Samoa, Colonel Logan, and the Native Contingent Committee. Logan argued that it would be a grave mistake to deploy Maori in Samoa. He argued that the Samoans looked on the Maori as an inferior race and their presence would be disruptive.

More to the point, he considered that because of their role in Samoa the Maori would need to be accorded the same treatment as if they were white, which would have an even more unsettling affect on the Samoans.[8] It is not certain what impact these views had on the deliberations between Army Headquarters and the Minister of Defence.

What was clear, however, was that the Native Contingent Committee believed that the contingent should not be split up and that it should proceed to Egypt. Ngata set out his principal objection to the splitting-up of the contingent based on the argument of tribal cohesiveness. He argued that splitting the group into two 250-man contingents would disturb the delicate balance of intertribal relations.

On the other hand, his colleagues, particularly Te Rangi Hiroa and Parata, saw some merit in mixing the tribal groups. It says much for Ngata's determination that the contingent was divided into two companies, A and B Companies, each with four platoons with membership based on tribal lines.

The men of the Auckland isthmus and North Auckland formed 1 Platoon. 2 Platoon was formed from the catchment area south of Auckland and inclusive of North Taranaki and including Ngati Maniapoto, Hauraki, the Tauranga tribes and Ngati Tuwharetoa of Taupo. Men from the West Coast, Waitotara, Wanganui and inland tribes from Taihape and Manawatu formed 3 Platoon. The last platoon of A Company, 4 Platoon, gathered its soldiers from Horowhenua to Wellington, and the South Island.

B Company's first platoon, 5 Platoon, comprised men from the Te Arawa tribes of Rotorua. 6 Platoon comprised men from Matata to the East Coast and Waiapu and included Mataatua and Ngati Porou tribes. 7 Platoon men came from Tolaga Bay (Uawa) and Gisborne, and the last platoon, 8 Platoon, comprised men from Mahia Peninsula, Napier and Wairarapa made up of Ngati Kahungunu tribesmen.

Both the Minister of Defence, Mr Allen, and Major-General Godley had reservations about sending Maori to Egypt. Allen had expressed his reservations to Godley after he had visited the Maori at their training camp at Avondale in Auckland. He was anxious about the Maori susceptibility to 'venereal and drink', and that they would want a lot of watching as he feared that the 'officers were not all they should be'. Godley, on the other hand, feared for their treatment at the hands of other European troops who might see them as no different to the local 'wogs' – the racist term used by the British to describe Egyptian traders. He thought that they might have been better deployed at the Western Front in Europe.[9]

While the political negotiations regarding the deployment of the contingent were being conducted, the business of recruiting and enrolment for service of the volunteers continued. The Native Contingent Committee had issued through the *Maori Gazette* a paanui (notice) calling for volunteers between the ages of 21 and 40 years willing to serve the King for the duration of the war. Meanwhile the Committee and the Defence Department made the necessary arrangements to inoculate the recruits on arrival and enrol them for service.

Avondale racecourse was the site of the first training camp. This had been set up by the Defence Department in mid-October 1914. Small detachments of troops from the Auckland and Northland districts were the first to arrive. 'On October 19 a party of 50 young men arrived from the South Island, and 36 from the Hauraki and Ngati Maniapoto tribe. On the following day, 92 recruits came in from the west coast (of the North Island), representing the tribes of Whanganui, Ngati Apa, Ngati Raukawa and Ngati Toa. These young soldiers were quickly followed by 90 men of Te Arawa from the Lake Districts, Maketu and Matata; Ngati Awa from Whakatane; Whakatohea from Opotiki and Te Whanau-a-Apanui and kindred tribes as far as Tikirau (East Cape). The famous fighting Ngati Porou followed; these young men from the Tai-Rawhiti villages from the East Cape southward toward Gisborne. The Ngati Kahungunu from Hawke's Bay and some more Ngapuhi from Kaikohe and other northern districts completed the 500 men in training under canvas at Avondale.'[10]

Cowan describes their physique as being 'the theme of praise by inspecting officers'. On parade 'they attracted great admiration for their stature, their muscular development and their alertness and soldierly bearing.'[11]

Other commmentators, while agreeing on the quality of the Maori parade ground performance were not as equally impressed by their physical turnout. Lieutenant Colonel W. G. Malone (Commanding Officer of the Wellington Battalion), seeing the Maori shortly after their arrival in Egypt (March 1915), described them as 'mostly big hulking gone-in-the-knees walking men. I think the War Lords don't quite know what to do with them. They look soft, and, I fancy, were not killed with work on the transports.'[12]

There is a great deal of truth in Malone's private comments. The Maori Officer commanding B Company of the Maori Contingent on Gallipoli was medically boarded after the contingent's first action, and 'found rather obese and constantly short of breath on slight exertion. Also he presented a history of what appeared to be some form of heart failure.'[13] Moreover, one of the Maori officers, wounded in the battle, weighed more than 125 kg.[14] Clearly, the physical selection criteria were not high, nor indeed were they strictly applied.

The Maori Contingent eventually left its training camp in Auckland on 10 February 1915 and sailed from Wellington for Egypt on 15 February 1915. Ngata claimed that frustration at the considerable delay – Godley had intended that the Maori receive only four weeks' training – led to a number of soldiers deserting.[15] He claimed that they became tired of waiting the extra weeks in Auckland. On arrival in Wellington, the contingent paraded at Newtown, where the onlookers noted favourably the Maori 'standard of drill and bearing'.[16]

On arrival in Egypt prior to deployment to Malta as garrison troops, the contingent immediately made an impact on the senior commander of the New Zealand Expeditionary Force. Godley noted that having seen them he and the rest of the division 'are disappointed that they are not coming with us.'[17] This was a major change for Godley, who had never intended the Maori to serve as combat troops.

Three days later, Godley, in his report to Minister of Defence Allen, advised that the Maori had 'behaved extremely well and have earned golden opinions by their smartness and bearing and general efficiency . . . I am sorry they are not coming with us.'[18] He also reported that the Army Commander had cabled Lord Kitchener at the War Office that it was the Maori, 'desire to serve and fight with the New Zealanders, and that he recommends that they be allowed to do so.'[19]

It was also at this time that the Maori Contingent met their new Officer Commanding, Major A. H. Herbert. Godley was full of praise for Herbert, who in his view was 'a gentleman, a man of standing, and was ardently very keen and interested in the job.' Herbert's appointment was resented by the senior Pakeha officer of the contingent, a Captain Ennis. When Godley saw the contingent off, Ennis, smelling of whiskey, complained to Godley that he should have been made the Major.[20]

The Maori desire to be employed as combat soldiers on active service rather than garrison troops was finally agreed to by the Imperial Government. One fishhook in the Imperial Government's directive was that the New Zealand Government was to provide 250 reinforcements every three months. Allen, on receiving the Imperial directive, cabled

Major Herbert in Malta asking whether 'the Maori at Malta desired to go on active service'. He immediately received the reply that the Maori were indeed anxious to serve on active service.[21]

It took a Ngapuhi soldier, Private Huirua, in a letter to his parents to express the exhilaration and elation of the Maori as they looked forward to active service. 'We are to move to the forefront of battle,' he wrote. 'We are to enter the scorching flame of the firing line.'[22]

The forefront of battle was Gallipoli. Already, since the landing of the ANZACS at Anzac Cove on 25 April 1915, many hundreds of Australians and New Zealanders had died in action against the Turks. Mudros harbour was the first stopping place for the Maori Contingent on its way to Gallipoli. Here they were transferred to a smaller boat which took them on the final stages of the journey to the front.

Te Rangi Hiroa described the excitement as the contingent approached Anzac Cove. 'As we approached we saw occasional flashes of light on the horizon and heard the rumble of artillery. Nearer still and the incessant crackling of machine-gun and rifle fire became audible! The Maori were all intensely excited. If there were any qualms of fear they were pushed down by the slogan that now they were to have the opportunity of vindicating the honour of their race. Youth without the experience of age flares high in courage.'

He continued: 'As we got closer in, bullets from the overs whined around and interest was evinced in those that came close. We dis-embarked into smaller boats that landed us at Anzac pier. Our feet were set on a distant land where our blood was to be shed in the cause of the Empire to which we belonged.'[23]

On 3 July 1915, some 69 days after the historic 25 April landing by the Anzac troops, the Maori Contingent, 477 strong, finally joined their Pakeha comrades-in-arms. They were attached to the New Zealand Mounted Rifles Brigade and were sent to No. 1 outpost which became known as the 'Maori Pa'.[24]

Earlier, when requested by British military authorities for any information on special dietary habits the Maori might have, Godley responded that he 'hoped that during their stay here (Gallipoli) there would be sufficient Turks taken prisoner or killed to go round!'[25]

While Godley might have been happy to receive the Maori, he was not so happy when he discovered there was serious trouble between Herbert and some of his Maori officers. In spite of the presence in the contingent of men of eminence and considerable mana, such as Te Rangi Hiroa and a Maori chaplain, Godley's initial response was to cable New Zealand for a second-in-command to act as a 'go-between'.

Herbert's problem stemmed from an apparent inability to communicate with the Maori soldiers while the Maori officers misinterpreted, sometimes deliberately, Herbert's orders. Godley, in describing the two Maori officers commanding the companies as being 'rather indifferent', had already decided where the fault lay.[26] The onset of the 6 August 1915 offensive overtook events. For the first time, from 6-10 August, the Maori Contingent were in action. Their casualties were high: more than 100 men were killed or wounded.

Godley reported to Allen that the men had won universal praise for their bravery. Captain F. M. Twisleton wrote that he had seen them in a lot of action. 'A man could not wish to lead better material in action, and I must say they are good stuff . . . I should say they are amongst the best bayonet fighters in the world.' Of their willingness to follow, he noted that 'with a leader they trusted, I am quite sure they would stand anything.'[27]

While Godley thought the performance of the junior officers and men of the contingent was exemplary, the same high opinion was not held of the two Maori company commanders. Godley's opinion was quite clear. He thought that the two officers in command of companies were 'quite useless' and they 'did not give the men a fair chance'. In his view the Lieutenant in charge of one company was ignorant of military matters, lacked experience and lacked a proper sense of responsibility. The more senior of the two officers-in-charge of the other company was, in Godley's opinion, singularly unsuited to command of men in the field. He blamed this officer for the disloyalty and obstruction which Herbert had met.[28]

Godley's solution to the problem was firstly to seek the return to New Zealand of the two company commanders and two other 'troublesome Maori officers'. In addition he decided to break up the contingent by attaching elements to the New Zealand Infantry Brigade so that half a company would be attached to each infantry battalion.

The storm of protest which followed these moves was to be expected. The Native Committee sided completely with the disgraced officers. 'Their racial pride was deeply involved.'[29] They exercised the one principal and perhaps only weapon in their arsenal: they threatened no further reinforcements until the matters were resolved.

Arguments over the status of the disgraced officers raged for months. The senior of the two company commanders was medically boarded before leaving for New Zealand. The other three officers were returned almost immediately to New Zealand. By December 1915, Godley had relented, in the face of increasing Government pressure and the continuous threats by Ngata and his colleagues to refuse to support further recruitment. He accepted the return to active service of the three fit Maori officers.[30]

The question of the continued unity of the Maori Contingent was viewed with even graver concern. The Native Committee unequivocally rejected Godley's reasons for splitting them up. Maori letters home complained of separation. 'Kua wehewehe matou' – we are separated – was the plaintive cry.[31] Godley's reluctant agreement to the return of the three officers gave force to his view that the soldiers should remain separated from officers in whom he had no confidence.[32] By February 1916 there seemed no way out of the deadlock.

As O'Connor, in his study on Maori recruitment noted, the formation of a New Zealand division gave Godley the opportunity he needed to solve the problem and break the impasse. He posted all the Maori to a Pioneer Battalion and added an equal number of Pakeha volunteers from surplus reinforcements. It was intended that all future Maori reinforcements would be posted into the Pioneer Battalion. Godley also indicated a hope that eventually it would be an all-Maori unit. The battalion was to be commanded by a Major from the Staff Corps and Te Rangi Hiroa was persuaded to transfer into a combat commission as second-in-command.[33]

Perhaps it was the relief that comes from the lifting of enormous tensions which saw the Native Committee accept without too much questioning the pioneer role given the Maori. Their principal role was that of providing a labour source for front-line infantry to build roads, erect wire entanglements and dig trenches. Given the great deal of fuss put up by Ngata and his colleagues, it seems curious that they should demur to the allotted second-class support role accorded the Maori.

After a short period of training, the battalion left Egypt for France and the Western Front, arriving there on 14 April 1916. They immediately moved to the Front where they began work on digging and repairing trenches. Te Rangi Hiroa described the Maori as cheerful diggers. They had been told by General Sir Andrew Russell, who commanded the New Zealand Division, that 'they were worth any two of the other pioneer battalions on the whole front.'[34] Constant patrols and small raids were mounted by the Maori to ensure that they dominated 'no-man's' land in front of the positions they were working on.

Soon after arrival in June 1916, the battalion was reorganised into two Maori companies and two Pakeha companies. Six months later a further reorganisation saw three Maori companies and one Pakeha company established. Finally, in September 1917, the Pioneer Battalion became a full Maori unit and was entitled the New Zealand (Maori) Pioneer Battalion. The badge of 'Te Hokowhitu a Tu' was readopted.

The unglamorous work of trench warfare did not go unnoticed. On the departure of the battalion in 1919, Russell paid a tribute to their efforts. He said that while their work in France may not have been as dramatic as the fighting on Gallipoli and 'therefore not so easily recognised by the public . . . their work on communication trenches and in the preparation of defence lines has saved the division many lives . . . the Maori have shown themselves to be brave and well disciplined, and to possess in a very marked degree that cheerful and willing spirit which goes so far towards the making of a good soldier.'[35]

While Maori soldiers clearly acquitted themselves well on the field of battle, not all tribes were supportive of the war effort. The Waikato tribes refused their support and no amount of persuasion by leading Maori elders, or coercion could budge them. Michael King in his biography, *Te Puea*, documents the Waikato position. While Ngata and his colleagues were activating, not altogether successfully, the traditions of Tumatauenga, 'Te Puea was reinforcing those of Tawhiao, prophet of peace.'[36] Waikato had a long memory and was not about to capitulate to the enthusiam of loyalty to the Crown.

Waikato's objections on the grounds of past grievances over land confiscation, pacifism and the belief they owed nothing to the Crown which had deprived them of much of their land placed an enormous strain on an already faltering recruitment system. Ngata, ever the realist, had already acknowledged the difficulties. It was clear to him that the rhetoric of the Native Contingent Committee was 'all wind and words'.[37]

An effort was made to bolster recruiting figures by including other Polynesian groups. The third Maori Draft of 314 soldiers included 148 Niue Islanders and 55 Rarotongans. This scheme was a bad mistake as the Niueans were unable to cope and proved more a liability than help.

When all attempts at persuasion had failed the Government was finally, in mid-1917, forced to extend the Conscription Act to cover Maori recruitment with the specific intention of 'press-ganging' Waikato into service. As King rightly observes, 'the record of the imposition of conscription on Waikato can only be described as shameful.'[38]

While the men of the Native Contingent did not fulfil the expectations of the Maori political leaders completely, it was nevertheless satisfying to them that they had begun the process of standing besides Pakeha in their own right. The fact that Maori had served as second-class labourers seemed to be lost on them. It was as if the price of citzenship was so important that sacrifices had to be made. In the end, the politicians ended up with a Maori Battalion. They had achieved their goal. In the context of the lengthening shadows of the British Empire, it was probably too much to expect that greater advances could be made.

Chapter 3

CALL TO ARMS

'I have accordingly the honour to inform you that unless not later than 11 a.m., British summer time, today, satisfactory assurances . . . have been given by the German Government . . . a state of war will exist between the two countries as from that hour.'[1] The failure of the German Government to meet the British requests plunged the world, for the second time in a generation, into the darkness of a world war.

New Zealand's response was swift. A proclamation was issued by the Government, at 9.30 p.m. on 3 September 1939, declaring a state of war with Germany.

In the months preceding the declaration, Sir Apirana Ngata, in anticipation of war, pressed for the formation of a Maori unit. Ngata, supported by his parliamentary colleagues and Maori organisations throughout the country, put pressure on the Labour Government to raise a wholly Maori unit for services overseas.

The Government did not act immediately to satisfy Maori demands. It was not until 4 October 1939 that it agreed to raise an infantry battalion comprised of Maori. This decision was taken after the expeditionary force, of nine battalions and support units, had already been agreed to and gazetted. The additional battalion was not to be entirely Maori, as envisaged by Ngata and his colleagues.

As in the First World War, the Government reserved the right to appoint Pakeha officers and non-commissioned officers to key positions in the battalion, with the important provision that Pakeha officers would be replaced by Maori officers when they had gained the necessary experience and when the opportunity arose.

Understandably, this policy drew an immediate and sharp response from Maori politicians and tribal elders. Ngata and his colleagues maintained that a number of First World War Maori veterans could provide the senior leadership for the proposed battalion.

Te Arawa of the Bay of Plenty and Ngati Porou of the East Coast demanded that the battalion be led by Maori only. Both these tribes had long been supporters of the Crown. In the 1860s and early 1870s they had unstintingly provided young men to fight with British and colonial troops against their rebel kin. When the call to arms sounded in 1914, they willingly committed the flower of their youth to battle on foreign fields. In 1939 they were once more in the vanguard in offering up

23

another generation of young Maori to Tumatauenga – the God of War.

The Army and the Government were unmoved by the Maori pleas. The Government reiterated its position: key positions in the battalion were to be held, at least initially, by Pakeha.

Ironically, the man chosen to lead the Maori was, himself, of Germanic extraction. Major George Dittmer, a 47-year-old professional soldier and member of the small New Zealand Staff Corps between wars, brought to his difficult assignment the experience of 20 years of regular service, including five years of active service during the First World War. A tall, prepossessing man with pronounced angular features giving little hint of humour, Dittmer had established a reputation for exacting a high standard of performance and behaviour from his subordinates.

Army Headquarters announced at the same time the appointment of a part-Maori, George Bertrand, as battalion second-in-command. This 48-year-old school master from New Plymouth was plucked from the Reserve of Officers to fill this challenging appointment. In contrast to his new commanding officer, Bertrand was a thin, scholarly man given to reflective consideration of the problems of war – seemingly the perfect foil to Dittmer, the strict disciplinarian. Like Dittmer, Bertrand had seen active service during the First World War during which he had been wounded three times.

In between the wars he had continued to serve in the territorial forces, reaching the rank of Lieutenant-Colonel in the Taranaki Regiment before being transferred to the Reserve of Officers. As second-in-command, Bertrand's duties lay largely in the administrative and logistic side of the life of the battalion. Major Rangi Logan recalls that he went about these tasks 'with a single-minded efficiency that boded ill for the lazy, the careless and the inefficient.'[2]

Into the hands of these two dedicated and experienced soldiers was placed the fate of some hundreds of young Maori men. They were joined in their task by Regimental Sergeant Major 'Ace' Wood. Born in 1915, Wood was a member of the small pre-war permanent staff. Aged only 24 years, he was committed totally to the drive of his Commanding Officer to maintain high standards of training and discipline.

Dittmer's first task was to recruit and train suitable officers and non-commissioned officers to man the remaining command and control appointments in the battalion. Army offices throughout the country were alerted to earmark suitable candidates, both Pakeha and Maori, for consideration.

In addition, Dittmer visited the mobilisation camps of the First Echelon, which already were training the first batch of 6 000 men for deployment overseas, to interview prospective candidates. At the outset, it was made clear that service with 28 (Maori) Battalion was not mandatory and that Maori officers and soldiers already serving with First Echelon Units could remain with them.

Rangi Logan was training with the 4th Field Artillery Regiment when the announcement was made that the Maori Battalion was to be formed. He remembered well the impact of the announcement.[3] At the outbreak of the war he was a farm cadet, having just returned from an agricultural course at Massey College and was working in a Napier wool store. When war was declared this slight, dapper and well-educated young Maori immediately signed up with the First Echelon.

A pre-war territorial non-commissioned officer in the artillery, he joined the 4th Field Regiment. When the Army directive arrived inviting Maori to register for service with 28 (Maori) Battalion, Logan was paraded before his Commanding Officer and asked what his intentions were. Despite his loyalty to the artillery his response was immediately to opt for service with his fellow Maori soldiers. 4th Field Regiment's loss was 28 (Maori) Battalion's gain.

In the short time available to him, Dittmer had to raise an initial draft of 146 recruits to attend a training selection course at the Army School's Depot, Trentham. By the end of November 1939 he had the required number of trainees. Among them were six officers of the Pioneer Battalion including Captains Harding Leaf and Rangi Royal.

Before joining 28 (Maori) Battalion, Leaf had already carved out a legend in the far north of New Zealand. As an officer in the Pioneer Battalion during the First World War on the Western Front, he had won a Military Cross for his bravery. The action for which he received his decoration illustrates both Harding's personal impetuosity and bravery and the characteristic behaviour of his fellow Ngapuhi, the northern tribe to which he belonged.

The Pioneer Battalion, which was attached to the New Zealand Expeditionary Force in France, was carrying out its essential task of trench maintenance when a major attack was about to be launched. Harding Leaf decided that 'only women watch a fight'; he joined the attack and won a Military Cross for his subsequent actions. In the words of Humphrey Dyer, Harding Leaf was a powerful man. 'He was a cavalier, a rollicking blade who did not have to seek adventure – he created it. For wherever he moved, as did the three musketeers, he provoked mischief and fun and, at times, desperate adventure.'[4] One year short of his 50th birthday, Leaf was one of the first to offer his services. In his book *Ma Te Reinga*, Dyer recounted how Leaf helped to recruit large numbers of Ngapuhi for the war effort.

He also described how Leaf's impetuosity and disregard for military discipline led Dittmer to seriously consider his return home just before the arrival of the main body of the 28 (Maori) Battalion in Palmerston North.[5] Dyer advised that to send Leaf home was to court disaster. Such was Leaf's influence that many of the Ngapuhi would have returned home with him. The matter 'was patched up and [it was] tacitly agreed that a certain latitude be allowed to a certain distinguished soldier in regard to leave of absence, on occasions.'

Captain Leaf's response to this reprieve was to immediately petition the Commanding Officer to allow his Great Dane, called Tiger, to accompany the battalion overseas as its mascot. All approved of the idea except the Colonel.[6] He was faced with two problems. 'One was feeding such a beast on the meat ration overseas; but of course such things have been managed. The second seemed to him insurmountable. Harding alone was difficult enough to control. Like a volcano, he carried an atmosphere of unrest, of upheaval, of a feeling that something even worse might happen at any moment. Even so, Harding was possible. But· Harding plus Tiger were quite impossible. So the Great Dane was sent home.'

Rangi Royal was another First World War veteran. Like Leaf he was to play a crucial role in the battalion's formative days.

The trainees in the first draft were recruited on the basis that all officers except Dittmer and Bertrand were to be regarded as student officers and the balance as student non-commissioned officers, with the prospect of approximately 20 being recommended for commissioning at the end of the course. The trainees began to arrive in Trentham towards the end of November 1939.

Boy Tomoana was a railways porter when the trainees began to arrive for their training.[7] He watched with pride and envy the confident swagger and enthusiasm of the potential officers and non-commissioned officers. Some of these were relatives and friends from Ngati Porou and Ngati Kahungunu of the East Coast and the Napier-Hastings areas. Little then did he realise that the business of war is a ruthless leveller of human society and that he himself would soon be a member of 28 (Maori) Battalion and that he would end the war as a captain, decorated for gallantry in Italy.

Trentham Camp, the camp chosen for the training course, was the home of the Army's School of Instruction. Located by the Wellington-Masterton trunk line 30 km from Wellington, the camp was a collection of old buildings and barracks which had been used in the First World War. This camp became the home for the initial group of Maori trainees from which the nucleus of the officers and non-commissioned officers of the 28 (Maori) Battalion was found.

Frank Rennie, a young soldier of the Permanent Staff, with three years' experience behind him, was appointed as Course Sergeant Major to teach the trainees drill, weapon training, and discipline. Raised in Christchurch with little previous contact with Maori, Rennie was given the very difficult task of trying to sort out the arriving troops. 'I had been given a copy of the nominal roll' he recalls, but he had no intention of trying to call it.[8]

The call to arms had prompted many Maori to revert to the use of ancestral family names. This stratagem allowed quite a number to enlist who were either under or over the recruitment age limit. Private Noema Poi turned 16 years of age on 16 May 1941, the day before the German attack on Crete. He had joined up at the age of 14 years.[9]

Rennie had no intention of attempting to match the tongue-twisting names on the nominal roll with the sea of brown faces – and the occasional white face – in front of him. He was rescued from his dilemma by 'two large, very well-built figures' who arrived on the scene – Captains Rangi Royal and Harding Leaf.

From then on, wrote Rennie, 'things began to fall into place. Captain Leaf put his arms around my shoulders and introduced me to the other officers, using such expressions as, "If you ever lose anything this so-and-so will have it." Captain Royal introduced me to the troops and said something in Maori which seemed to make some difference because they came to attention from then on.'[10] Together, Royal and Leaf helped this young non-Maori soldier over what might have proved for him an insurmountable obstacle.

Dittmer had less than eight weeks available to him to sort out his potential officers and non-commissioned officers. Demanding times required vigorous and ruthless methods and throughout the course those considered unsuitable were replaced. Every man who made it through the course remembered the exacting and, at times, almost impossible demands placed on their time.

The first demand placed on the group of largely raw trainees was a request from Sir Apirana Ngata for a 100-man guard-of-honour. Ngata wanted the Maori to provide a guard to take part in the ceremony to open the Maori Court at the Centennial Exhibition in Wellington. While Army Headquarters had approved the request, few expected the Maori to deliver the expected level of performance.

Perhaps in their naivety the Maori themselves failed to appreciate the enormity of the task ahead of them. The challenge had been cast before them. In traditional terms, it merely remained for them to accept the challenge. This is exactly what they did.

Rennie observed that, 'to compound the problem it was necessary to keep abreast of the syllabus for the course' and therefore 'the drill periods available for the preparation were limited.'[11] These limitations did not daunt them. Immediately after the challenge had been accepted, the Maori utilised every spare moment to practise drill movements. Before breakfast, during lunchtimes, late at night and even during breaks on route marches they practised their arms drill and rehearsed their movements.

In the three weeks available, the Maori recruits did all that was humanly possible to prepare for the guard. When the time came to carry out the task, the performance of the guard, commanded by Captain Rangi Royal, was outstanding. Frank Rennie recalled with pride the success of that occasion. In his view, 'although it was a tough assignment to produce a guard-of-honour in such a short time, the circumstances and the performance did a lot to settle the mixed tribal group into a corporate entity.'[12] He might have added that the performance also demonstrated the Maori capacity to respond at short notice to challenging situations.

Their performance in other areas was not always greeted with the same sense of pride – sometimes more with a sense of bemused amazement. On one occasion the trainees were sent home on long weekend leave, each issued with two sets of battledress. When the Sergeant Major met the returning trainees he found, to his amazement, that instead of having 146 on parade he, in fact, had 160, 'all in battledress – all looking like soldiers.'[13]

Sergeant Major Rennie was a victim of the Maori soldier's casual attitude to the niceties of good military order and discipline. As far as the relatives of the original trainees were concerned, they could see no earthly reason why they, too, should not join in the fun. Thereafter Frank Rennie maintained that he was never convinced that the original 146 trainees completed the training.

His last word on his experiences during this period are worth recording. 'Having this experience with the Maoris provided a new dimension in soldiering for me. Their boundless and infectious enthusiasm and their tremendous pride in their reputation as warriors was something I had to see to believe. I saw it again and again. Many times I was personally grateful for it.'[14]

During this period of training, the tune which was to become famous throughout New Zealand and overseas as the marching song of the Maori Battalion was put to music by the bandmaster of the Trentham Camp

Band. The song had its beginnings in Rotorua. Anania Amohau, its author, had shaped the tune during Te Arawa's preparation for the centennial year of the Treaty of Waitangi, to be held in February 1940.

There appears to be considerable confusion and a great deal of uncertainty about how and when the tune, words and music came together. Cody noted that Amohau first whistled the tune then sang it.[15] Captain Royal had some copies typed and soon the Te Arawa had its own marching song. The men of Te Arawa brought the song to Trentham in November 1939, to find it had preceded them. Rennie recalled a calm evening in November at Trentham when Amohau for the first time introduced the song.[16] Ern Edwards recorded that the song was composed in January 1940.[17]

Whatever its genesis, within a short period the trainees had quickly adopted the tune, with its now famous words, as their rallying marching song. Over the next five years it was to be sung in countless bars, music halls and wherever Maori gathered together. As well as being a stirring marching song it also served as a nostalgic reminder of home to all soldiers of the New Zealand Division.

Not all considered the song as a rallying talisman. Epineha Ratapu on the occasion of his retirement from employment many years after the war recalled, 'how unlucky the song "Maori Battalion" was for him and his mates. Wherever we sang it before battle, we'd lose chaps. If we prayed beforehand, we'd hardly lose anyone. That song just wasn't right for us.'[18] Rangi Logan disputes Ratapu's statement. He said that, 'D Company never sang it before battle. The thought never ever arose. It did not seem to be the appropriate time. We did appreciate a church service or even just a prayer by the padre.'[19]

While the potential officers and non-commissioned officers were training in Trentham, recruiting was continuing. Recruiting had begun on 9 October and by the end of the month over 900 recruits had been enlisted. Unlike the situation in the First World War where conscription was introduced in 1917 to include Maori, recruiting for Maori remained voluntary throughout the Second World War.

In some areas, especially the smaller communities, the enlistment of many of the eligible men of the community had potentially disastrous consequences for families and the community at large. And yet all understood the need for the men of the family to exercise the right to raise the war trail.

It had little to do with patriotic duty, rather it was the age-old tradition of maintaining the mana or the status of the family, the hapu (sub-tribe) and the iwi (people).

So strong was this urge to serve that many areas were left without the 'seeds' to carry on the next generation. The small settlement of Hiruharama (Jerusalem), on the East Coast of the North Island, gave up 66 of its sons and fathers to fight in the war and 13 of them died. The Moekes and the Pahaus were typical of many Maori families. They sent several of their number to exercise that right – one failed to return.[20]

The enthusiasm to enlist was infectious. Ben Porter, a taxi driver at the outbreak of the war, enlisted after taking a load of potential recruits to the recruiting station. Once there, he joined his passengers in the queue.

The seriousness of losing most of the males of any one family was realised during the withdrawal from the abortive Crete campaign. Six Maori officers and 144 other ranks were ordered to remain behind to protect Evacuation Force Headquarters. The difficult task of choosing who to stay was made easy by the men themselves deciding who had to go. Men with wives and children at home were encouraged to go. Senior males of family groups also determined which of their younger kin should stay on Crete and which should go.

It was decided, by Army Headquarters, that the 28 (Maori) Battalion would gather in Palmerston North on 26 January 1940. Some two days earlier, the officers and non-commissioned officers arrived from Trentham to prepare the camp and ready themselves for the onslaught. On the day, hundreds of Maori, raw in the skills of modern warfare, converged on Palmerston North, accompanied by relatives, tribal elders and friends, all willing to stay and help with training.

Cody noted that Dittmer was at the station to meet the first draft.[21] He further observed wryly that, 'it would be interesting to know what he thought when he saw his first recruits. Many had ukeleles, accordions and banjos and nearly all were dressed in the bright colours of their Sunday best.' It is little wonder then that 'the Major went a little pale' as he contemplated the task ahead.

It had been agreed that the battalion be organised on a tribal basis. A Company comprised mainly men from North Auckland (Ngapuhi and Aupouri). B Company was made up of men from the Bay of Plenty, Thames-Coromandel and Taupo areas with the bulk coming from Te Arawa. C Company was manned by men from the East Coast of the North Island, principally from the Ngati Porou tribe. D Company was a composite company with men coming from all remaining areas, including the South Island. The principal tribal component came from Ngati Kahungunu, of Hawkes Bay-Wairarapa. Headquarters Company was similarly a composite company with men drawn from the surplus of A, B and C Companies.

Very quickly the men exercised the prerogative of every soldier to provide a convenient label or nickname that typified the different companies and tribal groups. The men from the gumfields of the far north were called the Gum Diggers (Nga Kiri Kapia). Te Arawa, famous for its penny divers and guided tours through the geyserlands of Whakarewarewa, were labelled Nga Rukukapa (the Penny Divers). Those unfortunate men in B Company who did not belong to Te Arawa and who belonged to the neighbouring tribes of Mataatua had to grin and bear the label.

C Company men were labelled Nga Kaupoi (the Cowboys), largely because of their regular mode of transport in the isolated areas of the East Coast. D Company, not so easy to label, were initially called Ngati D Company and also the Foreign Legion. It was only later that Ngati Walkabout was used. According to Logan, this was a title introduced by the 9th and 10th Reinforcements.[22] Headquarter Company became The Odds & Sods.

As the battalion settled into its temporary camp at the Palmerston North showground, the enormity of the task of preparing for war quickly became apparent. The problem was twofold. Firstly, much valuable training time was lost in bringing the Maori soldiers up to dental fitness with three dental officers fully employed on this task.

Secondly, a great deal of effort had to be made to select and train the technical personnel needed to run the battalion. Specialists such as radio operators, drivers, mechanics and medical orderlies had to be trained from scratch. There was one area, however, where the Maori excelled and that was in the field of weapon handling. The mechanical skills and repetitious nature of stripping and assembling weapons was an area in which the Maori had few peers.

Within a fortnight of entering camp the battalion was required to provide a 500-man contingent for the centennial celebrations at Waitangi.

It was agreed that the battalion would represent all of Maoridom. The time spent in preparing for the celebrations and the four days spent at Waitangi made a significant dent in valuable training time. However, any lost time was quickly made up by recruits, who used every opportunity to practise.

As well as trying to cope with the enormous pressures of training, the recruits also had to learn how to cope with the very real problem of adjusting to the Army's code of military behaviour. Most quickly learnt that military justice, while not necessarily sympathetic to the ways of the Maori, was nonetheless dispensed fairly, firmly and promptly.

Some, like Private Charlie Shelford, seemed destined to be perpetually

31

arraigned before the Officer Commanding and Commanding Officer on a wide variety of charges. Described as 'a tall leanish chap, quiet, certainly not talkative and friendly, in fact almost inclined to be surly', Shelford was so consistently ill-disciplined that when the battalion left for overseas service, he remained behind in detention.[23] And yet when Shelford finally reached the Middle East he was so consistently brave in action he was awarded an immediate Distinguished Conduct Medal. However, it was no surprise to learn that he had to be released from the detention centre to receive his award.[24]

Life in camp was not, however, all work. From time to time, the Maori were able to spend their free time either in camp amenities or, more frequently, in Palmerston North itself. Mr Ern Edwards, during early 1940 was a social worker with the Brethren Gospel Chapels of Palmerston North. He recalled how he got permission to erect a large marquee on the Palmerston North showgrounds to take the place of the usual YMCA hut located in military camps.[25]

The marquee provided a quiet retreat for those who wanted it. More importantly, Ern Edwards and his helpers dispensed tea, coffee, sandwiches and cakes for supper every night. To ensure it catered for all ranks, the marquee was called 'Every Man's Hut'. An old organ was used to provide accompaniment to a short service held every evening. And every evening they sang the hymn 'Aue Ihu', which became one of the hymns sung at church services on the many battlefields traversed by 28 (Maori) Battalion.

The battalion's early association with the citizens of Palmerston North was not a happy one. In the early days they made such a nuisance of themselves while on leave that the civic authorities mooted banning them from town.

Colonel Dittmer responded by speaking sternly to the battalion and telling them that, 'before we go we are going to make Palmerston North sorry to see us go.'[26] This had the desired effect of improving relations and, indeed, at the civic function held to farewell the battalion, much was made of the cordial relations between the town and the solders.

Chapter 4

FAREWELL AOTEAROA

As the day of departure dawned over Palmerston North, the men of 28 (Maori) Battalion quietly went about their preparations. In a little over 13 weeks they had been subjected to an intensive round of administration, medical and dental checks and training. While they had performed well in parades and had worked hard to learn weapon training and tactical skills, it would be misleading to say that they were all prepared for war.

Over three months, George Dittmer and his new officers and non-commissioned officers had taken nearly 1000 raw recruits and hammered them into a cohesive infantry force capable of operating in formed and disciplined groups. The four rifle companies had the necessary foundation on which could be built the skills needed to sustain a fighting unit in battle. The technical support platoons of Headquarters Company, including the wireless operators and the logistics staff, however, needed much more training before they could be confident of providing the infantry with the full support modern warfare demanded.

Just before midday on 1 May 1940, the men of the battalion prepared to leave Palmerston North. Dressed in their greatcoats and lemon-squeezer hats, with officers carrying side-arms and the remainder of the battalion carrying rifles, they looked impressive as they marched for the last time before the citizens of Palmerston North.

Before entraining at the railway station for the four-hour rail journey to Wellington, officers and men were able to spend brief moments fare-welling relatives and loved ones.

The euphoria of the occasion understandably blotted out the realities of the future. Few realised that many of these men would not be returning. The campaigns in Greece and Crete alone would claim the lives of 84 men. Many more would be killed in action, wounded or be posted as missing-in-action in subsequent battles.

As the train pulled out of Palmerston North, relatives and friends mounted the waiting cavalcade of cars, trucks and buses and followed the troop train south to Wellington. On arrival in Wellington the troop train, 'with shuttered windows and guarded doors passed onto Aotea Quay, which was then closed against the crowd'[1] which had gathered hoping for another opportunity for a last few words.

The troops detrained and were led up the high gangway onto the *Aquitania* and then down into the bowels of the ship to 'F' deck, which was to become the battalion's home for the next few weeks.

The HT *Aquitania* was, in peacetime, a luxury liner. There had been little time to prepare her for war and her troop-carrying role. Imagine then the awe and pleasure of the Maori as they were shown to their quarters. Dyer described the *Aquitania* as a 'beautiful ship, long and graceful and thoroughbred . . . Her lounges and state cabins filled us with immense satisfaction.'[2]

Many of the battalion, including private soldiers, travelled in luxury. Officers and senior non-commissioned officers shared state cabins which were large and roomy with tiled bathrooms.

Colonel Dittmer was appointed as Officer Commanding Troops on board the *Aquitania*. In total there were nearly 3000 troops (including Maori) aboard the ship. Major Bertrand became acting Commanding Officer and Major Humphrey Dyer, ship's Quartermaster, for the duration of the journey. During the evening of 1 May 1940, other units embarked.

Thursday, 2 May, was a wet wintry day. By early morning loading was completed and the *Aquitania* threw off its moorings to move out into the harbour. As the ship left the wharf, the Maori on board bade farewell, many for the last time, to their friends and relatives. Their last contact 'was the sight of the crowd allowed on the wharf at the last moment, and the sound of the Ngati Poneke girls singing farewell songs, as the distance widened between ship and shore.'[3]

Boy Tomoana, who was fortunate to be on the wharf to farewell his friends and relatives, was overawed by the sight of the huge troopships and the hundreds of soldiers lining the rails. It was a sight that he never forgot and could recall clearly 45 years later.[4]

The *Aquitania* hove to in the harbour to await the rest of the convoy being loaded with the remaining troops of the 2nd Echelon. It was at this point that the Governor-General farewelled the troops on board the *Aquitania* by circling the ship in a launch. 28 (Maori) Battalion responded by singing 'Po Atarau' ('Now is the Hour') and shortly after this the ship moved down Wellington Harbour and out into Cook Strait and the open sea.

Squally weather conditions and rough seas greeted the *Aquitania* and her sister ships as they left the relative shelter of Wellington Harbour. For the first two days, as the convoy headed for Australia, all but the hardiest of the men suffered from sea sickness. Rangi Logan wrote, 'my memory of the first day was a decent swell which had an effect on some of the troops due to the fact that the *Aquitania* was a ship of great length and her motion was accentuated or exaggerated.'[5]

Those able to enjoy the luxury of their new surroundings ate their meals in the splendour of the *Aquitania*'s dining areas. One of these men was Warrant Officer Garrett Leslie Burke, a Pakeha, who had been appointed to the battalion as the Regimental Quartermaster Sergeant. Burke, who turned 29 years of age as the convoy left the coast of New Zealand, joined with a number of his new-found friends of 28 (Maori) Battalion to celebrate his birthday.[6]

The luncheon menu of the Warrant Officers and Sergeants read like a menu of the Waldorf Astoria. After soup Creme St Germain, the men were treated to an entrée of boiled haddock with sauce piment. For the main course there were three choices: curried chicken and rice or Salisbury steak as the hot dishes, served with a range of vegetables including creamed spinach, mashed parsnips and French-fried potatoes.

The cold cuts of meat were roast beef with horseradish sauce, pressed beef and oxford brawn. These dishes were served with lettuce, beetroot or mixed pickles. Sago or custard pudding helped fill out any empty spaces. Coffee was taken in the luxury of the ship's drawing rooms.

For most of the men of the battalion, used to a simple yet filling diet, the range of food was forbidding. Burke used his meal menus as a novel form of writing paper, and during the voyage of the *Aquitania* wrote a daily commentary of events on them.

However, even the best of hotel menus eventually begins to lose its savour. The monotonous regularity of the diet encourages even the most seasoned of connoisseurs to seek a change. When the *Aquitania* had been stocked for the journey an ample supply of titi, or smoked muttonbirds, was also included. After several days of travel, Dyer noted that many of the Maori were unperturbed at the monotony of the ship's fare. Indeed they looked sleek and self-satisfied. It did not take Dyer long to discover that one of the soldiers had raided the hold and stored in his cabin hundreds of muttonbirds. He had been doing a roaring trade with his fellow tribesmen.[7]

As soon as the initial bouts of seasickness were over, training in weapons use, lectures on organisation and administration and daily fitness exercises began in earnest.

Shipboard routine did not deviate much during the voyage. Reveille at 6 a.m. was followed by breakfast and a session of training. After lunch, two further sessions of training were carried out. Platoon and Company Commanders strove to ease the inevitable boredom. Two days out from New Zealand the convoy was joined off Sydney Heads by two ships carrying Australian troops. On the following day, 6 May, the convoy passed through the Bass Strait, picking up another ship full of Australian troops from Melbourne.

The convoy steamed into Fremantle on 10 May 1940. Because of her size, the Aquitania was one of two ships that had to anchor off shore. Urgent representations by Brigadier Hargest, who commanded all New Zealand troops in the convoy, defused a potentially volatile situation. At one stage it looked as if the troops on board *Aquitania* and *Queen Mary* might not be able to land. However, Hargest's actions secured the use of a number of craft to ferry the Maori and their fellow-soldiers ashore for a few hours of leave in Fremantle.

On the morning of the 12 May, the convoy set sail. Besides the main course of his luncheon menu, Warrant Officer Burke noted, 'Engines started. Just pulling out of Fremantle. Bound were [sic]'[8] Later he adds, 'we are off out into the Indian Ocean. Colombo next stop we hope but I have my doubts. I've heard rumours from the 3rd Officer of the *Aquitania* of which the troops knew nothing. I'll lay odds we go to the Cape and then England. What Ho.'

As the convoy ploughed through the Indian Ocean, the training routine continued unabated. By now the novelty of shipboard life had long since gone.

The Maoris were 'heartily sick of looking at two lines of ships ploughing through an endless ocean.'[9] Concerts, community sing-songs and other social activities provided some relief from the boredom. Illegal poker and two-up schools proliferated. For the less adventurous, the official housie games with a three penny limit were available.

For some, like Second-Lieutenant Wattie McKay, other avenues lay open to ward off boredom. Before enlistment, he had been a school teacher, and later a journalist. He was one of the very few Maori with overseas experience, having travelled to the United States as a journalist.

Dyer in his memoirs, *Ma Te Reinga*, written after the war, described McKay as a 'young man of rather short stature, well built, athletic and agile' who was 'nimble physically and nimble mentally'.[10] Accomplished at tennis and rugby football he also excelled at chess. He had been captain of the New Zealand Maori hockey team and was a low-handicap golfer.

Dyer described how McKay roamed the *Aquitania* looking for victims upon whom to test his skills.[11] 'His approach was unvarying and what usually happened was this . . . You would be comfortably reading a book, looking up now and then to watch the other ships of the convoy racing along in formation, and to wonder what the folk on board them were doing, when a bad, dark spirit would come behind you.

' "What about a little game of chess to pass the time? It was just a fluke that I won last time. You know, if you hadn't left that queen . . . !"

'If you were strong you would say, "No thank you, Wattie. I am happy; leave me in peace."

'If you were weak you would drift into the whirlpool; for a game of chess with Wattie was likely to become a maelstrom. Laboriously you would work out your plan and carry the war into his territory, while Wattie in the midst of a constant chatter would, with no apparent plan, move his pieces quickly over the chessboard. Your plan matured. In another few moves you would have him.

'Then perched on the edge of his seat with keen eyes and nervous hands on the game he would suddenly leap his pieces frantically over the board, and after a few convulsive struggles you lay helpless.

'Sitting back, rubbing his hands and with eyes twinkling with merriment, he would suggest that since you had just missed an important move some time back, we could reset the pieces as at that stage and try the finish again. But now you are adamant. He must find some other poor wretch to torment.'

The intolerable heat also began to exact a toll on the men of the convoy. Burke noted on the 14 May, 'its getting hottish'. He adds, 'God it must be hot in the engine room.' He concludes with an observation that 'one of the stokers has just committed suicide by jumping overboard, poor devil.' The following day the temperature hit 98°F in the shade. Burke noted that 'the Maoris are not standing up to [the heat] as well as we are.'[12] Another stoker commits suicide.

Three days out from Perth, Western Australia, a dramatic change of direction for the convoy was made. Instead of heading for Colombo the convoy now turned south-west and steamed for South Africa, with England as its new destination. At 11.30 a.m. on 16 May, all quarter-masters were called for a conference. Major Dyer briefed the quarter-masters on the changes.

Burke recorded that he and his colleagues would have 'to warn the men that they cannot have any returns at meals [and] troops to go on rations . . . it appears there is danger from Italy and we are now making for Prince Edward Island somewhere near Cape Town. It is a naval oil base and will take us from 10 to 12 days longer to reach there. Thus there is danger of running out of food.'[13]

Sweeping southwards in a wide arc to avoid minefields, the *Aquitania* and her sister ships slowly approached Cape Town. The Maori excitement was somewhat subdued as they were uncertain of their reception. Major Bertrand had paved the way for any disappointment or frustration by briefing the Maori on their likely reception by the white residents. They were told 'that their reception would probably be cool, and that if they were turned out of shops or had any other indignity thrust upon them, they were not to make a fuss' as it was the custom of the country.[14]

The majestic sight of Table Mountain, the towering rock, covered half-way down with mist, excited Burke. His excitement was dampened with the observation that once again 'this tub is too big to go into port so we lie in the stream watching the other ships tie up at the wharfs (sic). Hell.'[15] For two days the troops aboard *Aquitania* watched with exasperation and anger as other troops were granted leave.

The Pakeha soldiers on board *Aquitania* broadcast their feelings by chalking in various places the words 'HM Prison Ships'. The move of the *Aquitania* to the Port of Simonstown (50 km from Cape Town) allowed the units aboard to finally take shore leave. This right was not granted the Maori.

By contrast, the soldiers of other ships spent four days and nights in Cape Town being entertained by the local community headed by the Lady Mayoress and the Women's Auxiliary Service. On the final day in port the Maori were finally granted leave. However, the leave arrangements were under strict supervision. Brigadier Hargest had cabled the New Zealand Government for a grant of 50 pounds to allow the Maori to be transported to and from Cape Town.[16] It is hardly surprising that when they were finally let ashore they were 'tight lipped and nervous'.

While other Pakeha units on board *Aquitania* had been granted leave earlier, the Pakeha members of 28 (Maori) Battalion remained on board with, and shared, the frustrations, envy and anger of the Maori. Burke's irritation and frustration shows through with his record of the so-called shore leave (Wednesday, 29 May). 'Hell I could swear for an hour and not say the same word twice,' he wrote.[17]

He vents his spleen on Dittmer, whom he accuses of 'playing up to the Dutch'. He continues: 'We got ashore at 10.30, were bundled into buses and driven for miles around Table Mountain through the vineyards. Very nice but after being cooped up in a boat we wanted to stretch our legs on mother earth not be cooped up in buses. Anyway we reached Cape Town at 1 p.m. And then were marched for a cup of tea and a bun. "Hell." It was too much for me so I beat it. Before going for lunch we were told that we had to be back at the buses at 2.15 p.m. A whole hour and quarter to ourselves. Well, by the time the boys were let out of the drill hall they had exactly 25 minutes to themselves.'

As the convoy left Cape Town bound for England, Burke's resentment still smouldered. He continued to lay the blame at the feet of his Officer Commanding Ship: 'What a farce Dittmer made of it,' he wrote. 'Isn't he a basted(sic), pardon my French.'[18]

Burke's chagrin is understandable but his criticism is not fairly directed. Dittmer would have carried out his orders without any thought of passing some of the opprobrium onto his superior officer, Brigadier Hargest. The responsibility for any decision on the Maori leave lay with Hargest and not Dittmer.

Even if they were not able to enjoy the people and sights of Cape Town, a number of Maori were determined to take with them a reminder of their visit. Dyer recalled that it was a fine day when the convoy left Cape Town. He paid a visit to one of the Maori messes and after ordering a beer sat down to enjoy it. 'And then, believe it or not,' he wrote, 'I started to hear things and to see things. There was a scraping noise, and then under the table I saw something green and large and fearsome approaching my leg.'

' "Harding," I said, "is this yours? Has it a name? If so call it home."

' "Its name!" they roared and threw open the bathroom door.

'There, in the bath, on its sides, and on the floor, there swam and fought and clambered a multitude of enormous lobsters. Surely the waters of Cape Town must be the annual meeting ground of lobster patriarchs from many oceans. And now they waved defiance at their captors.

' "What are you going to do with those?"

' "Eat them. Two a day." And I was not invited.

' "You see," they explained, "we are feeding them and they may multiply."

'I noticed large lumps of bread, filched from the mess tables, floating round in the bath in which the tap was running slowly and from which, with each slight roll of the ship, water splashed on the floor.

'Knowing my responsibilities as a quartermaster I discreetly retired.'[19]

Steaming north for a further seven days, the convoy reached Sierra Leone. Here the Ship's Quartermaster, Major Dyer, had his work cut out to curb trade between the negro traders, who had paddled out to meet the convoy in canoes laden with bananas, oranges and many other varieties of fruit, and the Maori.

The fact was that the Maori had no money. They had not been paid since Cape Town, 'where like good soldiers they had all become bankrupt.' Dyer observed 'a lot of fruit coming up the stern but was unprepared for what was going down. Blankets, sheets, pillowslips, battledress trousers, sand shoes – other people's of course, from the next cabins.'[20]

It was Captain Leaf who helped restore order. When repeated yells to the traders to clear off failed to move them, he pulled out his pistol, took aim at the nearest canoe and fired. The traders hurriedly rowed to safety.

Colonel Dittmer had been standing watching Captain Leaf's actions. Captain Leaf, unperturbed, grinned and said to the Colonel: 'I am always a bad shot with a revolver, Sir. If I aim at a man I miss him. So I aimed at the biggest nigger and just put a hole in the canoe.'

As the convoy neared England, the soldiers were still unaware of their eventual destination. On Monday, 10 June 1940, the convoy received news that Italy had declared war on Great Britain. Things seemed grim for the Allied cause. The Germans had swept across France and had bottled up the remnants of the small British Expeditionary Force at Dunkirk. The Germans stood poised to launch themselves across the Channel.

Burke noted that 'we are in the war zone with an avengeance [sic], during the night another aircraft carrier, the Courageous, has joined us also HMS Hood and 8 little destroyers – so now we have a guard of 18 boats.'[21]

The following day, Friday, 14 June, news was received that Paris had fallen at 5 a.m. that morning; the Germans had advanced right to the English Channel and major evacuations had taken place on the south eastern coast of England. The convoy began to adopt evasive tactics, constantly changing course every few minutes. After dawn of the next day the Maori saw, for the first time, the wreckage of war.

The *Aquitania* passed close to the wreckage of a ship torpedoed earlier that morning. A dozen empty lifeboats and two with survivors were seen. 'The sea for about an area of 10 acres was simply covered with spars and wreckage.' At 11.45 a.m., Burke reports, the submarines have struck once more. 'We have just sighted an oil tanker dead ahead all ablaze.'[22]

Early in the afternoon the frenetic pace of activity continues, as all the ships of the convoy 'have gone hard a starboard and four of the destroyers have shot away to port side either they have seen something or the planes have reported something. Here's hopeing [sic] we get a bag.'

Early in the afternoon of Sunday 16 June 1940, nearly six weeks after leaving home, the long journey came to an end as the *Aquitania* dropped anchor in the port of Gourock, a few miles from Glasgow. For the soldiers the hardest part of the journey was the lack of news as to where the convoy was going, and what was happening in Europe.

In the latter days of the voyage the constant zigzagging and threat from enemy submarines had helped sharpen interest. All were thoroughly relieved to have reached their destination at last. Burke, in his final notes of the voyage, laments the fact that having travelled over halfway around the world, 'we still haven't entered a port where we could tie up.'

The battalion was to spend six months in the United Kingdom. During that time their training continued apace. Twice during the period, the German threat to Britain was sufficiently serious for the battalion to be placed on a war footing and deployed to battle stations. On the first of these occasions, shortly after the battalion's arrival, it became part of the general headquarters reserve based at Ewshott, in the Aldershot area.

With the fall of France, the imminent threat of invasion was on the minds of Churchill and his generals. 28 (Maori) Battalion was moved to join the Mixed Brigade which was based at Dogmersfield. Further training followed throughout July and August 1940. By September, the division had been judged fit for front-line duty.[23]

During September, the intended move of the New Zealanders to Egypt was cancelled and the division came under the command of 12 Corps, which had been ordered to take up defensive positions in the area of Folkestone-Dover.

It was during this period that the battalion sent four Officer Cadet Training Unit candidates to a preparatory course for entry into Sandhurst. Rangi Logan and Jim Tuhiwai were the first Maori to enter the famous military academy, followed later by Ruihi Pene and Henry Toka.

John Harper who was in the same intake as Pene and Toka, recalled that, 'Ruihi Pene handled it all as well as any of us and better than some. Henry Toka was very quiet and did not seem to take much interest in anything and nobody seemed to take much interest in Henry.'[24]

Writing many years after the experience of entering Sandhurst, Rangi Logan recalled vividly his first thoughts. 'I think it is appropriate that I speak of my feelings as the truck taking us stopped for identification at the main gates of Sandhurst. I realised that Jim [Tuhiwai] and I were the first of our race to cross that threshold.'[25]

Logan passed out from Sandhurst with an 'A Outstanding' pass.[26] At the end of the course he was invited to apply for a commission in the Grenadier Guards. While he thought seriously of applying, he first sought permission from his father. The cablegrammed response was 'No'.

By October 1940, the threat of a cross-Channel invasion had abated and the men of 28 (Maori) Battalion turned towards inter-unit sport and continued training, including route marches every second day. Extracurricular activities included a rugby game between a Welsh XV and a Maori team. The Welsh team won 12-3.

On 29 November the news arrived that the battalion would be moving to a warmer climate. While no destination was given, all bets were on Egypt.

Chapter 5

GREECE: THE FIRST TEST

The entry in the battalion's War Diary for Friday, 29 November 1940, reads as follows: 'The 28 (Maori) Battalion is to mobilise for overseas service (tropical climate) under supervision of the Aldershot Command by 0001 hours this day.'[1]

After months of shadow boxing, the battalion was finally on its way to the Middle East to join the First Echelon. Preparations for the redeployment began in earnest. Just over two weeks later, on 16 December, an advance party of two officers and 69 other ranks left for Egypt to prepare the reception for the battalion when it arrived.

In spite of the intense activity, time was found to celebrate what for most was their first white Christmas. The Battalion Diary records, 'the Christmas feast that the boys had on this day was comparable with the best ever had in NZ.'[2]

Perhaps the realisation that the time of comparative luxury was nearly over added impetus to the celebration. J. F. Cody, the Official Historian, noted that, 'Ration Ordinances prohibited the killing of meat of any kind except by authority . . .'[3] The presence in the neighbourhood of an agricultural college and the fact that all hangi were well stocked with pork indicates that this was one set of ordinances surely doomed to failure.

With festivities over, the battalion for the second time in its short life packed for a lengthy sea voyage and on the evening of 3 January 1941 it finally farewelled the Surrey countryside it had come to know so well. After entraining at Farnham, the battalion travelled all night across England, arriving at Liverpool the following morning.

As the snow fell, the Maori detrained and embarked on the troopship *Athlone Castle*. Dittmer had preceded his men and on his arrival at Liverpool docks he found two large barrels of mutton-bird (titi) addressed to the battalion. The barrels were in the open with nothing else near them. Without hesitation, Dittmer had the barrels appropriated and loaded onto the *Athlone Castle*. Shortly after boarding was completed, the *Athlone Castle* made for Belfast. Warrant Officer Les Burke noted dryly, 'the powers must have known something . . . because within three hours of leaving, the Fritz bombed the docks and played hell generally . . .'[4]

After eight months of preparation for war the battalion, under the ever-watchful eyes of Dittmer and his Regimental Sergeant, Major Wood, felt more than ready to face the enemy. Graded by the British as 'fit for war' they had a confidence in themselves, in their knowledge of weapons and minor tactics, and the ability to respond to challenging situations with innovative and unorthodox solutions.

Cody observed that the unit had now reached the stage when it realised the necessity for discipline of a high order.[5] Colonel Leonard W. Thornton in a report compiled after the war, noted 'that the properly disciplined soldier is one who possesses a clear sense of purpose, who has self confidence and confidence in his leaders and comrades . . .'[6] Clearly 12 months of intensive training and exercises had brought the battalion to this stage of preparedness.

D Deck was allotted to the battalion for training. Shipboard routine and regular training were quickly mastered with emphasis on route-marching and bayonet training. In addition weapons training and lectures in what to expect in Egypt were covered. Prior to the battalion's departure from Farnham, Dittmer had ordered that of the two pairs of boots issued to each soldier the hob nails were to be removed from one pair, so that the soldiers could continue their route-march training on board the *Athlone Castle*.

Each of the senior officers was allocated a specialist subject to lecture the soldiers. Rangi Logan was given the subject of aerial photography, a subject that he had studied at Sandhurst.

The *Athlone Castle* was one of 20 ships in the convoy which was accompanied initially by escort ships which reduced in number the further the convoy got from port. The direct route from England to Egypt via the Mediterranean was so dangerous that the convoy had to head south to Cape Town and approach Egypt from the relatively more secure route of the Indian Ocean.

As the convoy swung far out into the Atlantic, a severe bout of influenza struck the men and it took about a week for most to shrug it off. However, as the ships steamed southwards, the climate warmed and very soon both influenza and greatcoats were discarded.

On 25 January 1941, the convoy reached Sierra Leone, where for the second time the Maori soldiers made their acquaintance with canoe-loads of native traders.

They were also reminded of the infernal heat and mosquitoes. Burke wrote that it is 'no wonder they call it the "white-man's graveyard". There wasn't a breath of fresh air in the harbour and the temperature was 121° in the shade.'[7]

The stench of the mangrove swamps assaulted their nostrils. At night no one was allowed to sleep on the deck. One way to ward off the intolerable heat was to sip gin and tonic but the mosquitoes were more difficult to cope with. The convoy's departure from Sierra Leone four days later was greeted with great relief by all the troops.

As the convoy steamed further south, the Maori looked forward with some trepidation to the port visit to Cape Town. Would they be locked out of the city? Would they be allowed to go ashore under the same strict supervision as during the first visit? Neither was to occur for this time Brigadier Hargest sought advice from the authorities on what restrictions would be placed on the Maori. Their response was prompt and to the point. They would treat the 28 (Maori) Battalion 'in exactly the same manner as any other British soldiers.'

Burke described this happier occasion: 'We had a great time,' he wrote, and 'the whole of the troops had leave every day and what a whoopee time we had. The Cape people sure gave us the freedom of the city for 4 days.'[8]

The battalion's War Diary simply noted, 'Cape Town: leave 1500-2359'.[9] On their last night in town, the Maori were hosted at a civic function by the Coloureds (people of non-African origin such as Indians) of Cape Town.

The function was enjoyed so much that when the *Athlone Castle* weighed anchor the following day, three Maori failed to report back to the ship and were left stranded in Cape Town. They were later picked up by military police and rejoined the battalion in Egypt months later.

After an uneventful voyage up the east coast of the African continent, the *Athlone Castle* berthed at Tewfik Harbour at the entrance to the Suez Canal. Cody reported that the Maori were unprepared for the sights and sounds of the Middle East when they stepped ashore from the tenders which had ferried them from the ship. Sights such as that of 'indescribably filthy children and adults dressed in what looked like dirty white nightshirts . . . fighting like mad dogs when a coin was thrown among them . . .' shocked even the most hardened Maori.[10]

Tom Worral, a signaller with the battalion, clearly recalls the arrival. He described the amazement and disgust of the assembling soldiers as one Egyptian, in full view of everyone, pulled down his trousers and squatted.[11] 'There was much derision,' he wrote, 'as cries of "you pokokohua" pierced the air after the men recovered from the disbelief of what they had just seen.'[12]

After a six-hour journey by train, the troops arrived at Helwan. This sprawling, tented camp, interspersed with semi-permanent buildings, housing mess facilities, toilet blocks and administration centres, was to become the Maori base camp for the duration of the Greece, Crete and desert campaigns. The Maori were picked up at the station by trucks provided and driven by men of 27 (MG) Battalion and delivered to their own camp site some 5 km from Helwan.

By the early hours of 5 March 1941, the men were finally able to get to sleep. They had arrived and looked forward to reuniting with their comrades of the First Echelon who had been in the Middle East for over a year. What they did not know was that already the first units of the New Zealand Division had left Helwan for Amiriya, near Alexandria. They were in transit ready to sail for Greece.[13]

The following day the battalion undertook the first of its toughening-up route marches. Those undertaken during the voyage from England had helped toughen the feet but no amount of deck marching can ever prepare men properly for desert route marches. The first march covered 9 km. The battalion War Diary entry for 5 March 1941, merely noted 'first experience over sands'.[14] The hot, searing heat and the soft sand were a hellish combination. However, Dittmer was determined to toughen his men for battle. This was the pattern followed by the battalion over the next few days.

Even during times of tough energy-sapping training the Maori sense of humour and a penchant for the ridiculous was never far from the surface.

Captain Tiwi Love, later to become the battalion's first Maori Commanding Officer, was involved in one such incident. Love was at the time Officer Commanding Headquarters Company ('The Odds and Sods'). Rangi Logan described Love as 'a big man, not tall, of average height, but otherwise solid and compact.'[15] In Palmerston North the men very quickly nicknamed him 'the Bull'. The moment he opened his mouth, you knew why. He roared.

The Bull's Company Sergeant Major was his cousin, Warrant Officer Ben Ropata. Ropata, himself a big man, was well known in Wellington rugby circles. He recounted the following incident to Logan.

Love was leading his company on one of the numerous route marches undertaken during the first two weeks at Helwan. They had been marching for some time on this particular march when a voice from the ranks piped up: 'Captain Love?'

'Whaat?' roared the Bull.

'Fuck yer!' came the voice from the ranks.

The Bull stopped as if he had run into a stone wall. Charging out to the side of the column, and turning on the marching men, he roared, 'Headquarters Company Haalt!'

The company halted. 'Who said that?'

Significant pause.

'Step out the man who said that.'

No one moved.

'We will not move until the culprit owns up!'

Still no one moved.

Pacing up and down the halted column, glaring at the men, he turned to Ben Ropata, 'Sergeant-Major, find that man.'

It could only happen in the Maori Battalion. Being a cousin seemed to give Ben the licence to respond in a way that would not be tolerated anywhere else. His reply came back: 'Find him your bloody self. He was talking to you, not me.'

The poor old Bull was flabbergasted. As he stood silently thinking, no doubt, of some suitable rejoinder, suddenly there was a movement in the ranks. Joe Broughton of the Sigs Platoon marching just behind the Bull stepped forward.

'You, Broughton?' He roared eyeball to eyeball with Broughton.

'Yes, Sir. You said step out the man who said that; so here I am ready to take my punishment.'

'You're lying, Broughton,' he roared.

Now everyone knew it could not have been Broughton who had been marching the whole time just a few places behind Love, whereas the voice came from well back in the column. Moreover, Broughton had a soft high-pitched voice; not at all like the voice everyone had heard.

'Don't lie to me, Broughton,' he yelled once again.

'No, Sir, you said step out the culprit so here I am.'

'You're lying, Broughton,' said the Bull. He paced backwards and forwards along the column, glaring at the men, finally coming to a halt in front of Broughton. 'Get back into line.'

Broughton stepped back.

Glancing once more at the column of sweaty faces, black and non-commital, he let out one more bellow: 'Headquarters Company . . . Quick maaarch.' And once more they were on their way.

By 11 March 1941, just seven days after arriving in the Middle East the soldiers were ready for more ambitious exercises. The battalion took part in practising the advance manoeuvres as part of the 5 (NZ) Brigade group. At night the battalion practised forming for a night attack.

Time, however, was running out. Already the advance units of the division had embarked at Alexandria for Piraeus, the port of Athens. While the men of the 28 (Maori) Battalion had not been told officially of their next destination, there were sufficient rumours to give a good indication that they would soon be going to Greece.

In the meantime training continued at a frenetic pace. The arrival of the

4th Reinforcement Draft saw the battalion's numbers swelled by an additional 300 men. Even when not fighting, an infantry battalion suffers casualties through sickness. Once the wastage through sickness had been replaced, the surplus men were formed into an extra company under the command of Captain Fred Baker.

The new arrivals, including Charlie Shelford, who had been left behind in detention in New Zealand when the battalion had departed in May 1940, were quickly made welcome. Their training progressed at an extraordinary pace, largely through the determined efforts of their new comrades-in-arms.

Just over a fortnight after their arrival in the Middle East the Maori were once more on their way. This time they were to move to the transit camp of Amiriya, near Alexandria. Before leaving Helwan, Dittmer was faced with the difficult task of selecting those men who were to form the 'Left Out of Battle' (LOB) group. These were the men who were to remain in the base camp area. On the basis of approximately one company per infantry-battalion, the LOBs' tasks were to provide the nucleus for the buildup of a new battalion should the parent organisation be destroyed in battle, to protect the base area and, if required, to provide immediate reinforcements.

On 18 March, the battalion entrained for the transit camp at Amiriya, where their training continued. They were also issued with their tropical kit for the forthcoming campaign, which included 'Bombay Bloomers' and pith helmets. This kit was to have replaced the battledress that the soldiers had been used to.

Brigadier Clifton, in his book *The Happy Hunted*, has some interesting views on this form of dress. He describes the bloomers as 'frightful turned-up shorts'. He adds, 'Despite instructions to hand in battledress, all Kiwis wore it, packing the tropical gear, except the helmet. Only place for the confounded thing was on the head – hence the extraordinary spectacle of . . . New Zealand troops disembarking at Piraeus in battledress and pith helmets.'[16]

Clifton made another pertinent point about the preparations for the Greece campaign. The move to Greece was ostensibly a secret to all except for a few senior officers and planners. However, the reality was that most people seemed to know where the New Zealanders were going.

'Anyone who was interested,' said Clifton 'knew perfectly well, including the enemy! There were Gyppo and other money changers at most dock gates, and in Amiriya, peddling drachmae notes: "Very good money – veree cheap! You need, Kiwi – in Athens!"'[17] For the first time, but certainly not for the last, Maori were exposed to the very efficient local intelligence system.

The battalion remained at Amiriya for seven days before they embarked on the transport *Cameronia* for Piraeus. They sailed on the evening of 25 March. The following morning, they were told officially that they were bound for Greece. The news came as no surprise.

Freyberg's Special Order was read to all troops. 'In the course of the next few days,' the order read, 'we may be fighting in the defence of Greece, the birthplace of culture and learning.' He warned the Maori that the German was a 'brave fighter' and exhorted them not to underestimate the difficulties that faced them.[18]

Freyberg also gave words of advice to those who were facing the ordeal of battle for the first time, 'do not be caught unprepared'. These words struck a chord with Dittmer's men for he had repeatedly reminded them to be prepared for the unexpected.

The *Cameronia* berthed at Piraeus at midday on 27 March 1941. As no unit vehicles were available the 28 (Maori) Battalion had to march the 15 km to the staging camp at Hymettus. Here they spent the remainder of the day settling in. The following day most soldiers were able to take the opportunity to visit Athens.

Earlier in the day, the Reinforcement Company left the battalion and moved to the advance base, some 20 km from Athens. Here they would be responsible for providing security to New Zealand logistic and administrative elements. They also provided work parties to unload ships in the port.

A day later, on 29 March 1941, after a very brief stay, the Maori began the long journey to the north of Greece where they would be taking up their defence positions. While the men travelled by train the unit vehicles were driven the 500 km to the battle area.

The Olympus Pass was the battalion's destination. Detraining at the town of Katerini, the soldiers were able to gain a short respite before moving to their defence area protecting the entrance to the Olympus Pass.

From their positions, the Maori 'had a clear view of the highway but the foreground was thick with prickles and wild pears and cut by many high-banked streams.'[19] It was clear that once the enemy was able to close on the Maori positions they would then be able to infiltrate the broken terrain and thick undergrowth to attack the Maori positions.

The expected German attack on Greece occurred on 6 April 1941. By now the Maori soldiers had fully utilised the four days available to thoroughly prepare their positions. The rifle companies had developed weapon pits, erected wire entanglement around their positions and had distributed considerable quantities of ammunition to every position. Having done much to prepare themselves the Maori 'in spite of wind, rain and snow' were 'growing still fitter and becoming more conscious of the impending engagement.'[20]

By 9 April, the signs of the impending clash were growing. Salonika, which had been attacked by the Germans that day, was only 65 km to the north-east across the gulf. The billowing columns of smoke from the oil fires could be clearly seen. 4 and 6 New Zealand Brigades holding defence positions north of the pass were withdrawing. Refugees in large numbers also began to stream through the pass heading south to safety.

Over the next few days, while the Maori awaited the German onslaught, adjustments were still being made to their positions. In this period, 'B Company prepared three different positions, D Company had two days to prepare its final position and C Company had only one.'[21]

Cody observed that the soldiers seemed to accept these moves philosophically. They had become used to such moves during training in England.[22] Once the final adjustments had been made the Battalion was strung out over a 6 km area. Immediately north of the battalion's position lay the Mavroneri River. To the north-east the main highway debouched out of the pass and headed in the same direction towards Katerini. To the south-west rose Mount Brusti. To the south, rising very rapidly to its peak of 900 m, was Mount Olympus.

The War Diary entry for 15 April 1941 simply reads, 'This is the day which we first made contact with the enemy.'[23] Two men were wounded as a result of enemy artillery and mortar fire. The North Aucklanders of A Company were the first to engage the enemy. With the support of a platoon of heavy machine guns from 27(MG) Battalion, the Ngapuhi engaged a column of enemy vehicles approaching the pass from the direction of Katerini. The Germans were forced to debus. No serious attempt was made to force the New Zealand positions although there were obvious signs that the Germans were reconnoitring the approaches to the battalion positions.

War Diaries, particularly those with entries covering periods of action, are an interesting instrument of history. In an infantry battalion, the diaries are maintained and kept up to date by the Intelligence Officer and his Intelligence Section. Preferably, entries are made as events occur. Often, however, the 'heat' of battle will preclude the accurate and regular recording of events. In these cases, summaries of actions are written up when time permits. This may, in fact, occur some days after the events.

Sometimes, as in Crete, particularly when the Battalion Headquarters is not immediately involved in the battle, events may be recorded as they occur. This was the case, at least in the early stages of the battle, as the Germans closed up in the Maori positions on 16 April 1941. The diary noted, 'The enemy was early on the job this day.'[24]

Heavy mist and drizzle during most of the day, cloaked the movement of the Germans' advance units. It was not until 3 p.m. that, 'the Germans who could be seen approaching A Company were engaged with all available arms.'[25]

Unfortunately, the heavy machine guns of 27(MG) Battalion had been withdrawn from the forward positions in preparation for a planned withdrawal that night. Nevertheless, the volume of fire from rifles and bren guns forced the enemy to move westwards along the Mavroneri River gorge to try to outflank the battalion's position.

The Germans had decided to throw the force of Battle Group 1 of 2 Panzer Division against the New Zealanders holding the pass. The fierce resistance they encountered was unexpected. When it was clear that they were not going to 'bounce' the New Zealanders out of their defence positions, the Germans began to try to outflank the heavily defended positions.

On the Maori front, after failing to close with the Ngapuhi, the Germans moved further west and ran headlong into the Te Arawa and Mataatua positions of B Company where they received similar punishment. Continuing to probe further westwards, the Germans next ran into D Company's positions.

Major Dyer, the Officer Commanding D Company, had his hands full as he attempted to hold off the Germans and, at the same time, prepare for that night's withdrawal. One third of his company at a time were absent from the position as they carried their heavy gear up the hill to Battalion Headquarters. It was during this time of vulnerability that the Germans massed for the attack on D Company.

The German approach along the Mavroneri gorge was observed by D Company scouts who had been positioned in the gorge to provide early warning of an attack. The scouts were led by Corporal Jack Tainui. Tainui watched nervously as the Germans approached the forming-up place for their attack on his company. Running aggressively and using the cover of the rocks to best advantage, the Germans closed in.

Tainui shot and killed the first German, then another, and watched as he went down onto his knees to crawl away. He said later that in the heat of the moment he had felt tempted to finish the wounded German off. Perhaps realising his own vulnerability and the fact that he had just killed another man might have delayed his trigger finger. Anyway, he had second thoughts and thinking 'You poor devil. I can't do it,' allowed him to crawl away. Ironically, as he fought back into the company position he killed another German.[26]

In spite of Tainui's gallant efforts, the pressure continued to build. Shortly after he had returned to his position and reported a large buildup of enemy in the gorge, the attack began.

'In the fading light they scrambled out below 16 Platoon, D Company to deliver the most determined attack in the fighting about Olympus Pass.'[27] The attack was mounted by two companies of the II/2 Infantry Regiment. Firing their submachine guns and hurling grenades, the Germans trampled the wire entanglement in their first assault. After a temporary setback they attacked once more and succeeded in overrunning the forward pits, killing three Maori in the process.

Corporal Harry Taituha commanded the section which bore the brunt of the German attack. Before the battle, he had asked to be relieved of his duties as the Orderly Room Sergeant and dropped rank to corporal just so that he could be where the action was and to be with the 'boys'. By now badly wounded, he took cover behind a tree and gave the remainder of his section covering fire. It was his 'determined stand that permitted his section to pull back. He kept shooting until the butt of his rifle was blown off and he himself so seriously wounded that he was left for dead.'[28]

Private Ropata, of Wairoa, also refused to retreat under the weight of the German attack. He remained at his post, and 'fought on until he was mortally wounded.'[29]

As dusk gathered over the desperate struggle, the enemy Battalion Commander was forced to withdraw his men back across the Mavroneri River. The battle report of 2 Infantry Regiment noted that although the attacking Germans had knocked out several Maori machine gun positions, the volume of fire remained undiminished. Against this determined stand the Germans had little option but to call off the action. The report also paid tribute to the Maoris' excellent use of camouflage and their fire discipline.[30]

28 (Maori) Battalion had entered the battle for Olympus Pass untested, untried but eager to get to grips with the Germans. They had been together for over 15 months. The majority of the officers and non-commissioned officers had been together for nearly 17 months. They emerged from the pandemonium and chaos of the battle bloodied but unbowed.

The actions of 16 Platoon, D Company, were an affirmation of the battalion's skill at arms. It also confirmed their confidence in their capacity to withstand a determined German onslaught.

Dyer was proud of the efforts of his company. They had come through their first action magnificently. The 'Ngati walkabouts' of D Company more than rose to the occasion.

Immediately after the war, he recorded his admiration for the way the men of D Company responded to the test of battle. He wrote of 'Karetu, who killed at close quarters with his bren gun; Joe Hiroti and Carroll, the tommy gunners who went looking for more; Tom Hawea and Murphy, the mortar men who refused to be afraid; Fowler, the runner boy who was very frightened and yet very brave; Tapuke the battalion clerk, who appeared in our midst "Just come down to be with the boys, Sir".'[31]

But the last word of this battle is left to Jack Tainui. As the crescendo of the fire fight was at its height, Tainui, 'his rifle slung over his shoulder . . . grinning broadly', walked up to Dyer and said: "16 Platoon seems to be having a tough time, Sir . . . I'll go down and give them a hand?" Whereupon he went down to join the fight.

' "Bonnie Lad!" exclaims Dyer. "Who but a Highlander or a Maori goes so gladly to the fight.?" '

Their ordeal, however, was only beginning. Plans for the battalion's withdrawal from the pass were set for that night. Preliminary movement of heavier equipment had taken place during the day. Colonel Dittmer was, however, becoming concerned about the safety of two isolated detachments of men holding positions on the western flank of the battalion's defence position.

Lieutenant Ruihi Pene and his platoon from B Company had been deployed about 5 km to the west, to keep an eye on tracks leading into the village of Skotina. This group had been reinforced later on 16 April 1941, by another platoon under the command of Lieutenant H. Te O. Reedy, of C Company. Another detachment of 20 men under the command of Second-Lieutenant George Te Kuru was occupying a security position between the men at Skotina and the battalion's left flank.

Dittmer sent Regimental Sergeant Major Wood and a guide, Private Hoko of Rotorua, to try to reach the Skotina platoons.

Battalion Headquarters was not sure whether the isolated detachments had been involved in the attack which had been mounted against D Company.

Wood was told to give orders to the two platoons that they were to move at last light, to try to rendezvous with the withdrawing battalion on the pass road. For the Skotina men this meant a precipitous climb directly up Mount Olympus, over terrain that they had been unable to reconnoitre in detail.

Meanwhile, it had been planned that mules would carry the heavy packs of the men in the main body of the withdrawal over the mountain. When the time for the withdrawal arrived, neither the mules nor their handlers could be found. A withdrawal by night, under threat of enemy action, is arguably one of the most difficult phases of war. A withdrawal over mountainous terrain is even more difficult and with heavy packs the operation becomes extremely hazardous.

When darkness fell, the withdrawal began. Battalion Headquarters and C Company led the way to the first rendezvous point. Here they awaited the arrival of the remaining companies. The order of march was to be D and A companies followed by B Company, which was given responsibility for providing the rearguard for the move. From the beginning the withdrawal was complicated by driving rain and strong winds which made the tracks slippery and movement very difficult.

D Company, which had beaten off the German attack, was delayed for nearly an hour as it tried to locate a missing section. When all efforts had been exhausted in trying to locate Corporal Wipiti and his section, the company moved on up the hill to the rendezvous point.

The men moved up the mountainside, 'each man with his hand on the shoulder of the man in front.' Suddenly, the air was rent with the cry of one of the withdrawing men: 'E, Wipiti! Hoki mai?' (Oh, Wipiti, come back).[32]

As midnight passed, Dittmer knew that urgent action needed to be taken if the battalion was to escape the Germans' encirclement. He decided to take one of the many tracks available that would put the battalion well to the rear of the main gorge. He realised that if the battalion descended into the main gorge too early they could be caught.

The withdrawal that night remains clearly in the memories of those who took part. It has been described as a 'terrible nightmare'. 'In single file and for hours and hours the men of the battalion trudged across these miles of rugged, mountainous countryside with their backs bent under the heavy loads that they were asked to carry.'[33]

The successful withdrawal from Mount Olympus was the payoff for Dittmer's exacting schedule of physical and mental discipline. For the survivors, the march made 'perhaps, a more lasting impression on the minds of those who faced the ordeal than any subsequent experience of war.'[34]

Even in the midst of his own desperate tiredness, Dittmer realised that time had probably run out for the battalion. The New Zealand Engineers had set up a series of demolition charges along the critical sections of the pass to blow up bridges and narrow sections. The demolition of these would not only severely impede the Germans' progress but would also severely hinder the progress of withdrawing troops. To speed up the movement, Dittmer reluctantly ordered the dumping of heavy packs.

At 3.30 a.m. on 17 April 1941, the leading elements of the battalion reached the head of the pass just as the Engineers were about to blow the final demolition. As McClymont records in the offical history of the Greece campaign, 'It had been a very close call, for at 3 a.m. Brigadier Hargest had reluctantly decided that if the Maoris did not appear within the next half hour their transport would be withdrawn and the road blown.'[35]

The battalion was ferried back to the alpine village of Ay Dhimitrios where they went into temporary defence positions. Remarkably, Lieutenant George Te Kuru and his detachment of 20 men had made contact and were able to withdraw with B Company. The fate of Wood and the two Skotina platoons was not known for a short time. Their arrival at the road-head soon after the last elements of B Company was greeted with excitement. They had undergone an even more gruelling experience than the rest of the battalion.

Wood has written of the experience as 'unmitigated hell'. The conditions were intensely dark with visibility absolutely zero. They were unable to use their compasses because of the twisting and turning nature of the tracks used. They were unable to see the stars for help in determining direction.[36] Lieutenant Ruihi Pene describes the enormous difficulties encountered by the withdrawing troops. On one occasion they had no option but to climb straight upwards. 'We climbed this precipice packs and all by grabbing and clutching at trees and branches and hauling ourselves up foot by foot.'[37] Pene did not think that any of them would ever forget that night as long as they lived.

The losses sustained by the battalion in this initial phase of the Greece campaign were 4 killed in action and 18 missing. Corporal Harry Taituha was one of the four reported killed. In fact, he recovered sufficiently from his serious wounds to make an attempt to rejoin the battalion. He was captured a week after being wounded and he spent two years as a prisoner of war before being repatriated in 1943 to New Zealand.

Corporal Wipiti and his section who had been left behind had evaded the Germans for a week. As they tried to rejoin the unit, they were captured by the Germans and became prisoners of war.

The battalion's War Diary laconically notes for this phase of the campaign that the battalion had been involved in a five-hour tramp and that it arrived 'some hours late at the Pass rd'.[38]

For the next few days the battalion took up a number of hastily prepared and just as hastily abandoned positions as part of the overall Allied withdrawal southwards. On 22 April, the Greek armies to the north had capitulated to the Germans and now the mission of British troops was to evacuate the country. Dittmer had received orders that 5 (NZ) Brigade would begin moving south to the embarkation port. All movement was to be carried out at night.

On 24 April, 28 (Maori) Battalion arrived at its pre-embarkation site, near Marathon. At 9 p.m. that evening they arrived at Porto Rafti and boarded the transports.

Chapter 6

BATTLE FOR CRETE: COUNTER-ATTACK AT MALEME AIRFIELD

Dawn of Anzac Day 1941 saw the overcrowded SS *Glengyle* heading for Suda Harbour on the northern coast of the island of Crete. The men of 28 (Maori) Battalion, who had boarded the ship in the early hours of that morning, had gratefully accepted the food and hot cocoa provided and then collapsed where space could be found. For the previous nine days, since the sharp engagement at Olympus, they had been on the run. In the last days before embarkation they had been forced to hide by day and move by night.

The security and cocooning comfort of the ship gave the Maori soldiers the much-needed respite from their desperate tiredness. The spectre of death or capture, which had haunted them for the past days, lifted as the *Glengyle* left the coast of the embarkation port far to the rear.

In their moment of immediate relief many temporarily forgot the high price their battalion had paid for the abortive defence of Greece. Ten of their comrades, killed in action, would have to make a long and unfamiliar journey home to the spirit underworld via Cape Reinga in the far north of New Zealand. Eighty-three men, principally from the Reinforcement Company, had been stranded at Kalamata and were ordered to surrender. A further 11 men, wounded in action, were also made prisoners.

Among the many men left behind to go into captivity were six officers. Among these were Lieutenant Hemi Wiremu and Sir Apirana Ngata's own son, Lieutenant Henare Ngata. When the orders for the evacuation had reached them they had made their way to Kalamata Beach to await the return of the troop ships evacuating soldiers to Crete. Their wait was in vain.

Hemi Wiremu's worst moments during his four years of captivity occurred when he was captured. 'It was a Sunday morning – I remember I woke up about 5 a.m., we were near the beach and I looked up and on the surrounding hills there were German tanks sitting looking down on us.'[1]

This shy young man from Kaitaia in the far north of New Zealand had always loved the army and had been a sergeant in the Territorial Force prior to the war. After his release from Germany at the end of the war he went to England, met a British woman, married after only six weeks and settled for the rest of his life in England.

Henare Kohere Ngata was born at Waiomatatini on 19 December 1917. At the outbreak of war in 1939 he was employed together with Charles Bennett as an announcer by the National Broadcasting Service. He was captured by the Germans on 29 April 1941 and remained in POW camps for the duration of the war.

The only officer from the Reinforcement Company to escape capture by the Germans was Captain Fred Baker. Some mystery seems to surround how Captain Baker managed to arrive at the embarkation point without his troops who were all subsequently captured. Moreover, he arrived in Crete complete with his bed-roll. Rangi Logan recalled asking Baker 'how he managed to escape while the rest of his command were captured.' After the war, Baker made a point of giving Logan a detailed account of how he had evaded capture. He told Logan that he had been on a reconnaissance task when the situation in Athens deteriorated to such an extent that he decided to make his way independently to the nearest embarkation port.[2]

The battalion had sailed without Captain Tiwi Love and 40 men of Headquarters Company who had remained behind, through lack of space, to await rescue at a later date.

Fortunately, they successfully embarked two nights later and rejoined the battalion on Crete. Another 40 men managed to escape Greece by a variety of methods and made their way back to Egypt.[3]

In spite of these losses of more than 150 men, the battalion, with over 600 men, was still an effective fighting force. More importantly the Maori still carried the bulk of their weapons. At Porto Rafti, the embarkation port, they had been told by embarkation authorities to dump everything except arms. Corporal Ned Nathan of A Company remembers Colonel Dittmer countermanding these instructions and ordering the men to hold onto their equipment.[4]

Again, at Suda Bay, the Maori were told to leave their automatic weapons at the quayside. Again they demurred. Some days later when 5 (NZ) Brigade Headquarters called for a return of tools, automatics and other equipment held by each of its battalions, the 28 (Maori) Battalion 'disclosed its untold wealth to a brigadier almost bereft of military necessities.'[5]

While the men took every opportunity to rest, their efforts were disturbed by several attacks from German aircraft. Nathan recalled that after a while they became used to the strafing and bombing runs and would lie on the deck calculating the trajectory of fire and bombing patterns, taking evasive action when necessary.[6] The Maori also took the opportunity to vent their spleen by letting rip with every weapon they possessed whenever German aircraft came near.

The *Glengyle* arrived in Suda Bay on the afternoon of Anzac Day. From crowded decks the Maori soldiers saw a scene of rolling farmland against a backdrop of massive mountains whose tops were covered in snow.

From his logbook of the campaign, Signalman (later Second-Lieutenant) H. Mohi noted 'left Greece 4.30 a.m. Disembarked at Crete. Bombed while crossing, two raiders brought down.'[7] The battalion disembarked into ferries and on landing were greeted by a scene of total confusion.

The principal aim of the Port Authorities was to clear the arriving troops from the overcrowded dock area as quickly as possible and Dittmer and his officers assembled the battalion. The men presented a bedraggled picture. Many wore an ill-assortment of clothing and footwear. Some had webbing, others had none. A number still possessed helmets. All, however, possessed weapons. B Company still had in its possession a three-inch mortar which it had picked up on the Olympus Pass Road and had smuggled aboard the *Glengyle*.

When the men were finally assembled, the battalion began the march to its allocated defence positions near the town of Platanias. Mohi notes from his log that, 'they marched late this evening then slept on the side of the road.' Without blankets, the first night spent under Cretan stars was very chilly.

The next day the battalion moved through the olive groves to its assigned positions. The Maori task was to act as 5 (NZ) Brigade Reserve. The brigade task was to protect the airfield of Maleme, in western Crete. After some days around Aghya, the battalion was deployed to its final defensive location along the Platanias River.

On 3 May 1941, the War Diary noted the move to the new position around Platanias. The Maori were to defend an area between Platanias River and the village itself. Dittmer's orders from Brigadier Hargest were clear. The Maori were to contribute to the defence of Maleme Airfield some five miles west of Platanias, prevent the eastwards move of the Germans should they capture it, and oppose any German landing on the beaches which flanked 28 (Maori) Battalion's northern defences.

Dittmer decided to give to D Company the task of holding the Maleme -Platanias road. Major Dyer placed his troops astride the Platanias River. The Official Historian described the river as being 'about a chain wide and varied in depth from a few inches to waist deep, while its valley was half a mile wide at the coastal strip.'[8]

Headquarters Company, under command of Captain Tiwi Love, was given the task of holding the northern sector facing the beaches. This sector included the village of Platanias. Headquarters Company was normally the composite company combining the infantry battalion's support platoons, such as Signals and Mortars and its administrative elements.

Even though its soldiers were trained firstly as infantrymen they were not expected to fight as an infantry group. However, with the need to cover as much ground as possible, Dittmer decided to reorganise Love's company. Three infantry platoons were formed. The Signals and Mortar platoons, however, remained organised to carry out their specialist functions.

The remaining three rifle companies and Battalion Headquarters were located on the high ground to the south of Headquarters and D Companies' positions. C and B Companies overlooked the Platanias River defending enemy approaches from the west and south. Ngapuhi of A Company held the rear flank looking eastwards.

When Freyberg's force had arrived on Crete some eight days earlier, it was faced with a scarcity of nearly every major weapon and critical items of equipment. It was clear that a reallocation of essential items had to be made so that units would have a better chance of carrying out their tasks.

When 5 (NZ) Brigade called for an inventory of the Maori weapons and equipment, it was equally clear that 28 (Maori) Battalion would have to part with some of its stock of weapons. Mohi describes the anguish of having to part with his precious signals equipment. He tells how 'miraculously we salvaged most of our signals equipment in the retreat from Greece because each man had clung tenaciously to whatever piece of equipment he brought out as though his life depended on it.'[9]

On arrival in Crete with their precious equipment, the Maori signallers shared Mohi's sentiments at having to part with their equipment. He recorded 'it nearly broke our hearts there to have the brigade take most of the gear away for their own use, as communication equipment was so scarce on the island.'[10]

Major Dyer observed that the Maori will not readily part with a weapon he has fought with.[11] For this reason the redistribution of eight of the battalion's 27 Bren guns to other units was not taken kindly. Dyer argued that the Maori took the redistribution exercise badly and remembered it in later days when ordered to hand in weapons.

After preparing their trenches, which was a difficult task as there were few entrenching tools, the men were given the opportunity to see the sights. They watched the Cretans, most of whom were women, going about their everyday tasks, seemingly oblivious to the disaster which was about to strike. In many ways they reminded Mohi and his friends of their own wives and families when working their kumara patches at home many thousands of miles away. Often the comment was made: 'Rite tonu hoki ki a tatou wahine, ki nga kuia o te kainga . . .'[12]

Even though the Maori knew that an attack on Crete was likely, they began to relax and enjoy the interlude. The War Diary records that on 8 May 1942 officers attended a cocktail party in Canea hosted by General Freyberg in honour of the Greek officers on the island.

The following day 10 percent of the men were given leave. They took the opportunity to visit Platanias and Canea. In Canea there were a number of restaurants and hotels. While the variety of food was limited, the range of drinks available more than compensated, and many soldiers returned to their defensive positions much the worse for wear.

Only in the most dire circumstances is the firm grip of military discipline relaxed. As the organisation and training restored order and confidence, so was the inexorable military justice exercised. In the days prior to the German attack, two general courts-martial were convened and held in the battalion area.

However, the semblance of orderly routine was merely a gloss on the desperate state of the forces in Crete.

General Freyberg had been asked by General Wavell to take command of the forces on Crete. Freyberg had at his disposal a motley force of about 28 000 men. The original British garrison comprised one infantry brigade and 11 badly equipped and largely untrained Greek battalions. To add to his difficulties, Freyberg had to contend with Greek demands to raise a Cretan militia. The reality of the situation was that Freyberg had few enough arms and equipment for his own troops. To try to raise, arm and equip another force was impossible.

The Greeks' willingness to help knew no bounds. Even the convicts on the island wanted to make a contribution to the war effort. Freyberg received a letter from them telling him that 'every soul in Crete is looking with confidence towards you'.[13] The note of confidence in the allies finished with the convicts' offer of putting themselves wholeheartedly 'under any service, dangerous or not, provided that the cause of our allied effort is fulfilled.'

Against this background the 28 (Maori) Battalion went on with the task of preparing themselves for the German attack. Rifle sections, platoons and companies practised repelling attacks by land, sea and air. They practised their counter-attack drills. Officers and non-commissioned officers traversed every inch of their respective sectors. A regular and vigorous night patrol programme was put in place.

In the first two weeks of May 1941, the German Air Force concentrated its attack on shipping and the port and dock activities in Suda Bay, with the clear intent of disrupting the Allied buildup for the defence of the island.

From 13 May, the Germans increased the intensity and scale of attack including, for extra attention, the airfield of Maleme. On this day, Colonel Dittmer briefed his officers to expect an attack in the next four or five days. It was anticipated that leading waves of aircraft would carry out strafing and bombing of selected areas. The next wave of aircraft would then drop paratroopers into the cleared areas.

The Maori response to these tactics was specific. Soldiers were to engage the Germans from their weapon pits. Once an enemy ground attack looked to be developing, 'then the Maori were expected to leave the protection of their pits to deal with the threat. Should any formal advance be carried out, 'all tommy guns would go with the first wave so as to permit riflemen to get in with the bayonet.'[14]

Over the next few days the intensity of the air attacks increased. On 16 May, Dittmer ordered a full alert. Each man was to have his full quota of 100 rounds of ammunition and to remain in his weapon pit during the day.

During the course of the enemy buildup, few New Zealanders appreciated the value of intelligence being fed to General Freyberg. Earlier in the war the British had successfully broken the German code and they were able to intercept General Student's orders to his field commanders about the proposed operation 'Mercury' – the attack on Crete.

Hitler's Directive 28, which launched operation 'Mercury', was released on 25 April 1941 – the same day the New Zealanders were evacuated from Greece. Because 'the operation was novel, the country unfamiliar, the pressure intense', the Germans had a race against time to prepare for the operation.[15]

Ronald Lewin, in his book *Ultra Goes to War*, wrote that the 'signals flashed to and fro'.[16] Overall command of the operation was in the hands of General Lohr, Commander 4 Luftflotte. The actual air assault was the responsibility of General Student, and his 7th Air Division, whose gliders and parachutists were to form the bridge head on Crete. The assault force would comprise 10000 elite airborne troops.

Because of its crucial importance to overall allied strategy, the British took great care not to let too many people know of their breakthrough with Ultra, the codeword given the method by which the British had intercepted and decoded German radio transmissions.

The detailed contents of Student's intentions and capability were known to Churchill by 29 April 1941. He gave instructions to the head of the Ultra Team to keep Freyberg fully informed. However, Lewin noted that as 'Freyberg was not indoctrinated . . . [he] could not be fed "pure" Ultra.'[17]

Lewin suggested that Field Marshall Wavell, when he visited Crete shortly before the attack, would have 'probably established its complete authenticity by some continuing fiction.'[18] Thus, even if he was not aware of the details of Ultra, Freyberg was aware that the intelligence he was receiving was of the highest quality.

Dittmer's alert orders of 13 and 16 May 1941 coincided with the quality of intelligence Freyberg would have received. General Student had planned to launch his attack on 15 May, but because of delays it was postponed first to the 17th and then to the 20th.

The entry in the Maori War Diary for 20 May reads simply: 'This was the day of the invasion.'[19]

As Major Dyer pointed out, the German invasion was not unexpected, as their overall plans were known. However, when it did come 'it was spectacular and alarming'.[20] Mohi's record noted, 'our eyes and minds boggled with what we saw and heard.'[21]

What the Maori saw and heard was a demonstration of the awesome might of the German's first and last large-scale airborne invasion. Early in the morning, they had watched Messerschmitts attacking Maleme Airfield. The Messerschmitts had not restricted their attacks on Maleme, but also roved up and down the Maleme-Canea road.

When the German aerial assault began it caught many of the Maori outside their pits. Dyer records that most of his men had just completed breakfast when the invasion began. 'Messerschmitt planes continued roaring over our position at treetop height strafing the whole area.'[22]

Private Monty Wikiriwhi, watching the softening-up process from the Intelligence Sections Observation Post, recorded the observation that, 'It appears the invasion is about to be launched. The area round the aerodrome is being most intensely bombed and machine-gunned by countless planes of all kinds.'[23]

Freyberg was having breakfast when the invasion began. When he saw the gliders overhead and the parachutists dropping, 'He was very calm, and simply remarked: "They're dead on time." So it was clear that he had an impeccable source of intelligence.'[24]

During this initial period of chaos the Maori occupied their battle positions. Major Dyer and some of his Maori soldiers waded in waist-deep water across the Platanias River to get to their positions. Dyer's position was up a poplar tree near the Platanias Bridge.

Dyer's graphic description of the impending airborne assault is gripping. 'We looked spellbound,' he wrote, 'at the great wall of three-engined planes. The fighters and bombers had left the skies to the formation upon formation of troop carriers and troop carrying gliders.'[25]

From his vantage point, Mohi described how 'the air was filled with billowing parachutes of various colours, white, red, green and brown.'[26] As the parachutes collapsed on landing, they added a technicolour streak to the countryside.

Remarkably, the Maori were little more than spectators of the ferocious fighting during the first day of the invasion. The brunt of the assault was taken by the men defending Maleme Airfield.

While no enemy dropped in the Maori areas, some glider-borne troops were noticed concentrating on the beach about half a mile west of D Company's position. A platoon from C Company, commanded by Lieutenant Reedy and a platoon from D Company, commanded by Lieutenant Rangi Logan, were sent to deal with the enemy.

The Maori's first action in Crete was a total success. Reedy and Logan, and their men, stalked the small German force under harassing fire from German aircraft. In spite of the several planes circling and attempting to frustrate their mission, the Maori killed seven or eight German paratroopers. Two officers and eight other ranks surrendered.

Late in the afternoon of 20 May 1941, the fate of Maleme Airfield hung in the balance. Dittmer was ordered to send a company to Maleme to reinforce 22 Battalion. B Company was ordered to stand by to move. Captain Rangi Royal and B Company of Te Arawa left the battalion position at 7 p.m. Because he did not know the previously reconnoitred route to Maleme, Royal took the bold and hazardous decision to march directly down the main road.

As the company reached the area of 23 Battalion just short of the village of Pirgos, the Maori encountered and overcame scattered resistance from a number of Germans who, practising subterfuge, yelled out they wanted to surrender. At the same time a grenade was thrown, which wounded two Maori. Cody, the Official Historian, observed that the grenade thrown by a German paratrooper 'was the signal for, as far as is known, the first use of the bayonet by New Zealand troops in the war.'[27]

With a savage cry of 'surrender be fucked', the Maori charged. Twenty-four Germans were killed. A further eight Germans were killed before the Maori finally reached 23 Battalion's position. There they picked up a guide. Their route to Maleme was a circuitous one.

Skirting south between 23 and 21 Battalion, they were then led north to the village of Pirgos, where headquarters of 22 Battalion was sited. After finding that 22 Battalion was about to withdraw, the Maori returned across country, and then onto the road where they met the commanding officer of 22 Battalion. He told them to return to Platanias.

When Royal and his men of the Lake Districts and the Bay of Plenty region finally reached their own home base, they had completed an 11-hour odyssey. In darkness and over unfamiliar terrain, they had confronted Hitler's airborne elite. They had killed over 40 Germans. They were exhausted, yet exultant.

As the second day of the battle for Crete dawned the position was critical, as 21, 22 and 23 Battalions fought for control of Maleme; 28 (Maori) Battalion waited to play its role.

In the early afternoon of 21 May 1941, Captain Baker of D Company was ordered to take a force to survey the beach and clear the area of suspected German Headquarters elements. While they were engaged in this mission the Germans struck a direct blow at 28 (Maori) Battalion's positions.[28]

The low-flying Junkers disgorged from their bowels 5 and 6 companies of 2 Parachute Regiment. These men had been targeted onto the Pirgos-Platanias road. Twelve loads fell along the Platanias River. They faced D Company.

It was D Company that had received the full brunt of the German's attack at Olympus Pass. It was now D Company that had to deal with the first direct threat to the Maori defence positions.

As at Olympus Pass, the company was not at full strength. Captain Baker and his force (Lieutenant Logan's Platoon less one section and half of Sergeant Smith's Platoon) were still carrying out their clearing patrol. Logan said that he never saw Captain Baker at any time during the operation to clear towards the beach. Logan's task was to patrol towards Maleme; to clear the beach area of enemy and then return to base.[29]

Those paratroopers who lay in the open were shot where they lay. In some cases the Maori ran out among the paratroopers to deal with them.

Dyer described how the Germans, who had landed on top of the ridge overlooking D Company's position, were dealt with. 'Te Hou's soldiers took in the situation. Their enemy were on top of them among vines and corn and must be engaged.'[30] Fully aware of the danger of leaving their weapon pits, the Bren gunners 'abandoning their beautiful positions . . . carried their guns out into the open.' Dyer wrote of Mat Bailey, a small excitable man who 'ran through the vines like a madman using his gun as a tommy gun till he went down riddled with German bullets.' His fellow Bren gunner, John Whare, a tall, serious man, in a more methodical fashion destroyed the Germans nearest him before he too went down riddled with bullets.

Rangi Logan album

The first draft to leave Hastings, 1939.

Harris album

Tai Tokerau trainees shortly after their first parade, December 1939

Kate Walker album

Young men of Ngati Porou before leaving Ruatoria for camp. Moananui Akiwa Ngarimu (second left) would go on to win a VC, but at the expense of his life.

Harris album

A Company trainees, Trentham 1939. Centre front is Captain Harding Leaf.

Burke album

'For king and country': in camp at the Palmerston North showgrounds, February 1940.

Harris album

Harris album

Lieutenant-Colonel Dittmer at the farewell parade, Palmerston North, 1May 1940.

A group of soldiers on board the *Aquitania*.

Burke album

Two soldiers catch up on home news in England, October 1940.

Alexander Turnbull Library

Evacuation from Crete, 1941.

Rangi Logan album

5th Reinforcements march in to replace casualties from Greece and Crete, June 1941.

Rangi Logan album

Reta Keiha (left) with Rangi Logan.

Norman Perry album

A captured supply of white material being sewn into snowsuits for 28 (Maori) Battalion patrols, Orsogna.

Alexander Turnbull Library

Above: The 28 Maori Battalion ski school, Syria.

Left: Tiwi Love, appointed the Battalion's first Maori Commanding Officer in May 1942.

Below: Captured enemy equipment at Gazala, 20 December 1941.

Love album

Alexander Turnbull Library

Members of the Battalion training in Egypt.

Alexander Turnbull Library

Alexander Turnbull Library

Christmas dinner at Nofila, 1942.

Alexander Turnbull Library

The 28 (Maori) Battalion rugby team, winners of the Freyberg Cup, Tripoli, 1943.

Second-Lieutenant George Te Kuru led a counter-attack with the half platoon reserve. After clearing the open area before the ridge, he crossed the stream with his small force and moved up the ridge to engage the enemy. He was shot in the chest with a burst from an automatic weapon and 'went down as a good soldier wishes to go, with his face to the enemy at the head of his men.'[31]

For the remainder of the afternoon, the Maori cleared their positions of the threat from small pockets of paratroopers. As the evening of the second day of the battle drew near, it was clear that the loss of Maleme could be redressed only by a counter-attack. It was decided to commit 28 (Maori) Battalion and 20 Battalion to this task.

The Maori positions around Platanias were to be the launching pad for the counter-attack. Using the tar-sealed road to Maleme as the centre line, 20 Battalion would be between the road and the sea. Its task would be to clear the airfield. 28 (Maori) Battalion would attack between the road and south to a low ridge parallel to the road. Its task was to capture Point 107, the high ground dominating the airfield. The start was set for 1 a.m.

The Official Historian, Cody, noted that 28 (Maori) Battalion was considered the sole unit in 5 (NZ) Brigade fresh enough for the operation. In reality at least half of the battalion had fought hard all of that day. The men had had little to eat and no sleep.

The counter-attack by 20 Battalion and 28 (Maori) Battalion was a saga of missed opportunities. The operation got off to a bad start when 20 Battalion arrived late at the start line because of the late arrival of the Australian relief battalion which had been allocated to replace 20 Battalion in reserve.

Major Jim Burrows, who was in command of 20 Battalion had earlier sought permission from Division to leave before the Australians arrived to relieve him. This permission was denied because of the fear of a seaborne attack. Nevertheless, when the Australians did arrive, Burrows was able to gain permission to start the move westwards towards the start line for the counter-attack, with two of his rifle companies. The remaining companies were to join him as they were freed.[32]

It was not until approximately 3.30 a.m. that the counter-attack got under way with 20 Battalion's two rifle companies north of the road, which was the axis for the attack, and 28 (Maori) Battalion south of the road.

As the attack proceeded westwards towards Maleme Airfield, both battalions met pockets of enemy armed with machine guns. It was thought that these were remnants of the action of the previous day. As the New Zealanders neared the outskirts of Pirgos the advance elements found stiffening resistance and the enemy resistance became stronger and the volume of machine gun fire greater.

More significantly, the New Zealanders faced the prospect of fighting for the airfield in daylight. They had hoped that sufficient progress would have been made by night to enable the infantry to reach and hold the objective by daylight. Burrows' right-hand company, D Company, had managed to bypass major opposition and reach the perimeter of the airfield at approximately 7. 30 a.m. However, the remainder of Burrows' soldiers were bogged down in the outskirts of Pirgos.

By now Burrows had decided that to continue further to achieve the objective was not possible, so he gave orders for his remaining troops to swing in behind 28 (Maori) Battalion. Meanwhile, in the desperate fighting in and around Pirgos, the Maori had attempted to swing left around Pirgos. Here they were halted by heavy machine gun fire.

By midday of 22 May 1941, it became clear that the counter-attack could not proceed any further without fresh troops. Attempts to involve 21, 22 and 23 Battalions, who were holding the ground to the south-east of Maleme, were to little avail. The enemy had regained the initiative and had begun operations to recover lost ground.

28 (Maori) Battalion, together with its sister battalions, had been fought to a standstill. Along with the other battalions, most heavily engaged, the Maori had fought a number of fierce hand-to-hand battles with the Germans. Dan Davin, the Official Historian for this campaign, observed that, while all battalions had been involved in a similar manner, neither he 'the historian scanning the reports long after the event they describe nor the survivors to whom those events are still a vivid memory would hesitate to award to the Maoris of 28 Battalion the credit for the most conspicuous élan and valour shown on that hard day.'[33]

Chapter 7

FORTY-SECOND STREET AND WITHDRAWAL FROM CRETE

The failure to recapture the strategic Maleme Airfield spelt the beginning of the end of the Crete campaign. The attack had cost the Maoris a further 100 men killed, wounded or missing. Ngapuhi (A Company) mourned the loss of their two senior officers. Few wanted to believe that the legendary Captain Harding Leaf had gone to join his tipuna (ancestors).

His reputation was such that none of his men believed that he could be killed. Immediately after the war, Dyer wrote: 'But what of Harding? Was he killed, was he captured, was he in the hills? We never heard, not while in Crete, but we became convinced that he was dead. Already rumour was at work. The legendary leader was still abroad, leading a charge here, staying a retreat there; a burly jolly figure always in the middle of a fight.'[1]

Forty years on, Harding's fellow tribesman and at times co-conspirator Ned Nathan confirmed Harding's death.[2] It was he who found his friend and mentor surrounded in death by three of his kinsmen of the North. He had died as he lived, leading from the front, thus ensuring that those who followed would have an easier path to tread. He died in action, a true son of Tumatauenga, just five months short of his 51st birthday.

On the morning of 23 May 1941, the desperately tired men of 28 (Maori) Battalion waded back across the Platanias River and climbed up to occupy their old positions. Just as they had climbed out of the river, Lieutenant Tiwha Bennett of Headquarters Company was shot in the backside by a stray shot. 'Still able to walk, he had to put up with the jibes of his fellow officers – "shot in the arse, he must have been running away".' While much humour was derived from this incident, Logan noted wryly that his fellow officers for a brief moment had ignored the fact that they were all running away.[3]

They had been moving and fighting for over 36 hours. The Maori main body had been able to break off contact with the pursuing Germans, largely through the magnificent fighting and skilful manoeuvring of Major Dyer's rearguard.

In the meantime, while the battalion was involved in the abortive counter-attack at Maleme, its old positions east of the Platanias River were lightly held by Lieutenant Stewart and one platoon holding B

Company lines, Lieutenant Keiha and two platoons in C Company's area and Lieutenant Porter with 'a dozen walking wounded from 23 Battalion's Regimental Aid Post' manning A Company's area.[4]

These men were reinforced by Captain Fred Baker and a mixed force. Baker had been separated from the battalion after undertaking a house-clearing operation along the beach line. Rangi Logan strongly questions the Official Historian's account of Baker's separation. 'How could Baker have been separated if he had been with us? According to his account, he reached 7 Field Engineers about midnight. Why didn't he join us who were already there?'[5] Finally, Logan recalls, 'we joined the 28 Bn at dawn the next morning when we saw them going past. How come he didn't see them too?'

In the early hours of 23 May, as the Maori Battalion was withdrawing from Maleme to Platanias, Baker received orders from the Brigade Commander, Brigadier Hargest, to occupy the key D Company position. In particular he was ordered to hold the bridge over the Platanias River.

In the interim period, more German troops had parachuted into the area. An estimated 200 Germans were now in command of the bridge. Thus Baker's task to occupy now became one of capturing and retaking the bridge from fresh, well-armed airborne troops.

Baker's force comprised 60 stragglers from 20 Battalion, some engineers and a collection of Maori soldiers. When the attack got underway it very quickly became bogged down. The enemy, using captured Bofors, were too strong. Baker's force was pinned down and could get no closer than 500 metres. In his own words: 'I had about 90 men and no supporting fire except machine guns. The mortars were too much for us and eventually I had to call it off.'[6]

The operation might have failed but it achieved two important objectives. It distracted the Germans' attention from the returning battalion and, more importantly, it 'discouraged further movement forward for the rest of the day.'[7]

The short respite at Platanias gave Dittmer time to try to organise his battalion. Many men had been left behind. Some too seriously wounded to be carried were left with medical orderlies. A forced withdrawal under enormous pressure and the constant harassment of enemy pursuit meant, inevitably, that those wounded and unable to walk might have to be left to be captured by the enemy.

The Maori had lost their Regimental Aid Post at an early stage of the counter-attack. Captain Mules, the Regimental Medical Officer, had himself become a casualty and had joined the walking wounded. Maori wounded were carried to the Regimental Aid Posts of 21 and 23 Battalions.

As there was insufficient transport to carry those seriously wounded to evacuation points, it was clear that their capture was inevitable.

Cody noted that the 'doctors and orderlies of both units elected to stay behind with their wounded.'[8] They were, he continued, 'unselfish and gallant gentlemen'. Brigadier Jim Burrows, then Commanding Officer of 20 Battalion, recounted how, when passing 23 Battalion's Regimental Aid Post, he stopped to tell Ron Stewart, the Battalion Medical Officer, that the Germans could be expected in half an hour.[9] Stewart thanked him quietly and told Burrows that he understood the situation. 'He was obviously going to stay with the wounded men in his care and with him was the Battalion Padre, Bob Griffiths, who equally obviously was going to do the same.'

As Burrows pointed out, from a military point of view, their actions were quite wrong. In any case, soon after capture they would be separated from their charges. However, as he left the aid post he had no thoughts about what was right or wrong. Rather his thoughts were about 'two very gallant men whose sacrifice made us all feel very humble.'[10]

Throughout the remainder of the 23 May, the Germans probed and harassed, with mortar fire, the Maori forward positions. While theirs was largely a defensive holding operation, the Maori still had the energy and cheek to remind the Germans from time to time that they were not to be taken lightly.

A platoon of Maori was linked into the defensive positions held by 20 Battalion. Lieutenant McPhail of B Company, 20 Battalion, described how they watched the Germans approaching along the road and beach with 'something that looked like a Bofors gun and obviously digging in.'[11]

He continued: 'One of our tanks was in the courtyard of a house or blacksmith's shop but was very dubious about attacking the position, so Tui (Tiwi) Love got a Bren carrier, called for two or three Maoris and rushed the Huns. They had a heavy MG but Love mopped them up and then returned.' McPhail reckoned the Maori effort 'a good show'.

The German's persistent pressure forced the New Zealanders to continue the withdrawal further east to Galatas. As darkness fell, the 28 (Maori) Battalion left their positions and marched the 11 km back to their new positions. Although they were very tired, the Maori discipline never wavered.

The sight of the Maori Battalion moving particularly impressed Sergeant Basil Borthwick. He wrote: 'There seemed a never-ending column of them and they marched without sound apart from the creak of their equipment and the stamp of their feet . . . We felt better,' he added, 'after seeing them.'[12]

Captain Baker wrote, 'We moved back that night and had no actual fighting for two days although he (the Germans) gave us a very warm time with aerial dive bombing and machine gunning.'[13] Before leaving Platanias, the Maori had broken into an ammunition and rations dump to replenish stocks. While they had sufficient food, there was little water. Baker observed further that for 'two days I have mentioned we had hardly a drop of water.'

By now the battalion's strength was reduced by some 140 killed, wounded or missing. The Germans continued to exert pressure. At Galatas they attempted to breach the New Zealand lines and ran up against 23 Battalion. Galatas was lost and regained at the point of the bayonet. Although Maori were not directly involved, they were placed on standby to prepare for a counter-attack.

At 9 p.m. on 25 May, Maori began to move forward to prepare to push the Germans back. Meanwhile, at a brigade conference to discuss the matter not all were keen to commit the 28 (Maori) Battalion. Kippenberger wrote that Brigadier Inglis, Commander 4 Brigade, 'was anxious to use the Maoris in a night attack and recover the ground.' He continued 'it was clear to all of us that if this was not feasible Crete was lost.'[14]

Dittmer knew the task was a difficult one. Perhaps it was impossible. The terrain was unfamiliar, it was dark, there was no good start-line and there were numerous obstacles. Olive trees and vineyards would hamper progress and make control more difficult.

Nevertheless, when pressed Dittmer was willing to commit his remaining 400 troops. 'I'll give it a go' was his response to Inglis' question, 'Can you do it, George?' The arrival of Colonel Gentry, the Division's Senior Staff Officer, brought an air of calmness and objectivity to what was clearly a desperate situation. When Inglis explained the position, Gentry's response was an emphatic 'No!' 'The Maoris were our last fresh battalion,' he said. 'If used now we would not be able to hold a line tomorrow.'[15]

The Maori returned to their positions somewhat relieved they did not have to launch a major attack that night. The following morning, 26 May, the strafing and bombing continued. Being well dug in, the Maori 'escaped lightly though nerves were getting ragged under the constant punishment, the lack of sleep and scanty meals.'[16]

During the morning, a German patrol tested A Company's defences and got more than it bargained for. Captain Baker, now Officer Commanding A Company, reported how the Germans 'got right up to us and then we caught him on all sides and gave him a hell of a surprise. The ones who got away did not stop till they were at least a quarter of a mile away.'[17] In retaliation, the Germans hammered the A Company position with mortars.

That night, further orders were received to continue the withdrawal. This time the route for the Maori lay across country then back onto the main road east of Canea. Just before dawn, on 27 May 1941, the Maori arrived at a road known as 42nd Street. The street was a sunken road south-east of Canea and 3 km west of Suda Bay, the Maori arrival point in Crete just over four weeks earlier.

By now the channels of communication between Freyberg and his commanders had almost completely broken down. So much so that the Maori thought they were in a reserve position. In fact they were in a frontline position and there was no one between them and the rapidly closing Germans.

Dittmer realised the true position, after a short sharp exchange with General Weston, General-in-Charge of the Royal Marines. Weston had had an earlier encounter with the Maori which left him less than happy about New Zealand soldiers, especially Maori soldiers. He had been 'captured' on the afternoon of 26 May 1941 and was nearly shot by Lieutenant Charles Bennett and Private Monty Wikiriwhi when he was slow in identifying himself.

When he told Dittmer that the Maori should already be withdrawing south with the rest of the New Zealanders, Dittmer said that they would remain where they were until they were ordered to move by their brigadier. Weston left no doubt thinking that the Maoris' officers were equally as stubborn and unwilling to recognise sense as their soldiers.

Dittmer reorganised his men into a defensive position east of 42nd Street. A, B and C Companies occupied forward positions. D Company, Battalion Headquarters, and Headquarters Company were positioned further east in reserve. The New Zealanders agreed that if the 'unexpected happened and the enemy got too close they would open fire and charge.'[18] Given the tiredness of the troops and their state of morale it was the only course open. It was a bold yet necessary decision.

The 2/7th Australian Battalion, which was on the right flank of the New Zealanders, sent a runner to find out what the New Zealanders intended to do in the event of an enemy breakthrough. When told of the New Zealanders' decision, the Australians 'quickly returned with a further message to the effect that the Australians would be pleased to be associated in any such action.'[19]

The approaching Germans were about to test that resolve. 1st Battalion of the 141 Mountain Regiment was close at hand. Moving confidently they expected to cut the road west of Suda Bay. The battalion's War Diary

71

records that at '1020 hours 1/141 Mountain Regiment while moving through thick olive grove 2.5km west of Suda, visibility nil, came up against English mines unexpectedly . . . Four desperate enemy counterattacks were driven off.'[20]

What the Mountain Regiment's War Diary fails to acknowledge was that they were decimated, not by English mines, but by Maori, New Zealand and Australian bayonets. The action began with a series of explosions and a cloud of smoke from the vicinity of a nearby Engineers stores dump. As the terrain to the front of the Maori positions was covered with olive trees, the first direct evidence of the German presence was 'a ragged rattle of small arms fire, surprisingly close, and bullets mowing the leaves of trees.'[21]

By now the Maori had donned webbing and had fixed bayonets. Safety catches were released and the men took up positions ready to move.

It is very difficult to get a clear picture of those few seconds and early minutes of the bayonet charge. What is certain is that the Maori led it. What is more interesting is that it was not a pell-mell rush to get at the enemy. Rather it was a deliberate sequence of moves which culminated in the systematic destruction of a unit of Germany's finest airborne troops.

In the early stages B Company led by Captain Royal 'brandishing a bamboo walking pole like a taiaha in one hand and a revolver in the other and C Company following Captain Scott got into 42nd Street first and deployed across the battalion frontage.'[22] The enemy went to ground when confronted by a yelling, advancing line of Maori. B Company took casualties. Meanwhile A Company managed to get into the line of the attack and went for the enemy.

Captain Baker recorded that A Company took up the whole of the battalion front as the attack developed. 'Jerry tried to hold us back with everything he had,' wrote Baker. 'We walked all the way,' he continued, and 'jumped into his first positions, bayoneted or tommy-gunned them, then walked on to his next line.' Section after section of the enemy were wiped out in the face of the inexorable advance of the Maori bayonet charge. Baker's men behaved as if they were on parade and after they got to the second line the Germans started to 'crack and run'.[23]

While D Company had been sent back as reserve for the attack, the Company Commander Major Dyer remained to take part in the action. Dyer wrote after the action, 'I decided to stay, sending the company back under Lieutenant Logan. I called to two of my best section leaders, Cpls J. Hemi and Governor Mathews, to stay with me.'[24]

During the attack, 'Hemi rushed a bush, from which a Hun kept firing, and bayoneted the man. He said afterwards, "I wish I had shot him. The scream was dreadful." After a few yards we came to a wide shallow ditch in which a lot of Germans lay sprawled out. Some were obviously dead; some were wounded, many were doubtful. At Maleme we had suffered casualties by sparing three German tommy-gunners. After our passing they seized up their guns and fired at our backs.'

Mathews fired at the bodies and one jumped up. After that, 'everything dead or alive was made certain of.' Dyer wrote that this incident may have contributed to the story that the Maori had killed everything when they charged.

The Maori continued to sweep the area. They chased the survivors until they themselves came under fire from the forward elements of a fresh German battalion some 1 200 metres west of 42nd Street. Major Bertrand was sent by the Commanding Officer to recall the Maori. When he caught up with them he told them the 'old man was going fair dinkum crook'.

In *Myth and Reality*, John McLeod has written that 'It has been claimed that over 100 Germans were bayoneted in this charge . . . but this total is unsubstantiated.'[25] Bertrand, however, stated in his report of the action, that he counted over 100 bodies with bayonet wounds in front of the Maori.[26] This was to be the last of several major bayonet charges the Maori were to take part in on Crete. Later in other theatres they were to continue to use the bayonet as their special weapon.

Colonel Leonard Thornton was commissioned soon after the war to put together a report on the New Zealand infantryman in battle. The report was commissioned in response to a series of questions posed by the American War Historian Colonel S.L.A. Marshall who had just completed a book on the American soldier in battle.

In his report, Colonel Thornton wrote that the bayonet was a weapon of great moral victory. 'Even a resolute enemy will rarely fight to the last when faced with a determined bayonet assault.' Although its use in battle would be infrequent and fleeting 'its threatened use in battle remains a moral weapon of the first order.' Thornton's report goes on to observe that with highly civilised troops there would be an instinctive reluctance to use the bayonet in 'cold blood'.[27]

The Maori instinctive battle heritage was for close-quarter fighting. In Dyer's view, 'in all ages, the close-quarter fighting yields pride of place to no man, and has a feeling akin to contempt for arms that throw missiles at a distance, or for units which will not close with the enemy.'[28] Dyer supported Thornton's assertion that highly civilised troops do not make good close-quarter infantry. Good infantry, wrote Dyer, 'are born and reared close to the soil . . . Gurka, Highlander, Pole, Maori, etc.'

For all that, even the Maori at times needed to be encouraged to use the cold steel. Dyer recalled an incident on Crete, during an assault on a German, who was sheltering inside the top of a filled-in well. When Dyer and the Maori accompanying him reached the well, the German feigned death. Dyer said to the Maori, 'Bayonet him.' The Maori responded by thrusting his bayonet through the German, but turned his head away as he did it – apparently unable to bear the sight.[29]

In moments of crisis, the enthusiasm of even a few men for the bayonet will inspire the remainder to follow. 'The use of the bayonet in such a moment will frequently be decisive.'[30] The Maori use of the bayonet in Crete was decisive. The Germans lost 120 killed and 14 wounded in the attack. Unsettled by the unexpected sting in the tail of the withdrawing New Zealanders, they did not disturb the Maori for the remainder of that day (27 May).

In the absence of any orders from division, Commander, 5 (NZ) Brigade, gave orders to continue the withdrawal that night. At last light the Maori began the final move to the embarkation port of Sfakia.

To reach it they faced a daunting obstacle – the White Mountain. The road from Suda Bay to Sfakia 'traversed steep hills and went through mountain passes to one of the most inhospitable coastlines imaginable.'[31] The road rose to a height of 800 m where it dipped down into the Plain of Askifou and then dropped steeply and sharply down to the sea. 'In all some 40 miles over some of the roughest country on earth.'

By just after midnight on 27-28 May 1941, the battalion had reached the road junction heading south. Here A and B Companies were dropped off to deny the junction to pursuing German troops until 9 p.m. on 28 May. For the next two days and nights the Maori struggled over the arduous White Mountain. They were hampered in their march by the hundreds of stragglers also making their way to Sfakia. The road was littered with abandoned equipment. Major Bertrand, the battalion's second-in-command, 'whose military religion was march discipline', took over the 'stragglers platoon'. These were men who had dropped off the main body. There were not many of them and under Bertrand's command they continued to march.

Bertrand recalled that, so far as he knew, the Maori did not lose a single man on this 'most arduous and nerve straining move . . . though many of the men must have been very near breaking-point at times . . . Everybody was determined to ensure that no Maori was left behind.'[32] He continually harassed his officers about the troops' march discipline. Logan was so fed-up with his continuous barrage that he had to move away from him.[33]

The walking wounded had left 42nd Street under the command of

Captain Baker and made their own way ahead of the main body to Sfakia. They rejoined the battalion just before the final climb over the White Mountain.

Meanwhile, A and B Companies, which had dropped off to provide rearguard protection, had been attacked and forced to withdraw. The way in which they evacuated their wounded exemplifies their determination to save them. B Company had two stretcher cases, one seriously wounded and a number of walking wounded. Four men were each detailed to a stretcher. They were ordered to throw away their rifles. As the company withdrew under pressure, the two stretcher cases, Privates 'Darkie' Hall and Ted Leonard, pleaded to be left behind so that they would not hamper their comrades' chances of escape. 'The bearers' answer was to throw away the stretchers and carry the patients.'[34] They succeeded, against all odds, in reaching Sfakia.

On the morning of 29 May 1941 the two rearguard companies caught up and rejoined the battalion. When finally the Maori reached the embarkation point they received the news that the 28 (Maori) Battalion allotment for immediate embarkation was 230 all ranks. Dittmer's protests were overruled. The final order was that Major Dyer, five officers and 144 all ranks were to be left behind to protect Force Headquarters. They would be evacuated later with Force Headquarters.

D Company soldiers all volunteered to stay behind to make room for others. Rangi Logan, Jack Tainui and Governor Mathews decided to make the selection. According to Logan it was decided, 'Married to go, no argument, and then single ones. Tainui and Mathews were both married but they, point-blank, refused to go.' Logan had to order his batman, Jim Koti, to go. 'He performed and cried but I insisted. I gave him my watch (mother's present), a valuable Rolex Oyster, and my money belt.'[35]

Ngati Porou, which had come through the recent fighting relatively unscathed, was required to provide one officer and 50 other ranks for the rearguard. In all, ten Bren guns and 11 tommy guns, in addition to rifles, were allocated to the men of 'Suicide' Company. At dusk on 30 May 1941, the 'Goers' moved off to the embarkation beach. The 'Stayers' sat quietly mulling over their fate.

The task of the Embarkation Authority was an extremely onerous one. Hundreds of leaderless stragglers were camped on the beach, all waiting to try to get off. Late in the afternoon of the next day, the Maori were required to form an inner cordon to hold off the stragglers.

In the meantime they had met a small band of Maori walking wounded. Dyer's orders, however, were strict and definite that not more than 150 Maoris (i.e. the nominated men of Suicide Company) were to embark. In Dyer's own words, 'we heartlessly turned back a party of 13 Maoris who appeared.'[36] It must have been a traumatic experience for them to turn back their men. Fortunately Brigadier Hargest came upon the wounded Maori and marched them up to Dyer and ordered him to attach them to his strength.

At midnight, the remaining Maori were called to embark. At 2 a.m. on 1 June 1941, the last man of Suicide Company left Crete.

Chapter 8

DESERT FIGHTERS

The survivors of the Crete campaign reached the sanctuary of the Middle East in early June 1941. Very quickly the men were caught up in a round of medical inspections, kit reissues and muster parades. Dittmer and his senior staff knew that the first few days in base camp at Amiriya were crucial. The men had to be handled with care. They had been fighting and withdrawing for nearly 10 weeks and many had lost relatives and close friends. The best remedy was to keep them occupied and busy.

Within days, the Maori were entrained at Alexandria for the move back to Helwan, near Cairo. Here Dittmer formally paraded the men and spoke to them of their actions in Greece and Crete. After the parade the men were given seven days' 'survivors' leave.

The majority headed for Cairo. For many, the first ports of call were the doss-houses, in the red-light districts of Cairo. Few tarried there. As Noel 'Wig' Gardiner in his book *Freyberg's Circus* observed, 'For some it was perhaps a short, sharp session, then on to some quiet, shady bar with their mates; somewhere where the soft music played and the amber stella kept on flowing till the faloose (money) ran out.'[1]

The impact of the losses sustained by the battalion did not hit home fully, until the special church parade held shortly after the men had returned from leave. Padre Harawira, the battalion padre who had shared the trials and tribulations of the Greece and Crete campaigns, spoke movingly at the church parade, held on Sunday, 15 June 1941. Remembrance of the dead and thanks for deliverance were the themes of the service.

Padre Harawira chose as his text for the sermon, 'Oh death, where is thy sting?'. Thirteen officers and 219 other ranks had been killed or captured in Greece and Crete. Of this total 71 men, including 5 officers and 66 other ranks, had given their lives. Few of the battle-hardened veterans remained untouched by the service. When the funeral hymn 'Piko Nei te Matenga' ('In solemn grief we bow our heads') was begun, many shed a tear for their departed comrades and relatives.

The campaigns in Greece and Crete had cemented bonds of kinship which already were strong before the baptism by fire. A shout of 'Tatou tatou', ('all for one and one for all') was sufficient for Maori bystanders to commit themselves, without hesitation, to the assistance of a beleaguered comrade. It was a time to relive recent events and to exorcise painful memories. It was also a time to remember, in reflection, those who had fallen and gone to join te tini me te mano (the legion of ancestors who had gone before).

Newly arrived men of the 5th Reinforcements, who had been training at Maadi Base Camp, were marched in to build up the battalion's strength. In all, 11 officers and 240 other ranks joined.

After a few weeks of base routine the veterans started to become restless and bored. A disciplinary routine order was published on 1 July 1941, which noted that 'too many men are wandering around the lines. In future such personnel will be collected and sent on a long route march if they are absent from training parades without a reasonable excuse.'[2]

For the next three months, the Maori trained for desert operations. Compass training was critical. In England, Greece and Crete navigation had been a relatively simple matter but in the desert, where there were no village signposts or, indeed, people to seek directions from, the art of compass navigation became crucial. In addition, the Maori also trained in night approaches for dawn attacks. After the defensive operations of the Greece and Crete campaigns, they looked forward to conducting offensive operations on their own terms.

The desert presented an inhospitable face to those who were about to live and fight in, on and under it for the next two years. And yet, like the jungle, once it was understood, it could also provide shelter and defence against the enemy. Cody described it as 'a land of bare stones and drifting sand, of escarpments and defiles, of low ridges and shallow depressions.'[3] It was also a land of unbearable heat during the day, and cool temperatures during the nights but above all it was a land of flies. 'They were everywhere (and) shared our meals, committed suicide in our tea and used our bodies as playgrounds for the remainder of the day,' laments an entry in the War Diary.[4]

The desert was bereft of roads, and trucks were driven on compass bearings. Armoured vehicles 'fought whirling battles in the dust and smoke and infantry were pawns on a thousand square mile chessboard.' The desert is described as 'a general's paradise of parry and thrust, where formations had no front or rear or flank and where sudden reversals of fortune could lose a battle after it had been won.'[5]

For the Maori, fighting in the desert was mainly a series of approach marches to designated objectives, principally by three-tonne lorries. As movement was conducted mainly at night, the journeys were a nightmare of jolting and twisting as the drivers tried to avoid patches of soft sand or, alternatively, piles of rock.

On arrival at the debussing points, the Maori would then prepare for the attack. After the attack they would have to consolidate their positions on the objective and dig in as quickly as possible to be ready for the inevitable counter-attack or bombardment.

The routine during daylight hours was very restricted, particularly if the Maori slit trenches were under enemy observation. Thus breakfast and dinner were taken before first light at dawn and after last light at night. Lunch was usually a snack taken in the slit trench. To ward off the unbearable heat during the day, groundsheets were erected over the slit trenches.

At night the whole area would come alive as men moved about under the protective shelter of darkness. Slit trenches were deepened, patrols aggressively patrolled no-man's land, and men took advantage of the cool temperatures to relax and catch up on rest. The one significant consideration that all desert veterans recall is that nightfall brought with it a relief from the flies.

Since Crete, there had been a number of changes in the battalion's officer and non-commissioned officer ranks. Major Bertrand was posted to New Zealand. His replacement as Battalion second-in-command was Major Dyer. At the junior level of command, many of the Greece and Crete veterans had fought their way into positions of responsibility.

The battalion was therefore an excellent mix of the experienced and the new. For a number of the 'new' young officers, it was a testing period as they came to grips with their platoons. The 'old hands' reserved final judgement on the new leaders until they had observed them under combat conditions. Trial by fire was the sole test to confirm their standing.

In early September 1941, the 28 (Maori) Battalion was moved by train to El Alamein, some 100 km west of Alexandria. From here they were loaded onto trucks and deployed into the area known as the Kaponga Box, approximately 30 km south-west of Alamein.

The purpose of this deployment was to prepare a fortress area in the Western Desert as part of the defence of the valley. Kaponga Box was a 'ten square mile semicircle of low, steep-sided ridges'[6] which was strategically located between the coast to the north on one flank and the Qattara depression on the other.

Road construction was the principal task set for the Maori. They were required to assist in the formation of a 15 km stretch of road connecting Kaponga Box and El Alamein. As the Official Historian noted, because of their inexperience in such matters, the Maori consulted with the Engineers to find out what length of road should be constructed each day.[7]

The Engineers suggested that a working party of 90 men should be able to construct up to 100 metres of road. The Maori quickly accepted the challenge and after the first day's work one company had completed a staggering 400 metres of road construction. During the period, Middle East Command decided to produce a pamphlet on road building in the desert. 'They duly arrived, watched us for a day and decided that they couldn't possibly produce a pamphlet based on our methods and results as, to use their own words, "we were mad".'[8]

In October 1941, the battalion was on the move again, this time some 130 km further west to the defensive position of Baggush. The Maori were inexperienced in large-scale moves by vehicles at night, so after the advance to Baggush there followed six weeks of intensive training in mobile operations and attack, by day and night.

Dittmer addressed his troops and emphasised 'the importance of dash, initiative and intelligence'.[9] The War Diary reported that among all ranks there was a gradual 'keying up of spirits, a certain buoyancy of feeling in expectation of action at last.'[10] On the next day 8 November 1941, the War Diary recorded that, 'Battalion bayonets were collected today and sent away to be sharpened.'[11]

In the six months since Crete, the battalion had been reorganised and strengthened and the Maori looked forward to closing with the enemy. In Greece and Crete they had been on the back foot; here in the desert they had an opportunity to call the shots. The strategic plan called for the New Zealand Division to carry out an outflanking manoeuvre across the Libyan frontier, isolating the frontier forts of Sollum and Capuzzo, and to capture the small, but strategic, German resupply port of Bardia.

In spite of the urgent preparations to ready themselves to face the enemy, the New Zealanders were not above indulging in a game of rugby on the eve of departure. In the Maori War Diary, above the entry which notes the bayonets being taken away for sharpening, is an entry describing an international rugby match between the New Zealanders and the South Africans.[12] A good percentage of the battalion attended the match, which was won by the New Zealanders.

The diary entry for same day, 8 November, observed that 'the assembled men presented a juicy target to an enemy bomber' but, the entry continued, 'jerry did not know we were having a gala day in honour of our national game.'

Three days later, the Maori left Baggush on a divisional exercise which was, in fact, the preliminary move in an 18-month-long operation to drive the enemy from North Africa. Major Dyer and the left-out-of-battle men (in total 62 from all ranks), watched as the battalion moved off towards the 5 (NZ) Brigade assembly point.

In the early hours of 23 November 1941, exactly six months after the failure of the counter-attack on the Maleme Airfield, the 28 (Maori) Battalion were again in action against the enemy. Their task was to seize the frontier post of Upper Sollum at the top of the strategic Halfaya Pass, thereby cutting off German and Italian traffic along the coast road between Sollum and Bardia.

After a vehicle approach to the objective from the south-west, the Maori debussed at Fort Musaid, some 3 km west of the objective. The attack was led by C and D Companies who 'surged through light rain in the stillness before a cold dawn' to successfully capture the barracks. Over 250 prisoners were taken with only minor losses to the Maori. The poor quality of resistance was explained when it was found that the troops belonged to 4 Italian Labour Unit, a line-of-communication unit responsible for providing work gangs.

In the daylight that followed, the Maori exuberance at mounting their successful attack was dampened with heavy casualties being sustained from enemy artillery fire. The shellfire 'on inhospitable ground caused several deaths and wounded many men.'[13] By the end of the day the Maori casualties were high – 20 dead and 34 wounded. Dittmer who had been wounded in the earlier assault was evacuated and command of the Maori devolved, temporarily, to Captain Tiwi Love.

In the confusion immediately following Dittmer's injury, Major Sutton of 8 Royal Tanks took temporary command. It has been suggested that Maori casualties 'would doubtless have been fewer had some of the Maoris restrained their high spirits and investigated their new surroundings more cautiously.'[14] Private Bill Hoko was observed riding a tracked motorbike along the escarpment in front of C Company in full view of Halfaya provoking a lot of fire from enemy heavy guns.[15]

Over the next two days the Maori prepared their positions against a counter-attack. B Company was redeployed to occupy Fort Musaid, a pile of rubble, 3 km to the west. Its role was to act as a link between 28 (Maori) Battalion, on the coast, and 23 Battalion, further west of Fort Musaid, at Fort Capuzzo. 23 Battalion had also deployed a small force into the western part of Musaid. By first light, on 26 November 1941, they were ready. Later that day a reconnaissance patrol sent to the south 'came streaking back with speed'. Their report was short, graphic and blood-curdling. 'They're coming in bloody thousands.'[16]

An enemy column, Ravenstein Group, part of 21 Panzer Division, had been ordered to attack towards Capuzzo from the south and break through to Bardia on the coast, which held much-needed ammunition, petrol and other supplies. The enemy column split into three, one column aimed directly at Musaid, another spilling around to the east and the third column moving further west to attack Capuzzo.

Captain Royal had given strict orders to the Te Arawa company not to fire until directed. The enemy's eastern column, fired upon as they neared Musaid, were forced to dismount. By accurate Bren and 2-inch mortar fire, Royal was able to hold up the enemy advance for a whole hour.

The column which advanced directly at Musaid was engaged and halted by 2-pounder anti-tank portees and artillery. As night fell, the main weight of the attack continued to fall on the eastern flank of Musaid. During the fighting, the enemy were able to move further east and slipped large numbers of vehicles through the gap between B Company at Musaid and the remainder of the 28 (Maori) Battalion at Upper Sollum.

Dawn revealed the 'vigour of the defence, particularly in front of the Maori, where seventy-six German dead were counted and seven prisoners, most of them wounded, were taken.'[17] The Maori had lost two killed, four wounded and two missing. It was a very satisfying victory against considerable odds.

The long-awaited clash with experienced German troops had taken place. For Te Arawa, utu for their losses in Greece and Crete had been extracted. Moreover, their discipline and determination under fire against a mobile German column was exemplary. Captain Love, in temporary command of the battalion, had assumed from the noise and movement at Musaid that B Company was overrun and destroyed.

Three days later, B Company was relieved at Musaid by its neighbours, 23 Battalion. On 30 November 1941, Royal and his men returned to Upper Sollum in triumph. They arrived in style, 'with a long string of cars, motor cycles, tanks and sundry other vehicles.'[18] Meanwhile, the remainder of the New Zealand Division which had been fighting for its survival further west at Tobruk was withdrawing. At Sidi Rezegh and bel Hamed it had suffered crippling losses. The Maori were ordered to redeploy to Menastir as part of 5 Brigade blocking force west of Bardia.

The main purpose of this operation was to stop supplies from Bardia reaching Afrika Korps. 5 (NZ) Brigade defences were therefore facing east towards Bardia with 28 (Maori) Battalion taking up the reserve position. In reality, the Germans were interested in getting supplies into Bardia from the west. Thus, the Maori position in reserve, facing towards Bardia in the east, had its back to the most likely German approach. Perhaps appreciating the need for all-round defence, the battalion planned its defences for a potential attack from the west.

The Germans decided to launch Geissler Advance Guard to break the blockade and force its way into Bardia from the west. In command was Lieutenant Colonel Geissler of 200 Regiment of 15 Panzer Division. Troops under his command included Headquarters of 200 Regiment, 15 Motor Cycle Battalion, a company and a half of anti-tank guns and a troop and a half of 33 Artillery Regiment.

On the morning of 3 December 1941, an enemy force of about a hundred vehicles with artillery was reported. The column approached cautiously and halted 3 km short of the Maori defensive positions on the lower slopes. Geissler's advance elements were expecting trouble from the high ground of the escarpment. They did not anticipate any trouble from the lower slopes. D Company, which faced the likely assault, held its fire. The men kept out of sight in their slit trenches and maintained excellent fire discipline. 'It was a situation of a kind the Maoris delighted in, and they kept the enemy in entire ignorance of their proximity.'[19]

The descendants of Heke and Kawiti from the North, and Ngaiterangi of Tauranga, had they been aware of their history, would have recognised that the Germans had walked into a trap, just as the British had during the wars of the North with their attack on Ruapekapeka, and just as General Cameron had during the battle for Gate Pa.[20]

The lead enemy vehicle was well past the Maori forward pits when Lieutenant Matehaere shot the officer standing on the running board of the lead vehicle. This was the signal for a murderous rain of fire to pour down onto the German column, with very heavy casualties inflicted on the forward elements. A valiant attempt by the Germans to press the attack failed and 'within an hour the enemy was in full retreat and the front was strewn with blazing vehicles.'[21]

While German casualties were heavy, enemy detachments on the right flank attempted to outflank the Maori positions. In the late afternoon, and supported by 2-pounders from 32 Battery, the Maori counter-attacked and cleared the ground with bayonets. By nightfall it was all over and the enemy had been completely routed. The Official History of the New Zealand Artillery noted that 'the gunners had given useful support, but the honours of this action clearly belonged to the Maoris.'[22]

The German report for the action noted 8 men wounded and 231 missing. Geissler Force was virtually wiped out. Maori casualties were two killed and nine wounded. The jubilant Maori could not believe their successes. In the space of 10 days the battalion had fought and won two battles. This, at a time when the rest of the division had taken a mauling at the hands of Rommel's Afrika Korps.

After this action, 5 (NZ) Brigade was ordered back to the Sollum-

Capuzzo area for regrouping. It was understandably 'a highly delighted 28 (Maori) Battalion, loaded down with trophies of the chase . . . which led the column back to its old area.'[23]

Here, Captain Love handed command of the battalion to newly promoted Lieutenant-Colonel Humphrey Dyer and marched out to hospital. Before he handed over the battalion, Love addressed the men and complimented them on their outstanding performance. He also reminded them that, as Maori prisoners of war had been well treated by the Germans following the Musaid Battle, they should reciprocate.

As Cody noted, this message was 'regarded as a piece of amiable eccentricity on the part of the CO.'[24] No one would harm a prisoner as long as he surrendered expeditiously and acted correctly.

On 10 December 1941, the Maori were on the move westwards past Menastir, the scene of their recent triumph, and on toward Gazala. 5 (NZ) Brigade was to move west towards Gazala but not get involved in serious fighting without permission.

Seventeen miles west of Tobruk, the battalions were given their tasks. 23 Battalion was to move down the main coastal road. The Maori were to move along a track on the escarpment overlooking the coast road. 22 Battalion moved further south.

The 28 (Maori) Battalion's first objective was (Point 209) Sidi Mgherreb, 'a slight rise dominated by a little hill hardly more than a pimple on the desert.'[25] It was a very strong position, protected by a minefield on its left flank and by a line of 26 anti-tank guns, interlaced with machine guns and mortars on its right.

The defenders of Point 209 had already destroyed the greater part of a British battalion. Nearby, were the remnants of a British tank regiment which would not move until the infantry had cleared the way.

The Maori method used to clear this formidable position was extremely simple, tactically unorthodox and, yet, highly dangerous. The whole battalion mounted in 'soft-skinned' trucks had charged the position. Again Ngapuhi impetuosity was to the fore. Lieutenant Ben Porter, in the vanguard, made a quick decision when enemy shells began to fall among the moving vehicles. He told his driver to 'step on it'. The speed of the column accelerated from 7 to 40 miles an hour. The Maori thundered up and into the position with A Company on one flank and B Company on the other.

Meanwhile the startled Italians, whose anti-tank weapons were still firing at where the Maoris should have debussed, were so staggered by the tactic used they stopped firing altogether. Two hundred prisoners were captured in the initial attack by B Company.

Later that day, as some A Company soldiers 'were out on a "ratting" mission to secure souvenirs, they were surprised by the sudden appearance of a couple of Ities out of a dugout – the boys fired a couple of shots above their heads and, wow! Ities seemed to come from out of the ground. No 7 Platoon collected 1 000 in all.'[26]

An astonishing total of 1 123 prisoners and a large range of war materials were captured. Maori losses were 5 killed and 11 wounded.

The captured men were from 62 Regiment of the Trente Division. Evidence of the Italians' determined resistance to earlier attacks was seen in the many dead British soldiers, lying, with bayonets fixed, near the gunlines. The Maori success was due in part to the Italians' preparations for withdrawal. However, Porter's unorthodox tactics were a major factor in explaining the Maori achievement.

Two days later and 12 km further west, the Maori were in action again. The objective was Point 181, which was a horseshoe position with its open front inviting the attacking Maori to enter. Dyer attacked in the early hours of 14 December. In little over an hour the Maori had dealt the enemy a severe blow. After beating off the counter-attacks, they held the position. A further 382 prisoners from the Parvia Division were taken. As Murphy later observed, 'the Maoris lost only three killed and 27 wounded, remarkably few in view of the thorough and skilfully laid out defences which daylight revealed.'[27]

It was during this action that Private Charlie Shelford won his award of DCM. 18 Platoon, after coming under enemy fire from its left flank and right rear, was halted. Shelford volunteered to silence the enemy behind the platoon. In spite of being wounded three times by grenade splinters, he achieved the task. In the action he attempted to use his captured Spandau, which had been damaged by an enemy grenade, and he was forced to use his own grenade to subdue the enemy. He captured 4 officers and 36 other ranks and for this action he was decorated.

Rangi Logan, who was Company Commander of D Company, was approached by Shelford's platoon commander, Second-Lieutenant Jim Matehaere, who discussed Shelford's deeds. Logan recalled that he said that 'it's worth a VC' and he and Matehaere wrote the citation. Later Logan said, 'how it came to be an immediate DCM I cannot understand. I can't believe that Jim and I changed our minds, or was it altered after it left my hands?'[28]

Daylight of 14 December also revealed three positions similar to Point 181, in an arc from west to north. The ambitious task of taking two of these obstacles was given to the Maori. Because of the complexity of the position it quickly expanded into a major operation, and the Maori were supported by 22 and 23 Battalions and a Polish Brigade, which had the additional task of pushing past 28 (Maori) Battalion's left flank and heading for Gazala. When the Polish Brigade arrived later in the afternoon they proceeded to disarm members of 18 Platoon D Company, thinking that, as they were armed with Spandaus and Lugers and wearing German greatcoats, they were German native troops!

Zero hour for the attack was 3 p.m. A Company, supported by D Company, was given the task of capturing Point 154. This they did, again using unorthodox tactics. Porter had noticed that a surrendered Italian 750 kg truck, used by the Maori as a ration truck, was never molested by the enemy. Also, as his men wore a mix of Allied and enemy clothing and carried enemy weapons, they could be mistaken as 'friendlies'.

He had his men issued with a hot meal, then ordered them to sling weapons and to straggle towards the enemy positions eating. The ruse succeeded. When the men neared the Italian positions, they formed quickly into three lines of disciplined infantry, and charged.

The rest of the battlefield was not so easily subdued. C Company were pinned down until direct artillery fire allowed them to attack. By last light, the Maori had gained their positions but losses were heavy: 10 men killed and 39 wounded. Over 200 prisoners had been captured.

The Italians had, however, not finished the battle. Dyer had just finished arranging with brigade for reserves to assist his men when he received news that an estimated 800 enemy were massing for a counter-attack on A Company.

Lieutenant Ben Porter, in racing to get back to his company, was thrown off a motorcycle and badly concussed. The Ngapuhi Company was, thus, without its commander. However, Ngapuhi spontaneously left their pits and charged the enemy. Nearly two-thirds were mowed down by the advancing enemy. While the cost was extremely high, with 58 men killed or wounded, the Ngapuhi's courageous action halted the enemy in its tracks. At dawn the following morning they had gone.

'With a vengeance the Maori were making up for the time they had spent cooling their heels at Upper Sollum,' wrote Murphy. He continued that 'first at Menastir against the Germans and now against three successive Italian divisions they were compiling an impressive list of successes.'[29]

In this action, Jack Tainui was killed. Tainui had been the first Maori in Greece to close with and kill the enemy and he had been a tower of strength in Crete. Now at Point 181, leading 17 Platoon battle he was hit in the stomach by an anti-tank shell and was mortally wounded.

As he lay dying, he called for a Bren gun and magazines. His last words were, 'Give me the gun. You load the magazines.' The men of D

Company buried him in the rocky ground where he fell. They covered his grave with his spent cartridge shells.

When the fighting was over, Lieutenant Colonel Dyer, who had been Tainui's Company Commander at Olympus Pass on 16 April 1941, and was now Commanding Officer, asked the Assault Pioneer Sergeant to make a plain cross. The words inscribed on the cross were: 'Sgt Jack Tainui – Maori Friend'.

Dyer then asked Logan, Tainui's Company Commander, for a 'good Maori' to accompany him to Tainui's grave. Logan sent Tomoana. Dyer wrote, 'I was glad of that. Tomoana had come to his own people from another battalion and had already proved himself a good soldier.' They found his grave. 'A small mound on a rocky rise, facing the rising winter sun and the long road home.'[30]

They raised a large stone at the head of the grave and set the cross. Then with small stones they enclosed the grave, the cartridges and the patch of blood where he had fallen.

Tomoana recalled how Dyer then asked to be left alone. He moved away and watched in wonderment, this lean, tall, stern Pakeha mourn the passing of a Maori soldier.[31]

Dyer wrote, 'I will not tell you what I experienced there, but I will tell you that a brave man lies at peace. He would not change it, nor would he have us weep, who passed so suddenly from strife to rest.'[32] In the stillness of the desert, both men wept.

The campaign which had begun on 18 November had by 17 December 1941 exhausted itself. The Medical Officer and Company Commanders reported that the men needed a spell. The battalion's casualties for the campaign were 78 killed or died of wounds, 151 wounded and 13 prisoners (10 of these were also wounded).

Chapter 9

SYRIA: COLONEL DYER DEPARTS

When the battalion arrived at Baggush, two days before the new year of 1942, it faced, once more, the task of rebuilding its strength. Of the 28 officers who had begun the First Libyan campaign just one month earlier, 15 were killed, wounded or captured. Over 225 other ranks had been killed, wounded or captured. After the campaigns on the Greek mainland and Crete, the battalion's 'wastage' – the technically clinical military term to describe men lost in action – had been made up by reinforcements, comprising 13 officers and 219 other ranks. Now, a further several hundred reinforcements were required to bring the battalion back up to its fighting strength of approximately 750 men.

The whole process of getting the battalion ready for action had to be repeated again. After Crete, the Maori had the luxury of six months to rebuild itself. In view of Rommel's penchant for the unexpected, no one knew how much time was available. A sense of urgency seized the New Zealanders as they hurriedly absorbed the new reinforcements, re-equipped and began the battle training needed for survival.

However heavy these problems might have rested on the minds of the senior commanders of the battalion, the men were keen to forget, for a while at least, the trauma of battle. New Year's eve was celebrated in style. Ignoring the blackout regulations, the Maori built bonfires and let off steam in the only way available to them. They fired their weapons, mortars, Verey flares and anything else they could get hold of. It was a 'blow-out' in grand style. The remarkable thing was that no one was hurt. The authorities, perhaps appreciating the need for such actions, did not pursue the matter.

In early January 1942, the Maori moved to Kabrit where they spent two months in reorganising and rebuilding the battalion. The familiar routine of training, route marching and muster parades quickly brought the men together. Soon, however, the men, and particularly the veterans, began to get bored with the familiar pattern of activities. They began, once more, to look forward to the next action.

Veterans of combat often have a view that, as they have been through the fires of hell, they know it all. From this perspective, it is perhaps understandable for them to baulk at the constant retraining inflicted on them after gruelling battles and campaigns. And yet, despite their frustrations, most realised that the development of an *esprit de corps* had to begin at a basic level. If nothing else, it helped refocus the mind and body on the skills of survival needed after lengthy periods of leave.

During this period, Lieutenant-Colonel Dittmer, who had been wounded during the battalion's first action at Upper Sollum, paid a farewell visit to the battalion. He had been taken from Sollum to the New Zealand Medical Centre, near Sidi Rezegh. On 28 November 1941, the Medical Centre had been overrun by the enemy and a thousand prisoners, including Dittmer, were 'in the bag'. During the confusion, Dittmer managed to rid himself of his badges of rank and he joined a group of other ranks.

With the help of Captain Lomas, of 4 Field Ambulance, Dittmer then engineered an escape from captivity and led a group to safety by heading deep into enemy territory and then outflanking them by heading south.[1] For his services, he was awarded the DSO and was mentioned in dispatches. On his return to New Zealand he commanded 1 Infantry Brigade Group from April 1942-August 1943.

The decision, in late February 1942, to deploy the Maori, along with the New Zealand Division, to Syria, came at a time when the men were beginning to get restless and bored with the monotony of the desert training routine. Even regular leave periods in Cairo had begun to pall. The move to Syria, to frustrate a potential German thrust down through Turkey and Syria, was warmly welcomed.

Syria was a land of stark contrast to the deserts of the Middle East. The Maori were deployed in the northern end of the Bekaa Valley, in northern Syria. They were struck, on arrival, by the severity of the Syrian winter, welcomed as they were by the last blizzard of the season. It burst on them before they could begin work on their defensive positions. Heavy rain and gales blew down ill-secured tents and, to compound their miseries, 10 cm of snow fell.

By the end of March, however, the weather began to clear and the Maori got on with the job of building a barrier against the expected invasion from the north. The hard work and the ample rations helped toughen the men and build up their confidence. The revitalised desert veterans were keen to get to grips with the enemy once more.

As their morale rose, the Maori were challenged and defeated in two areas of activity in which they thought they had no peers. Their reputation for scrounging took a severe drubbing. The local hill tribesmen, to whom thieving was more a 'religion than a pastime', taught the Maori how to do it without getting caught.[2] After the Arabs had removed a large quantity of gelignite from a truck in which a number of Maori were sleeping, all agreed that drastic action was necessary.

The Maori set up grenade booby traps under movable, attractive items which proved to be a more successful deterrent than Lieutentant-Colonel Dyer's efforts to persuade the locals. The company's property was safe, however, only after nine of Dyer's officers were invited to dine with the Muktar, the village chieftain.

The dinner invitation from the Muktar provided the Maori officers with an opportunity to excel in an area that they thought they were very good at: their ability to consume large amounts of food. However, in this area also, the Maori were doomed to failure.

As the nine officers sat down to the dinner they were suitably impressed with the 'starters' of coffee and pheasants, followed by the complete hindquarters of a sheep. But then came the side of a sheep, garnished with entrails. When most of the officers had eaten enough, they found the feast was only half over. The courses were each accompanied by huge dishes of rice, dishes of boiled greens, bread, honey, curd and olives. This was all topped off with garlic salad and two cups of tea. Finally the meal ended with more bread and coffee.

All but one of the Maori failed to impress the Muktar and he expressed his disappointment at their poor showing. The secret of the exercise, however, was to try small portions of everything. The Maori had fallen victim to trying to eat as much as possible of the dishes that they preferred.

Rangi Logan was the only Maori who succeeded in mastering the protocol. Because he could speak French, Logan had been appointed Maori Liaison Officer to the village. He had worked with the Muktar's nephew, who took great delight in teaching Logan the correct protocol: he had tasted all the dishes, even those he did not fancy. He had also taken the opportunity on occasions to catch the Muktar's eye, bow towards him, and issue an appropriate belch of satisfaction indicating that the meal was excellent.

The Muktar was so impressed with Logan's performance that he called together his followers and publicly announced that from that time on Logan was to be treated as his son, which meant that the villagers were not to steal anything from D Company's lines. His announcement did not, however, mean that the rest of the battalion's lines were similarly out of bounds. For these actions in Syria, Logan's men always claimed that Logan was the rightful holder of the title of the 'Muktar' – a title which Lieutenant-Colonel Peta Awatere later claimed as his.[3]

The Battalion Commander, Humphrey Dyer, saw the issue from another point of view. He observed that some 'of our officers were invited to a feast by the Muktar. Our younger officers enjoyed taking delicacies out of the huge bowl and even tried to emulate the approved Arab technique, of which I believe loud belching to show one's approval or satisfaction formed a part. Rangi [presumably Logan], our stage artist, excelled himself.'[4]

While in Syria, Divisional Headquarters asked Lieutenant-Colonel Dyer to submit a confidential report on the enemy equipment still in the possession of 28 (Maori) Battalion.

'Lists of astonishing length and variety were turned in by the companies, with the transport driver heading the field. Their trucks were rolling arsenals, for they remembered Capuzzo, and had taken steps to deal with such a situation should it again become necessary.'[5]

Dyer believed that captured enemy weapons were an essential part of the battalion's arsenal, particularly anti-tank weapons and long-range mortars.

Following the battle for Sollum in late November-early December 1941, Brigade Headquarters requested the handing-in of captured enemy weapons. Dyer 'felt justified in retaining a selection of anti-tank weapons and long-range mortars, for it was common knowledge that many men had been scooped up by enemy tanks because of the absence of anti-tank weapons.'[6] Accordingly, he handed over two truckloads of weapons and the rest became a secret reserve.

Early in 1942, before the move to Syria, Dyer was once more asked to hand in any captured weapons in the possession of 28 (Maori) Battalion. Again, Dyer failed to respond fully to the instructions. 'He compromised by delivering up two anti-tank guns and a number of automatics.'[7]

The third formal request in Syria for Dyer to hand over the weapons was the final straw for both sides. Dyer believed that there had been a breach of trust between himself and his soldiers. He believed that he owed it to his men to retain the weapons for their protection.

Finally, he asked to be relieved of his command, and on 13 May 1942, nearly two years and two weeks after the battalion had marched out of Palmerston North, he left the battalion for base duty in Maadi Camp. Shortly after that, he was sent home. Dyer's own commentary on the matter is typically brief and to the point. He wrote 'there had been a serious conflict between the Maoris and Divisional Headquarters over the handing over of captured enemy weapons. Of course Divisional Headquarters had won.'[8]

For a period of just over five months, Humphrey Dyer had command of the battalion. Like Dittmer, Dyer was a strong disciplinarian. He had an abiding love for his soldiers and, though he expected much of them, he was also equally determined to stand up for them on what he considered to be matters of principle. No one who has read his book *Ma Te Reinga*, which tells the story of the men of D Company, could ever doubt the enormous respect and love he had for his men.

If Dyer had a flaw, it was that, at times, he was too impetuous and lacked judgement. Over the issue of the enemy weapons he took his beliefs to such an extent that, even if he had been right, he left the military hierarchy little room for movement and the inevitable consequence was that he lost command of his battalion.

Sad though the circumstances of Dyer's departure were, the news that he was to be replaced by the battalion's first Maori Commanding Officer was greeted, both at home and in the battalion itself, with jubilation. Major Tiwi Love had, for a period of some weeks, already held command of the battalion during the Sollum and Gazala battles.

The political importance of his promotion was not lost on Freyberg who cabled the news back to the Minister of Defence who released the cabled message to the public of New Zealand. Freyberg's message read: 'Feel that you would like to know that on the recommendation of the Brigade Commander and with my full concurrence Major ETW Love has been appointed with temporary rank Lieutenant-Colonel to command the Maori Battalion. First time Maori has commanded the battalion.

'As you know the battalion has done excellently in Greece, Crete and Libya. Maori officers have been good leaders in the field and Major Love has done particularly well while in temporary command. I feel confident his appointment will be justified.'[9]

The Minister of Defence added in his public release: 'I am sure the Maori people will learn with considerable pleasure of Colonel Love's appointment and promotion.'[10]

Rommel's sudden attack on the Eighth Army in Libya cut short the Maori stay in Syria. In late May, the Africa Korps had launched a surprise attack on the Allies, which drove the Eighth Army back towards Egypt. By mid-June 1942, the New Zealanders were on the move, with urgency, back to the Western Desert. By now the Eighth Army was in full retreat. As the leading elements of the New Zealand Division moved westwards towards Mersa Matruh, some 400 km west of Cairo, they met dense convoys of Eighth Army transports streaming in the opposite direction, towards El Alamein.[11]

For the fourth time in its existence, the 28 (Maori) Battalion would be fighting for its survival. The plan for the New Zealand Division was that it should hold Mersa Matruh. Freyberg objected to this proposal as he did not want to be tied down. He preferred that the New Zealanders be allowed to conduct a mobile campaign against the advancing Germans.

Meanwhile, the Maori had arrived at Mersa Matruh on 19 June 1942. The utter confusion and panic they were confronted with was manifested in the orders and counter-orders received. Few seemed to know what was going on. For five days in a row, 28 (Maori) Battalion were required to shift their positions in and around Matruh.

Before leaving Mersa Matruh on 25 June 1942, the battalion was required to send one of its rifle companies back to base camp at Maadi. This decision flowed from an Eighth Army memorandum which pointed out that a division could not be adequately supported by its anti-tank guns and field artillery as there were too many infantry units. The memorandum recommended that infantry battalions should be reduced to three rifle companies.[12]

D Company, which had been in the forefront of every campaign, was chosen to return to base. On 25 June 1942, the Maori moved south to take up its defensive positions. The defensive position was sited at Minqar Qaim, an escarpment 25 km south of the coast. Fleeing columns of British vehicles were ample evidence that Rommel was almost on them. They needed little incentive to prepare their positions. The rock hard ground, however, did not allow for the construction of slit trenches. Instead, the Maori used rocks to build up sangars, or rock walls, to provide protection against enemy small-arms fire.

From the early hours of 27 June 1942, the Maori on the escarpment watched as endless columns of German vehicles moved east along the coast road. It was clear that the Africa Korps knew of the presence of a major threat on their southern flank. It was only a matter of time before they moved to deal with it.[13]

During the day, several attempts were made by German groups to test the division's perimeter. All day long, columns of tanks and lorries lapped around the northern and eastern rim of the New Zealanders' positions. By last light, 21 Panzer Division had succeeded in encircling the New Zealand Division. The only way out was to break through the German encirclement.[14]

Just before last light, a company of German infantry debussed in front of the Maori positions. Lieutenant-Colonel Love's request for a few prisoners of officer rank was eagerly taken up by Ngati Porou of C Company.[15] From their reverse slope positions, the Ngati Porou could not see what the Germans were doing to their front. They could hear explosions. These could have come from German attempts to lift the minefield in front of the battalion. The question was what to do? The answer came from an unexpected quarter.

Private Ted Wanoa suddenly left his position and charged towards the enemy, loosing off snap shots as he went. Second-Lieutenant Bully Jackson, Platoon Commander of 14 Platoon, C Company, ordered a section to follow him and took off after Wanoa. The ensuing firefight drew the rest of the platoon into the action. Without orders, the remainder of the company left their sheltered positions to join the scrap. Captain Keiha, the Company Commander, had no option but to follow his company into battle.[16]

When the irate Company Commander arrived at the scene of the fight, the fight was over. He found 20 Germans lying shot or bayoneted and 14 prisoners. While the raid did not produce any prisoners of officer rank, it did produce three senior non-commissioned officers of 1 Battalion, 40 Lorried Regiment. Cody has suggested that the whole action started because Wanoa had a past debt to repay the Germans and had decided to take his revenge directly.

Wanoa had been captured in Crete. He had escaped from a prisoner-of-war camp and had left Crete by submarine. Whatever the reason, this small battle was another example of the fearless, albeit foolhardy, manner in which the Maori soldiers often operated in the heat of the battle.

Chapter 10
MINQAR QAIM TO MUNASSIB MASSACRE

Late in the evening of 27 June 1942, the inevitable orders for the break-out from Minqar Qaim were issued. Lieutenant-Colonel Love arrived back from the Brigade Orders Group at midnight. He had only 30 minutes to give orders, collect his patrols and be at the start line. With the best will in the world it was impossible for the Maori to make the deadline. It was not until 0130 hours that the Maori finally reached the start line. It was an ironic twist, for the Brigade Commander was Jim Burrows, whose 20 Battalion was late for the counter-attack at Maleme on Crete.

The reasons for the lateness were beyond the control of the respective commanders. At Maleme, Burrows had been late because the Australians were not on time to relieve his battalion. The Maori were late for this battle because of the time constraints placed on Colonel Love.

For the break-out, the Maori were allotted the right of the line. 20 Battalion held the left of the line and 19 Battalion held centre position. When the Maori arrived, all three units moved off without further command. 'With bayoneted rifles at the high port and Bren and tommy guns ready for action the brigade stepped off.'[1]

As the New Zealanders closed with the Germans, the brunt of the fighting was faced by the two Pakeha battalions. The Germans holding the gap through which the New Zealanders had decided to go were of the lst Battalion of Rifle Regiment 104. They had chosen the wrong place and the wrong time to be there. In the subsequent action the German battalion was practically destroyed as a fighting unit.

The Maori met light resistance on their front. This may explain why one section commander decided to take his section and head across the entire brigade front to where 20 Battalion was fighting a major battle, on the extreme left flank. Brigadier Burrows recalled seeing the Maori section commander with his section, 'running across our front to join the 20th in their sector'.[2]

At that very moment the brigadier and his party let off a Verey flare. Without hesitation, the Maori section commander and his men turned and charged at Burrows and his men, as in their experience only the Germans used flares at night. 'Fortunately,' said Burrows, 'our head-quarters runners had a violent flow of kiwi invective which checked even the Maoris'.[3] Nevertheless it was an anxious moment for the Brigadier.

By 9 p.m. the following evening the Maori had succeeded in reaching the El Alamein line, over 150 km to the east. This was to become the final line of resistance against Rommel. Some days later on 5 July 1942, enemy planes struck without warning killing the Maori second-in-command, Major Chesterman, Lieutenant Hamiora and 14 other ranks. Twenty-one men were wounded in the same attack.

Six days later, during preparations for an attack on Ruweisat Ridge, Lieutenant-Colonel Tiwi Love was mortally wounded by an artillery air burst. He died later that night. The battalion had lost its first Maori Commanding Officer – a gallant officer and man of enormous character. Another Maori chief had left for the long journey home to Cape Reinga to join his ancestors. The men heard of his death in the simple way in which death is always notified in Maoridom – 'kua mate a Tiwi' ('Tiwi has gone').[4]

Tiwi Love commanded the battalion from 13 May 1942 until he was killed in action on the El Alamein front on 12 July 1942. In that brief period of command the 'Bull' never had the opportunity to put into practice the years of military training and experience that he had accumulated.

Before the war he had served for 15 years as a Territorial Force officer and had been promoted to command a company in the 1st Battalion the Wellington Regiment (City of Wellington's Own). At the outbreak of war he was transferred to the temporary staff to assist with the mobilisation of the 28 (Maori) Battalion. He joined the battalion in November 1939. For a short time in Palmerston North, Love commanded D Company before being transferred to command Headquarters Company.

With the postponement of the Ruweisat attack, the battalion was temporarily withdrawn from the battle line and redeployed back to a rear area where it was joined by the new Commanding Officer, Lieutenant-Colonel Fred Baker. The reason for the withdrawal of the battalion from the front line is not difficult to understand. Brigade Headquarters were no doubt concerned that the battalion's two senior officers were dead and the third in seniority was back at base.

The adjutant had been seriously wounded in the same attack which had wounded Love. There would have been a natural concern at the capacity of the remaining officers to command and lead the battalion during very difficult times. Similar concerns had been expressed when Love, as a captain, had taken temporary command of the battalion following the Upper Sollum attack. However, Love had gone on to lead the battalion very successfully in four tough battles.

The Maori were sent back to the front line on 18 July 1942. Four days later, in the midst of the defence of the Alamein line, the Maori received 100 reinforcements. It was a difficult time to receive reinforcements but it was better to accept some lack of battle training than do without the advantage of the additional soldiers. Being expert at on-the-job training, the Maori moved quickly to accelerate the learning process for the new arrivals.

The period spent in the defences south of El Alamein was one of the most critical for the New Zealanders. As Kippenberger wrote, 'Summer was at its height and the flies at their worst. Strengths were so low that there was little rest for anyone. We were depressed and cynical. The men's faces were gaunter and more strained each week and there were many cases of jaundice.'[5]

Even the Maori, whose success rate was very high, were becoming more strained during this period of waiting.

It was during this extremely trying period that the 28 (Maori) Battalion Padre wrote home to New Zealand telling of the plight of the troops. Padre Wharetini Rangi had arrived in the battalion lines on 9 July 1942. On 5 August, he wrote home to his wife, telling her to forward his letter to Sir Apirana Ngata. Ngata sent the letter to the Prime Minister, adding that the sentiments contained in Rangi's letter supported the contention of the Maori tribes that the men of the Maori Battalion be returned to New Zealand as soon as possible.[6]

Rangi tells of conducting a round of services with the men. Against the backdrop of German shelling, he describes a church parade held at 6.30 a.m., for 82 soldiers.

It was, he said, 'a scene full of pathos . . . Our hearts were with you at home. The longing of these men to come home to their native land is most intense from officers to the rank and file. This is the spirit that pervades them all . . . It is not that they fear the enemy or have lost confidence in themselves.'[7]

Rangi's letter continues that the men had fought through four campaigns. They had seen their ranks thinned by death, wounds and sickness. In Rangi's view the men also were of the view that all their most capable leaders, 'the men who inspired them most', had all either been killed or had returned to New Zealand and had thus 'left them orphaned'.[8]

During the remainder of August the Maori continued to wait for the Germans to attack. At the same time the winds of change were sweeping through the Allied ranks. Lieutenant-General Bernard Montgomery had arrived to take command of the Eighth Army.

He arrived on 12 August 1942. Next day he took command and immediately began the much-needed revamp of the Eighth Army. His first order was that there was to be no further withdrawal. All troops were to strengthen and hold existing positions. The Maori on the eastern end of the El Mreir Depression strengthened and extended their positions.

Kippenberger, who commanded 5 (NZ) Brigade, decided to use the Maori to capture prisoners and frustrate an anticipated German attack scheduled for 25-26 August 1942. It was an occasion full of firsts. It would be the first time the Maori had attacked under Kippenberger and it would be Baker's first action as battalion commander. Above all, it would be the first offensive action carried out by the Eighth Army under Montgomery's command.[9] Baker decided to make it a matter requiring his personal attention. He led the preliminary patrol to check the route and terrain and identify the objective.

Kippenberger also took a very personal interest in the planning and preparations. He noted that planning was not a Maori strength and later they asked his headquarters to prepare the plan. He was concerned that the heavy concentration of artillery fire (it had been decided to use 144 guns, the complement of two divisions' worth of artillery, to support the attack) and the Maori bayonets would kill all the Italians.

Kippenberger, therefore, warned the Maori that he wanted 'prisoners and not scalps'. As he watched the preparations, Kippenberger was pleased at the cheerful and business-like way in which the Maori went about their preparations. 'The men were delightful, laughing and talking with one another, working busily at oiling and cleaning and polishing their weapons and all giving the most cheerful grins.'[10]

The two-company raid was undertaken by Ngapuhi, led by Porter, and Te Arawa, led by Pene. Before leaving for their mission the men held a service. Kippenberger writes, 'the Maori padre spoke with them, most eloquently and impressively. Then he said a prayer, very moving in the utter silence.'[11]

At the expected time, the patrols returned. Forty-one prisoners were captured. From the patrol commanders' reports it was estimated that two enemy companies were destroyed. The Maori casualties were higher than expected, caused by the men overrunning the supporting artillery fire. The prisoners were shaken by the shellfire and the ferocity of the Maori attack. Ronald Walker, Official Historian for the campaign, wrote that the raid 'was considered a model on which future operations of this sort should be based.'[12] Kippenberger reported that all the following morning ambulances were seen moving into and out of the depression.[13]

In retaliation for the raid, the Italians unleashed a murderous artillery barrage onto the Maori positions on the morning of 27 August. An estimated 2 000 rounds of artillery were fired into the Maori lines. Remarkably, the Maori were able to avoid major casualties by hiding in their slit trenches. There was only one casualty when one man was killed by a direct hit on his trench.

Following the battle, Bernard Montgomery and Horrocks, the Corps Commander, sent warm messages of congratulations. Later, on the evening of 27 August, Lieutenant-General Horrocks visited the Maori lines.

Late in August 1942, intelligence was received that Rommel's last offensive would be launched against the southern flank of the New Zealand positions. The Maori were deployed, together with the remainder of 5 (NZ) Brigade, to the south to meet this threat.

When it became clear that Rommel had shot his bolt and that the anticipated offensive would not take place, Kippenberger was given orders to attack and seize the northern edge of the Munassib Depression.

The Maori were given the task. As ever their approach was novel and unorthodox. Baker decided that Keiha and Ngati Porou would throw a screen across the whole Battalion frontage (1 000 metres).[14] On heavy contact with the enemy, Keiha's C Company would then go to ground and act as a launching base for the assault companies. A Company and D Company who would pass through and capture the objective.

The Munassib attack is a classic example of the chaos resulting from the 'fog' of war. It is also a classic example of the initiative and determination of the Maori soldier when left to his own devices to get on with the job. Predictably, when C Company struck opposition on the assault, they continued to attack. Very quickly all effective control of the company was lost. Keiha was in the embarrassing situation of carrying out mopping-up operations with his Company Sergeant Major, batman, two stretcher bearers, two of his own riflemen and two stragglers from A Company. Instead of halting to form the firm base as planned, the rest of his command had joined A and D Companies in pressing the attack.

At just after 2 a.m., Baker was able to report back to the Brigade Commander that the objectives had been achieved 'after violent and most bloody fighting'. By now the Maori had got out of control. They had continued on beyond their objectives and carried on into the Munassib Depression, 'directly contrary to their orders'.[15]

A Company, under its dashing commander Ben Porter, in following up the withdrawing enemy 'swarmed down over the floor of the Depression attacking all who tried to oppose them and destroying numerous trucks with grenades and Bren fire.'[16] They were helped in this task by the majority of the men from C Company who had followed so that they would not miss out on the action.

D Company, under Peta Awatere, had begun to veer west as soon as they had reached the lip of the Depression. As their assault continued they went further into the area which should have been covered by the 132nd British Brigade.

The attack by this brigade on the right flank of the Maori Battalion had failed badly. As D Company moved further to the west, the battle broke down from platoon into section clashes. 'It was a fight in which sections and platoons worked in coordination with outflanking movements and frontal attacks, and the Maoris aptitude for such battle was allowed full play.'[17]

As dawn neared, individuals, sections and platoons began to filter back to the Depression. Most realised that they needed to be reorganised before first light. Kippenberger became increasingly concerned about the welfare of the Maori, fearing that they would be encircled by German tanks during daylight and destroyed. Consequently, he moved reinforcements nearer to the Depression.

Meanwhile, the companies in the Depression had managed to link up. Both Porter and Awatere agreed that they needed to be further east, dug-in and ready to receive the expected counter-attack at dawn. As the men prepared shell scrapes on the lip of the Depression, Baker, who had by now linked with his men, moved his headquarters about a kilometre to the rear.

When dawn broke, the stragglers of the battalion were still making their way back to the new positions. With his concerns mounting as the morning wore on, Kippenberger decided to withdraw the Maori behind a defensive area prepared by 22 Battalion. A smoke-screen was to be laid down to help the Maori withdraw. As the smoke-screen built up, Baker called for volunteers to go forward to give A and D Companies the message to withdraw.

Several men volunteered. Baker picked two men whom he knew would try their best to get through to the forward companies. Both headed off into the area where the smoke-screen was drifting. One of the men seemed to be having trouble with his pants. They were torn, split down one side, and flapping around his legs. He paused momentarily, ripped them off with a vigorous tug, threw the now-useless trousers to one side, and made off at high speed into the smoke.

A very short time later he reappeared at even greater speed. Lieutenant-Colonel Baker yelled out to him to ask whether he'd lost his way, or even lost his nerve. 'No, sir,' he yelled back at the Colonel, 'Just forgot my paybook!' Whereupon he bent down, yanked the pay book out of the pocket of his discarded trousers, tucked the book into his shirt pocket and disappeared once more into the smoke.[18]

One of the runners reached D Company and they immediately began their withdrawal. Porter, of A Company, had become apprehensive as the morning lengthened. Down below them in the Depression, they could see activity and movement. Realising that the Germans would certainly mount a counter-attack, he sent a runner back to Battalion Headquarters asking for a smoke-screen to be arranged, so that the company could withdraw when the tanks attacked. Kippenberger's planned smoke-screen began to fall soon after.

As Kippenberger observed later: 'Porter was a very shrewd, experienced officer . . . He guessed the purpose of the smoke-screen and withdrew through it with the tanks on his heels.'[19]

The battalion's casualties for this operation were listed as 5 killed, 54 wounded and 18 missing (later some of the missing were accounted for). Kippenberger wrote that, 'the Maoris had made a brilliantly successful attack and had killed quite an exceptional number of Germans. They had however, got badly out of control and were lucky to have got out without disaster.' In his view, 'splendid troops as they were and easy for a hard commander to handle, the Maoris needed an iron hand.'[20]

After speaking with every Maori Company and platoon commander, Kippenberger came up with the staggering estimate that the Maori had killed at least 500 Germans. This figure was questioned but, as Kippenberger points out, the Maori were not boastful in laying claim to enemy killed. Moreover, Kippenberger himself had seen an exceptional number of dead in their path. Little quarter was asked. Little was given.

In addition to the Brigade Commander's congratulations, the Maori received recognition from Freyberg who sent the following message to Kippenberger: 'I send 5 Bde my congratulations on the successful attack of night 3/4 especially to Lt Col Baker and Maori Bn. for their exploits in the Munassib Depression.'[21]

Horrocks also sent a message to Freyberg paying a special tribute to the battalion for its efforts.

To add to the confusion of the night attack, it was found that the enemy were employing new tactics. 'They were lying doggo in their slit trenches until our infantry were past and then were shooting at them from the rear.'[22] To combat this development, the battalion decided in future operations to employ reserve forces to mop up after the attacking elements.

101

After the Munassib battle, the battalion was withdrawn from the lines for a 10-day leave period near the sea. Leave to Cairo and Alexandria was available. The remainder of the month and early October 1942 was taken up in preparing for the battle for Alamein – the turning-point in the desert war.

Chapter 11

EL ALAMEIN TO TRIPOLI:
YEARNING FOR HOME

The battle for Alamein (Operation LIGHTFOOT) opened on the night of 23 October 1942, with a massive 1 000 gun barrage. The Eighth Army under its new commander, General Montgomery, was about to begin the task of ejecting Rommel and his Africa Korps from the continent of Africa. The Maori role in this battle was, uncharacteristically, a minor one. Split between the two assault brigades, 5 and 6 (NZ) Brigades, with two companies attached to each, their mission was to follow behind each brigade to 'mop up' any opposition left.

'Mopping up' is the technical military term used to describe the act of destroying, eliminating or capturing any enemy strong-points or pockets of resistance left after the main assault groups have moved through an area. Usually the orders to the assault elements will have a provision in them directing the assault troops to bypass enemy opposition. Any delay in stopping to deal with stubborn resistance could jeopardise the impetus of the overall attack.

The principal role of the attackers is to seize the laid down objectives. It is for the mopping-up troops to deal with residual resistance.

It is difficult to determine or understand why the Maori were left out of the main attack. Their pre-eminence in attack and their outstanding ability to capture their objective was indisputable. Perhaps their failure to obey orders at Munassib the previous month may have worried Kippenberger.

Whatever the reason, for the first time since their service with the division, the Maori were separated and not allowed to act under their own unified command. Interesting enough, although not surprising, the companies allocated to 6 (NZ) Brigade for a time actually bypassed the assaulting troops. Given the nature of their task, the Maori casualties for this operation were exceedingly high: 6 killed and 53 wounded. Two men were listed as missing. The majority of these casualties had been caused by enemy artillery fire and mines.

Dawn on 24 October 1942 showed that the attacks across the divisional front had achieved most of the objectives. However, the breaches required to allow the heavy armour to break through had not been made. In 5 (NZ) Brigade over 560 casualties had been sustained by the attacking force of three battalions. While there was still much fighting to be done before the break-out from Alamein had been achieved, for 5 (NZ) Brigade, except 28 (Maori) Battalion, the battle was over.

At midnight on the last day of October, Lieutenant-Colonel Baker was summoned to an urgent orders group at Brigade Headquarters. The battalion was detailed to provide flank protection, during a planned attack, for 151 Brigade of the British 50th Division.

Despite its heavy casualties in the Alamein battle, the 28 (Maori) Battalion was considered to be the freshest and the strongest unit available in the brigade to support the British attack. For the task, the Maori were placed under command of 151 Brigade.

The brigade's task was to attack westwards with another British brigade, to breach the enemy's lines and to provide the heavy armour with the corridor they needed for the break-out.

For Baker, the experience of dealing with the British was a most unhappy and frustrating experience. Later he wrote that it was 'the most unsatisfactory Bde or other conference' he had ever attended.[1] Orders were indefinite and critical details were sketchy or non-existent. Moreover, the nature of the task left the Maori exposed.

Their task was to protect the northern or right flank of 151 Brigade, which was the right assault brigade. As the attack was in westwards direction, this meant that the Maori right or northern flank would be exposed. For such a strategically important mission, the lack of detail was appalling. When Baker arrived at the start line, the Australian Brigadier, from whose sector the attack was being launched, did not know what was going on. Nor indeed was he aware that his own forward troops had to be moved back before the barrage began.

The code-name given this operation was SUPERCHARGE. On this operation hung the success of the Eighth Army's break-out hopes.

In the early hours of 2 November 1942, the attack began. Very early on, Baker received serious wounds. His second-in-command, Major Hart, was mortally wounded. Thus after only a short while, the command elements of 28 (Maori) Battalion had been knocked out. Meanwhile, the companies were fighting their own battles. Ngati Porou, advancing on the extreme right, hit the enemy at close range after moving forward about 400 m. They had little time to do anything other than charge.

Cody quoted Montgomery as describing the action as 'a real killing match as the company stabbed, grenaded and tommy gunned its way through an area thick with machine gun and anti-tank guns'.[2] Because of the intensity of the fighting, the company lost its cohesion. Small parties of Maori were left to their devices to capture or destroy the enemy strongpoints in their way. The fighting was so intense that one of the forward platoon commanders of C Company arrived at the objective with only five men. The other forward platoon commander arrived at the objective with 10 men.

Te Arawa of B Company, even though it followed 15 minutes after the first wave of Maori, had to fight all the way to the objective. Bennett, the Company Commander, describes how at one spot they were opposed by a wall of fire. 'We all broke into the haka "Ka Mate! Ka Mate!" ("Tis Death! Tis Death!") and charged straight in with the bayonet.'³ It was, he said, the most spirited attack he had taken part in.

A and D Companies had come through the attack relatively unscathed. Despite the harrowing experiences faced by C and B Companies, the Maori were able to gain their objectives and dig in. As dawn broke, they waited for the expected counter-attack. B Company was in an exposed position. It was, said Bennett, 'unsafe to poke your head out above ground level.' He was not, however, apprehensive about the presence of enemy infantry. His principal concern was from the threat from German armour.⁴

The Maori remained all day exposed to enemy observation. The expected counter-attack did not eventuate. What Bennett and his men did not know was that Rommel himself was desperately trying to plug the gaps that had opened up in his defences.

Later that day (2 November 1942), Rommel gave orders for the withdrawal of his forces to the west. Also later that day, Major Charles Bennett, of Te Arawa, discovered that he was the senior officer remaining in the battalion. Rangi Logan was sharing a shell hole with him when the call came from Kippenberger for Bennett to take command. As he left to go for a briefing, he turned and said to Logan, 'I leave this to you. I have to go back and take over.'⁵

Lieutenant-Colonel Fred Baker had always been an enigma to some of his fellow officers.⁶ He was only an eighth Maori and he did not always readily identify with his Maori heritage. When the Official History for 28 (Maori) Battalion was being written, after the Second World War, Kippenberger wrote to Freyberg suggesting that, because of his limited amount of Maori blood, Baker might like to consider himself as a Pakeha commanding officer. The history shows Baker listed under the Maori commanding officers.

In a letter home to his cousin, while he was convalescing after the Greece and Crete campaigns, Baker wrote about Maori soldiers as if he were an interested observer rather than one himself. He noted, after a lengthy explanation about the Greece and Crete campaigns, that 'the greatest surprise of all of course was the Maori. Even though I was with them, before the show I was probably one of the greatest Doubting Thomases of all.'

Baker had expected the Maori soldier to excel at bayonet charges and offensive action because, he wrote, 'It was in their nature, as we knew it, to show that sort of flash of spirit. With the rigid discipline we have maintained in the main body I expected that we would be able to control them in those situations. Both of these surmises proved correct.'

However, what Baker did not expect was 'the almost stoical way they sat down under the strafing that he (the Germans) gave us in our trenches and when out on the move.'

Baker closed his letter by telling his cousin that he 'had always intended to get back to my old crowd until this show but I am not so sure now. I believe quite a few officers from other battalions are looking for a job with us now.'[7]

For all of the uncertainties expressed about Baker by some of his fellow soldiers, including Rangi Logan, what cannot be disputed is Baker's record of successes with the battalion. In his four months of command he had taken the battalion through a series of highly successful operations. For his agressive leadership in the field he was awarded an immediate DSO.

Lieutenant-Colonel Bennett assumed command of the battalion on 2 November 1942. Kippenberger observed that Bennett was 'a member of a well-known Maori family. He was only 26, the youngest officer to take a command and the first who had not been a soldier of some sort before the war.'[8] Kippenberger was not correct about Bennett's age – he was 29. Nevertheless, he was still a young man to be given senior command in the New Zealand division.

On the night of 2 November, Bennett collected together his new command and resited them to face a threat from the north. He found that three of his companies had lost their commanders during the attack of the previous evening. After reorganising themselves they once more awaited the enemy counter-attack, not realising that Rommel had already started his withdrawal from the Alamein line.

Maori casualties during the attack had been heavy – nearly 100 men from an already depleted battalion. Twenty-two men had been killed, 72 wounded (including eight officers) and four missing. By now the strength of the battalion, like its sister battalions in 5 (NZ) Brigade, had reached a critical level.

The rifle companies of the brigade had an average strength of 50 to 60 men. No reinforcements were available. At full strength each company had 5 officers and 100 men. Thus the bayonet strength of an infantry battalion was its 20 officers and 400 men. The remaining approximately

330 men and officers staffed Battalion Headquarters and Headquarters Company.

In an attack, the Commanding Officer would take with him from this group a small Tactical Headquarters comprising the Intelligence section, which marked out the start line for an attack and was responsible for providing direction during the attack; radio operators to maintain communications with the assaulting companies during the attack, and stretcher bearers.

Kippenberger wrote that in an attack 'the remainder could not and did not come forward until gaps in the minefields were cleared and the situation stabilised; of course most of the transport and administrative personnel were never required in the forward area during the attack.'[9]

For these reasons nearly 90 percent of casualties fell on the rifle companies. Thus it would not take more than one or two major actions to severely hamper the effectiveness of an infantry battalion.

Kippenberger believed that rifle company strengths of 50 were adequate for defensive operations as the main killing power was provided by well-sited guns. On the other hand he reckoned on 'nothing less than 80 percent per company was sufficient for an attack.'[10]

The Maori had sustained in the space of 10 days nearly 160 casualties. In the attacks on the 23-24 October and 1-2 November, they had lost 28 men killed, 125 wounded, and six missing. Even if the battalion had been at full strength this tally would have represented just under 50 percent of its bayonet strength. The battalion was not at full strength.

Fortunately there was little fighting required over the next few days. By 12 November, the last enemy soldiers had been pushed out of Egypt. Montgomery's message to the troops paid tribute to the 'soldiers of the Empire', who had made it all possible. He reminded them that the task was not yet finished and promised them that there was 'some good hunting to be had further to the west in Libya.'[11]

During December 1942, and most of January 1943, the New Zealand Division pursued Rommel westwards. Despite being badly beaten, Africa Korps refused to behave as expected of defeated troops. From time to time they turned and reminded the New Zealanders that even during a withdrawal they could still pull the occasional surprise. With skilful manoeuvres, they fought their way back to the borders of Libya.

It was, however, only a matter of time before they were pushed out of Libya as well. On 23 January 1943, the 28 (Maori) Battalion entered Tripoli at the end of a 2 200 km pursuit. 'For the first time in months the troops were in an area where water, cool fresh water, was plentiful.'[12]

Here the battle-weary men of the New Zealand Division rested, licked their wounds and gathered their strength. It was here that the Maori were able to take full stock of the toll of the second Libyan campaign. For some, the results of this stocktake were depressing.

The officers of Ngati Porou decided to write to their mentor and fellow-tribesman Sir Apirana Ngata. It seems that the letter signed by Major Keiha, Battalion second-in-command, and senior Ngati Porou officer, Padre Wanoa, the battalion padre, Captain Awatere, Company Commander, C Company and the platoon commanders, was in part a response to a letter from Ngata to them seeking certain information.

They wrote, 'It was your letter that reached to our innermost beings, and roused to an appreciation of the things you have put for our consideration.'[13] Ngata's letter to the Ngati Porou officers probably stemmed from the earlier letter sent to Ngata by Padre Rangi suggesting that all was not well and that the men would not be averse to going home.

The letter begins by lamenting the loss of the two Maori colonels, Love and Baker, and acknowledging the appointment to command of the Bishop's son (Bennett). Keiha and his colleagues suggest that it matters little who the colonel is as the Maori are locked into the Allied plan over which they have no control.

Here they have suggested that because there is a total commitment to achieving the aims of the overall Allied plan little consequence would be paid to the losses of 28 (Maori) Battalion. The officers next set out to document the severe state that C Company is in. Of the 100 original soldiers, only 22 are left. Some of these men have been 'wounded three or four times and it is their spirit only that enables them to carry on.'

All of the different reinforcement batches have sustained major casualties and the remaining men of these groups have been wounded at least once or twice. The final batch of reinforcements, the 7th Reinforcements, had been committed to the battle of Alamein where their losses had been heavy. The majority of the wounded in C Company during the Alamein actions had been from this draft.

The Ngati Porou officers paint for Ngata a dismal picture of the state of the men of Ngati Porou who have joined the battalion. Because of the high casualty rates, replacements for the battalion have to be found by clearing out the base areas of anyone capable of holding and firing a weapon. The officers express grave concern that the wounded men recovering in base camp at Maadi 'are the ones to take the place of men, who may be put out of action in the days ahead.' They cannot be restrained, continues the letter, 'by officers or guards or administrative officials at base, because of their desire to rejoin.'

In addition to the men in hospitals, there were also numbers convalescing. When reinforcements were called for it was common practice for many of these men to volunteer for reinforcement drafts to be sent forward to the front line, even if they were not fully fit. The result of all of this, write Keiha and his colleagues, is that C Company is full of that 'kind of man'.

The letter next deals with the question of compassionate leave. In essence, Keiha and his colleagues seek a commonsense measure of returning to New Zealand the remaining brothers of men killed in action. They note that the matter has 'not been considered by those in command'. They tell Ngata that they have asked Bennett to allow men of Ngati Porou in this category to return home.

Finally, to complete the survey, the officers provide Ngata with details of their casualties since the Greece campaign. They advise him that men from the Tairawhiti area have sustained the following losses: in the Greek and Cretan campaigns 18 men were killed, 30 prisoners taken and many were missing. From the first Libyan campaign, 22 men were killed and 5 were taken prisoner. In the second Libyan campaign, 27 men killed, 8 prisoners and 2 missing. Thus, over 100 men from C Company had been lost. In addition, 40 men had been invalided home from wounds sustained during battle.

As the letter points out, 'If the Maori Battalion is regarded from this angle the figures are tragic. They had not been seriously considered by the companies hitherto, because of the many changes in administrative officers.' The stay in Tripoli had allowed the battalion finally to overhaul its records and provide more accurate statistics of the losses in the various campaigns.

Having placed their survey before Ngata, the officers of Ngati Porou rest their case, leaving to Ngata and the Maori people the decision whether to press for the return home of the battalion or leave it overseas. It is clear, though, where the Ngati Porou sentiments lie. They tell Ngata that the campaign in Tunisia could be over by the time he receives their letter.

Should the campaign for Tunisia be ended then, 'This is enough for us, the Maori Battalion. The tramp of Japanese feet is resounding on Hawaiki. Already the thunder of the feet of the Americans and the English reverberates on the soil of North Africa.' Thus the Maori would have done their job.

For Keiha and the older officers it is time for them to make way for the younger men. This sentiment is expressed to Ngata in the form of a Maori proverb: 'The strands of the old net are sagging with use. It is for the young ones, who are straining to lift the weapons of the god of war, that we are pleading.'

The letter ends with the advice that the remaining companies of the battalion are in a similar position to Ngati Porou. Only Ngati Porou and Ngapuhi (A Company) are fit to fight another campaign. Keiha and his fellow-officers also advise Ngata that 'officers of the other companies have been consulted and they are all of the one mind.' But, the letter continues, 'they keep their mouths shut, because there are no elders of their tribes to receive their views.'

The letter writers do inject a note of caution by emphasising that perhaps another reason why the other officers wish to keep quiet is because 'they do not wish it to be said that they threw up the job they so strenuously pressed to do.' This latter point does not constrain the Ngati Porou. 'We of Tairawhiti have no hesitation in putting the case before you. We have been in three great battles; there is no man here with a sound body to take our places, that we may rest. There is only one place in this case and that is home.'

Captain C. N. D'Arcy, the 28 (Maori) Battalion Medical Officer, wrote on the 'Psychology of the Maori Soldier'.[14] He noted that, 'After the Tunisian campaign and the return to New Zealand of the three echelons, it was evident there were still many men of the 28 (Maori) Bn who were completely useless as soldiers. Many had been in a great deal of fighting but were now battle weary.'

D'Arcy went on to describe how he arranged for 25 men to be medically boarded and returned home. They were, he argued, more of a hindrance than a help and they always upset the other men. 'When the time for action came they were always left behind in the B Echelon.'

The timing of the C Company letter coincides with the period that D'Arcy writes about and it is therefore not surprising that Keiha and his fellow Ngati Porou officers should take the stance they did. It is interesting to note that none of the other senior officers from the battalion who were there at the time can recall such a letter. Nor can they recall having ever discussed it amongst themselves. Indeed for Rangi Logan it came as a complete surprise.

Chapter 12

MEDENINE AND TEBAGA GAP: DEFIANTLY FACING THE ENEMY

Towards the end of the desert campaign the Maori were involved in two battles – the Medenine incident and the battle for Tebaga Gap. The first of these was a defensive battle, in which the battalion received the full weight of a panzer attack. The second battle, the attack on Tebaga Gap, led to the posthumous award of the Victoria Cross to Second-Lieutenant Moananui-a-kiwa Ngarimu for extraordinary personal gallantry.

Both battles exemplified the enormous depth of skill and professionalism reached by the Maori. Despite having fought a brilliant defensive battle at Medenine, however, the Maori themselves did not consider it any great feat. Cody suggested that the reason for this was that 'there were no trophies of the chase – not a Luger or a Spandau or even a pair of binoculars.'[1] Cody's suggestion is too facile. By its very nature a defensive battle is an orchestration of all of the elements of war. With the right piece of ground, time to prepare positions and the full weight of supporting arms (tanks, artillery and minefields), a defensive area can be made extremely formidable.

In its baptism of fire around Olympus Pass, some 23 months and numerous campaigns earlier, 28 (Maori) Battalion had repulsed a determined German attack. In a defensive battle, the soldier does not have the same degree of flexibility to initiate independent action. For the Maori soldier, whose temperament was more suited to the cut and thrust of attack operations, the defensive battle did not allow the same scope to exercise his aggressive fighting spirit. Nevertheless at Musaid and Menastir in late 1941, the Maori had demonstrated superb defensive qualities.

Lieutenant-General Bernard Montgomery considered Medenine 'the perfect example of a defensive battle in its setting, its conduct and its outcome.'[2] So much so that after the battle he suggested his senior commanders visit the Maori Battalion area. As Cody quite rightly pointed out, 'A suggestion from the Eighth Army Commander was equivalent to a command.' For a time, the area swarmed with colonels and brigadiers.

What ended as a highly successful defensive battle had its genesis in a plan for an Allied offensive.

In late January 1943, the advance elements of Montgomery's Army stormed into Tripoli. The entry of Allied troops into Tripoli was the

111

culmination of a 2 400 km pursuit which began in the breakout from Alamein in October 1942. Montgomery's grand design was to push forward light forces to the real line of strength – the Mareth Line. Here they would maintain contact with the enemy until the Army was ready for an all-out attack.

The Mareth Line was originally built by the French to protect its Tunisian territories from the Italians in Libya. It was a formidable barrier, relying for its strength on 35 km of broken hill country with a few navigable paths through strategic passes. It posed a major obstacle to wheeled transport.

During the months of January and February 1943, pressure was maintained on the Mareth Line while the Eighth Army continued its preparations for the attack. In the meantime, 28 (Maori) Battalion went about the business of enjoying the respite from war. The Carrier Platoon of 28 (Maori) Battalion had led the New Zealanders into Tripoli and it was intended that the platoon lead a stage-managed entry into Tripoli.

This intention was clearly not made known to the 51st Highland Division, which stole a march on the Maori and took possession of the city some hours earlier. The price of being upstaged was second pickings for hotel accommodation. In spite of the set-back, the Maori were able to make themselves very comfortable.

While preparations were being made for the attack, the battalion had time to beat off a determined bid by the Divisional Signals to win the divisional rugby final.

Initially, Rommel had left the defence of the Mareth Line to Italians while he took his panzer forces north to attack the Americans, who had landed north of Tunisia with the intention of fighting south to link with the Eighth Army. Following 10 Panzer's successful foray against the Americans, Rommel turned south to reinforce the Mareth Line and launch an offensive against the British.

Once Rommel's intentions were known the alarm bells began to ring. In spite of its larger forces, the Allies still had a residual fear of the Desert Fox. 28 (Maori) Battalion's daily routine was, at short notice, rudely interrupted and it was ordered to ready itself for a move. Cody, in the battalion's Official History, noted that at '10 a.m. on 1 March the troops were returning from a lecture by Captain Thomas (23 Battalion) on "Prisoners of War and Escaping"; at 11.30 a.m. everybody was packing up and checking over ammunition supplies.'[3]

Twelve hours later, at 11.30 p.m., the battalion embussed and just after midnight began the 300 km drive to the Medenine area. The battalion was ordered to occupy a defensive position on the right flank of 5 (NZ)

Brigade's area. The Mareth Line was some 15 km west of the allotted defence position.

Lieutenant-Colonel Charles Bennett, who had left Tripoli ahead of the battalion, accompanied the Brigade Commander's Reconnaissance Group. On arrival at Medenine, he had received his orders and had spent the remainder of the time available carrying out his own reconnaissance. Satisfied with his efforts, he awaited the arrival of his men. In a thesis prepared after the war for the degree of Master of Arts, Bennett described the arrival of his battalion. 'The first vehicles of the Maori Battalion reached the rendezvous ten miles from Medenine at 1745 hours on 2 March.'[4] Here they were met by Bennett, who intended to lead them straight to their positions. The end vehicles of the column, however, did not arrive until almost five hours afterwards. Realising that it would be better to move at first light, Bennett ordered the men to debus and rest.

Bennett was enthusiastic about the forthcoming battle. He considered the area allotted to the battalion was 'admirable' for defence purposes. While the Maori had been well tested in the defensive phase of war, they were required at Medenine to camouflage their exposed positions using all the skill and cunning they could muster.

Between the Maori forward defensive positions and the Matmata Hills some 15 km distant lay a 'flat even plain extending without interruption to the very foothills.'[5] Bennett considered that the terrain would 'provide excellent concealment for dug-in positions and essential transport.' In his view 'with judiciously sited positions held by disciplined troops it was quite conceivable that no sign of occupation could be observed even from the front.'[6]

Brigadier Kippenberger, Commander 5 (NZ) Brigade, shared Bennett's confidence. Each battalion position he wrote, 'had a depth of about a mile, with three rifle companies forward and six pounders echeloned in depth',[7] then occupied single rifle pits with seven to eight metres between pits. Each section occupied a front of about 60 m, which, in Kippenberger's view 'no amount of shelling would do much harm'.[8] He also insisted on concealment of the highest order, stating that 'a post spotted is a post destroyed'.[9]

The few days spent digging in were sufficient for the seasoned Maori soldiers to ready themselves. In the early hours of 6 March 1943, increased activity from the direction of the Mareth Line signalled a major German initiative. Shortly after breakfast Kippenberger was called by Bennett and invited to drive to the Maori position where he would see the sight of his life. He arrived to find 'Charlie . . . standing at his headquarters, admiring 10 Panzer Division deploying to attack.'[10]

The German division's initial movements had been masked by darkness and, in the early dawn, a thick fog. Soon, however, it was clear that the Germans were intent on a major push. As tanks, guns and troop transports debouched out of the hills and onto the plains the Maori waited expectantly.

At about 8.30 a.m., 28 (Maori) Battalion had reported 10 tanks and 30 trucks moving on the unit's right front. When the tanks reached the boundary of a dummy minefield, set up to deceive the enemy, they took the bait and swung towards the high ground.[11] The tanks were engaged by two six-pounders from 73 Anti-Tank Regiment RA, sited in the Maori defence position. Four shots were fired and four tanks were knocked out of action.

The Maori Mortar Platoon, not to be outdone, engaged a fifth tank and blew off its tracks.[12] Sensing that they might miss out on the action, a patrol from A Company stalked the immobile tanks and captured a company commander and fourteen other ranks of 7 Regiment, 10 Panzer Division. While the Germans later attempted to launch a major infantry attack on the 5 (NZ) Brigade's position, this was easily repulsed by New Zealand artillery. The battle of Medenine was effectively over.

Some eight days later, the battalion was on the move again. Montgomery had decided to try to punch a hole through the Germans' coastal defences. At the same time he proposed a giant left hook around to the west of the Mareth Line defences targeted on Tebaga Gap. New Zealand Corps was assigned this task.

On 12 March 28 (Maori) Battalion joined 5 (NZ) Brigade, moved southeast towards Ben Gardane and then south-west approximately 80 km from Medenine to a staging area in readiness for the New Zealand Corps' left hook attack on Tebaga Gap. They remained here for a week and tried to avoid detection from German reconnaissance aircraft and vehicles. Throughout this period, the plans for the eventual objective were kept secret.

Finally on 18 March 1943, Brigadier Kippenberger gave a briefing on the general plans for the attack. On 25 March, after he had failed to force the Mareth Line along the coastline, Montgomery decided to 'shift the weight of the attack to the New Zealand Corps area.'[13]

New Zealand Corps was 'to smash a breach in a daylight attack so timed that 1 Armoured Division, at the end of its tremendous march, would drive straight through the Hamma Gap without pause.'[14] This operation was named SUPERCHARGE II and Lieutenant-General Horrocks was placed in command of the attack.

5 (NZ) Brigade was given the task of right assault brigade. 6 (NZ)

Brigade had the task of left assault brigade. In the 5 (NZ) Brigade sector, 28 (Maori) Battalion was right assault battalion. On 5 (NZ) Brigade front, '28 Battalion holding a frontage of 1 400 yards on the exposed right flank had the most difficult task, namely the capture of Point 209.'[15]

The battalion's plan of attack was A Company under Major Porter right assault company; B Company under Captain Sorenson left assault company with C Company under Peta Awatere 300 m behind and spread across the battalion frontage. D Company was reserve company on the right flank.

The attack began on time at 4.15 p.m. The battalion followed the armoured vehicles, and progress was steady until the tanks attempted to climb Point 209. As they 'sheered off to go round it, an 88 mm cleverly placed behind the hill knocked out five in succession.'[16] The right assault company, A Company came under heavy fire from Point 209 and went to ground.

Peta Awatere immediately committed C Company into an attack on the feature. They thought they were attacking Point 209. In fact they were attacking a lower feature of Point 209 subsequently called Hikurangi. Hikurangi 'was strongly held and a bitter fight ensued on its slopes. The barrage had gone over, the tanks in the vicinity had lost interest or were out of touch and the Maoris had to fight it out themselves.'[17]

Awatere, in summing up the situation, decided to attack the feature with all his platoons. 13 Platoon, under the command of Lieutenant Bully Jackson, was to attack from the right. Lieutenant Haig and 15 Platoon were in the centre with the task of attacking towards the crest. Lieutenant Moana Ngarimu and 14 Platoon were to attack from the left flank.

The attack began at 5 p.m. From this moment until dawn the next day when he was killed repulsing an enemy counter-attack, Moana Ngarimu demonstrated qualities of extraordinary bravery and leadership that led to his being awarded an immediate Victoria Cross.

Much has been written about the battle and the facts are well covered in the official histories. However, it is interesting to look at the battle through the eyes of the two key witnesses who provided the sworn testimony which subsequently led to the award of the Victoria Cross.

The statements were sworn before Lieutenant Colonel Charles Bennett some days after the attack at Gabes, a coastal town some 50 km north-east of Tebaga Gap where the battalion rested after the attack. The process of determining the award had, however, begun already. Even as Ngarimu was fighting for his life, Bennett had determined in his mind that the outstanding leadership shown by Ngarimu deserved the highest consideration.[18]

This thinking was confirmed for Bennett just after Ngarimu had been killed. Kippenberger had called into the battalion area on the morning of 27 March 1943, to be briefed on the situation. He noted that 'Charlie Bennett was well forward in a slit trench, 200 yards from the foot of Hikurangi . . . C Company of the Maoris was where I had seen it the previous night hanging on just under the lip of Hikurangi. Charlie said that Ngarimu had been killed about daylight and he thought he had earned a VC.'[19]

One of the sworn statements was provided by Private Waihi. He stated that Ngarimu had led the attack up the hill and had preceded some of his men. By the time Waihi's section had reached the top of the hill, Ngarimu had already cleared the area of two machine-gun posts. 'We were attacked a lot of times by the enemy after we got to the top of the hill but Mr Ngarimu always told us to stick to our posts.'[20]

The repeated counter-attacks by the Germans as they tried to dislodge Ngarimu and his men from their positions took a tremendous toll in casualties and Waihi noted, 'Once some of my sec [tion] broke during the night but Mr Ngarimu rushed up to us and yelling out to us to follow him led us back to the top of the hill again.'

During the night, Ngarimu and his men ran out of grenades and he immediately ordered them to improvise by using stones to simulate grenades. 'We ran out of grenades and our officer told us to use stones.'

As dawn rose, the situation became desperate. In the meantime, the company commander, Peta Awatere, had been evacuated and Lieutenant Jackson was in command. Jackson was the second key witness who provided evidence of Ngarimu's bravery. 'I established my Coy HQ just in the rear of Mr Ngarimu's platoon,' wrote Jackson. From here he moved forward to the crest where he found that Ngarimu had been wounded 'in two places, a wound in the shoulder and one in the leg.'[21]

When Jackson ordered Ngarimu to the Regimental Aid Post, Ngarimu insisted that he should stay till the morning. During Jackson's conversation with Ngarimu, the Germans launched another attack. 'Mr Ngarimu immediately stood to and engaged the enemy who were only a few yards from him.'

'After he had used his grenades I saw him pick up some stones and he used these as grenades. At the same time he rushed up to the top of the hill firing his tommy gun at the enemy who could be clearly seen.' When Jackson rejoined Ngarimu at the top of the hill, he saw some enemy dead lying around. He was counter-attacked many times during the night but he was always there to lead his men. 'I did not actually see him killed the next morning but when we went to get him we found him lying near the four or five German dead right at the top of the hill.'

116

At dawn, 7 Company of II/433 Regiment, which had lost a considerable number of men during the night attacks on Ngarimu's position, was reinforced by two other platoons. They then launched their last counter-attack. This was watched anxiously from the bottom of the hill by Jackson and Bennett. 'Ngarimu was seen waving his men on, tommy gun in hand, and then at last was shot down on the crest.'

The Germans had effectively played their last hand. Later in the morning, a number of German surrendered. Sensing that the moment was right, Bennett decided to make the final attack at 3 p.m. By 5 p.m., the attack was over. A total of 231 Germans were rounded up. It was clear that the German battalion was at its last gasp, having neither ammunition nor transport, with large numbers of wounded, and no hope of relief.

28 (Maori) Battalion lost 22 killed and 77 wounded. W.G. Stevens noted that the proportion of killed to wounded was slightly higher than normal.[22]

Chapter 13

TAKROUNA:
'THE POLITICS OF BRAVERY'

To those men of the Second New Zealand Division who fought in the battle for Enfidaville, the last major operation on the African continent, the name Takrouna recalls memories of some of the bloodiest hand-to-hand fighting of the desert campaign.[1]

The price of victory was, however, very high. Out of the 17 officers of the 28 (Maori) Battalion who crossed the start-line at zero hour, ll p.m. on 19 April 1943, only 5 were not killed or severely wounded. Over a third of 104 other ranks were killed, wounded or missing.

Kippenberger, in his foreword to the Official History of Takrouna, wrote that the battle for Takrouna 'came at the end of a severe 10 months' campaign, when the division was at the peak of its efficiency as a fighting machine but signs of strain were beginning to appear. None of the troops engaged had taken part in fewer than two battles, Medenine and Tebaga Gap, and the great majority in many more.'[2]

With the loss of so many officers early in the piece – within hours of the attack commencing the Advanced Dressing Station reported to Kippenberger that 11 of the Maori officers, including all of the company commanders, were already wounded[3] – the battle for Takrouna became a vital testing ground for the leadership qualities of the Maori soldier.

Wards wrote that the battle gave expression 'to the outstanding qualities of those who direct and wage the battle: qualities of firm leadership, of sound infantry craftsmanship, of determination, and of sustained courage.'[4]

The heroic deeds of a handful of Maori soldiers were no less outstanding than those of their comrades-in-arms some three weeks earlier at Tebaga Gap, where Ngarimu's platoon captured and held Hikurangi.

By the 15 April 1943, the Second New Zealand Division had closed up to the main enemy line of resistance in the Enfidaville area, some 110 km south of Tunis. The Eighth Army plan had been for the New Zealanders to 'bump' the enemy positions, which were located in mountainous country beyond the town of Enfidaville. When this attempt proved unsuccessful, Eighth Army was directed to 'exert the maximum pressure' to allow time for the American 2 US Corps and British First Army, north of Tunis to carry out a major offensive to capture Tunis, thereby ending the war in Africa.[5]

Lieutenant-General Montgomery's orders required him to achieve the twofold objective of drawing the enemy's attention away from Allied activities north of Tunis and to deceive the enemy as to where the main attack was to come from. He directed the Second New Zealand Division to strike from the south and west 'directly into a series of precipitous ridges and spurs that overlooked Enfidaville.'[6]

Freyberg gave the task of capturing Enfidaville to 6th (NZ) Brigade. To Kippenberger's 5 (NZ) Brigade, which included 28 (Maori) Battalion, he gave the task of capturing Takrouna and Djebel Bir. Kippenberger, in describing his own preparations for the attack, noted that he 'spent a lot of time forward with the battalion commanders, studying the ground and working out a plan for attacking our formidable objective.' While the brigade patrolled vigorously, no prisoners were taken and information on the enemy positions and strengths remained vague.

On 18 April 1943, Charles Bennett, Commanding Officer of 28 (Maori) Battalion was finally given an indication of what objectives the Maori were to capture. Kippenberger told Bennett that 'the Maori Battalion would be responsible for taking Takrouna.' Given this warning, Bennett was able to take his own officers forward for a reconnaissance.

Moreover, on the evening of the 18th he sent out patrols to probe and test the defences around Takrouna. In all cases the 'patrols reported back that the enemy positions were being held strongly. At the foot of Takrouna they seemed to be digging in; they could hear sounds of shovels.'[7]

The Takrouna feature, rising 300 m above the plain, comprised three distinctive parts. Dominating the feature was the summit. On top of the summit was a stone village believed to be of Berber origin containing a domed mosque. In the subsequent battle this area was known as the 'pinnacle'. A ledge running off in a southerly direction from the pinnacle contained a number of stone houses. The side of this ledge dropped steeply to the floor of the plain. This part of the feature was known as 'the ledge'.

The ledge was the part of the feature nearest the 2nd New Zealand Division and it was from there that the initial and subsequent attacks on Takrouna were to be launched. The final part of the feature, known as 'the village', jutted out to the west from the pinnacle and sloped down to the Zaghouan road.

Bennett's efforts to find out more about the enemy strengths on Takrouna and Djebel Bir – the 28 (Maori) Battalion's objectives – were unsuccessful. Major-General W. G. Stevens, in the Official History of the Campaign *Bardia to Enfidaville*, writes of the mood of optimism throughout the Eighth Army. The Army 'approached this last corner of Tunisia flushed with victory and full of confidence, for the farther it had advanced the speedier had been its victories. There was only this last pocket of enemy troops to brush away and the Army would have completed the task it had begun at Alamein.'[8]

The lack of certainty about the enemy experienced by 28 (Maori) Battalion, combined with the prevailing spirit of optimism observed by Stevens, had the effect, almost, of casting caution to the winds. This did not mean that planning was any the less meticulous, as always in the back of the minds of experienced commanders like Bennett was the thought that unexpected difficulties might arise.

W.G.Stevens noted that in spite of reservations from Brigadier Kippenberger about the forthcoming attack, 'the general feeling remained, as one of the battalion commanders explained to his officers, that the whole thing "was a piece of cake".' Charles Bennett confirmed this impression. He said that the Maori 'really did think it might be a bit of a cakewalk.'[9]

Monday, 19 April 1943, was as Kippenberger recalls 'a perfectly beautiful day, all the land bright with spring flowers and the air balmy and clear.'[10] Bennett's orders for 28 (Maori) Battalion were finalised and his orders group were called forward to a vantage point where final verbal orders were given.

Bennett's plan for the 28 (Maori) Battalion was determined by his two main responsibilities which were the capture of Takrouna and Djebel Bir. He decided to use three companies forward and one in reserve. The reserve company was to do the mopping-up, push on to the Zaghouan road beyond Takrouna, then turn around and take Takrouna from the rear.

The decision to take Takrouna from the northern slope was based on the better access from this direction onto the pinnacle. An attack from the south would have required the assaulting troops to attack up a steep and at times precipitous ledge before continuing up and onto the pinnacle.

Bennett chose Te Arawa (B Company) to bear the brunt of the initial assault on Takrouna. Ngati Porou (C Company) was to move in the centre and pass to the east, or right hand side of Takrouna; and Ngapuhi (A Company) was to be on the extreme right with the task of capturing Djebel Bir. D Company (the composite company) was given the task of reserve company for the initial assault with a second phase task of attacking Takrouna from the north.

The attack began with an artillery barrage at 1 100 hours. Shortly after their advance, the forward companies of 28 (Maori) Battalion began to take casualties from heavy enemy mortar and artillery gunfire, booby-trapped minefields and pockets of enemy resistance.

On the left flank of the battalion attack, B Company, under the command of Captain C. Sorenson, 'after hacking its way through the cactus hedges with machetes, got as far as the south-eastern end of Takrouna' where it was stopped in its tracks by a murderous hail of gunfire from enemy positions on Takrouna.[11]

By now the 28 (Maori) Battalion's attack had stuttered to a walk. Lieutenant Wikiriwhi, the battalion's Intelligence Officer, was sent to find out what the holdup was. He reported back to Bennett the difficulties being met by Sorenson and the Te Arawa men. Bennett gave instructions for B Company to bypass enemy opposition, move around the eastern or righthand side of Takrouna, and to link up with Ngati Porou which was trying to reach the Zaghouan road.

Meanwhile, Bennett himself, on hearing heavy gunfire still coming from the southern end of the Takrouna feature, moved to that location to reinforce his bypass instructions to B Company. 'He found it still pinned down by the heavy fire from Takrouna.'[12] He sent instructions to the supporting tanks attached to the battalion to engage and suppress enemy fire coming from Takrouna and directed the bulk of B Company to move to link up with C Company.

One platoon under the command of Sergeant Johnny Rogers, a 27-year-old school teacher, was left at the base of Takrouna to carry out the original plan of making a feint attack up the slopes to draw enemy attention. The pitifully small force of 12 men under Roger's command with a 30-year-old labourer, Lance Sergeant H. Manahi, as second-in-command, sat in the lee of the imposing objective and worked out their plan.

Rogers had been given instructions by his commanding officer to keep the enemy's heads down. What made these two very mature and experienced senior NCOs decide to forgo the easy option of carrying out the allotted task without moving from the secure positions they occupied? After all, in their existing positions they could easily engage the enemy and bring effective fire-power to bear without inviting further casualties to an already depleted platoon.

Even 41 years later when asked why they decided to attack, Manahi did not have a clear answer.[13] One suspects that the two NCOs decided to have a 'crack at the top'.

They decided to split their small forces and attack with one section from the south-east (Rogers) and one from the south-west (Manahi). Before they began the attack they were joined by a 'stray' sergeant, W. J. Smith, from 23 Battalion, and Captain S.F. Catchpole, an artillery observation officer.

In the initial assault, which was launched at dawn of 20 April, the ledge and the pinnacle were largely undefended. The enemy had positioned troops on the lower slopes, little expecting the New Zealanders to make headway. The 11 men and 3 sergeants working in their two groups attacked uphill against mortar and small-arms fire.

Italian soldiers of the Trieste Division had been given the task of holding the position even if surrounded. General Messe, Commander of the 1st Army (German-Italian), had decided to use Takrouna as an independent strong-point whose function was to break up the Allied attacks. He entrusted this task to General La Ferla, Commander of the Trieste Division, whose response was that he accepted the task and had extracted from the garrison commander an oath that 'Takrouna would be defended to the last man.'[14]

Against the determined assault of battle-hardened New Zealand troops, led by experienced NCOs, the Italians, after initially offering fierce resistance, quickly capitulated. Private Hinga Grant, of Mourea, Rotorua, rounded up 60 Italian prisoners around the base of Takrouna.

While the lower slopes were being cleared, Manahi with three men reached the base of the ledge. A sheer rock face topped by stone buildings held up further movement. Meanwhile Sergeant Smith and Private K. Aranui of Rotorua, using telephone cables, had scaled the rock face to gain access to the ledge where they surprised, and accepted the surrender of, a German wireless operator and an artillery observation officer.

By mid-morning, the first phase of this remarkable operation was complete. Rogers and Manahi had deployed their limited forces in a defensive position against an expected counter-attack. The enemy mortars and artillery had by now begun a heavy concentration of artillery and mortar fire on the pinnacle and the ledge. Johnny Rogers and five of the original assaulting party were killed during this bombardment.

After two attempts to get messages to his battalion had failed, Manahi himself went down to seek reinforcements, ammunition and stretcher bearers to carry the wounded off Takrouna. He managed to find Lieutenant Walton Haig of C Company, who agreed to provide a section. With these men, some stretcher bearers from the battalion's Regimental Aid Post and food and ammunition, Manahi, for the second time made his way back up the slopes onto Takrouna.

On his way back to the ledge and the pinnacle, Manahi met the officer from the medium regiment who advised him that achieving the objective was no longer possible and that he should return to his unit.[15] Manahi, however, ignored the advice and continued up to the ledge and pinnacle where some of his injured men still lay. He posted reinforcements to cover all approaches to the ledge and pinnacle. Meanwhile the arrival of a platoon of 21 Battalion, commanded by Lieutenant Shaw, helped strengthen the position.

It was now 3.30 p.m., more than 15 hours after the attack had started. Just as Shaw's men were settling into their positions – the last members of the platoon were still moving onto the ledge – the enemy launched the long-awaited counter attack.

The attack was carried out by Italian reinforcements of the Folgore Division who had been 'rushed to the northwest corner of Takrouna in 12 trucks.'[16] They attacked from the village, moving along the base of the pinnacle and onto the ledge. The attackers were, however, caught between Manahi's men on the pinnacle and Shaw's men on the ledge. In Manahi's words, 'they were like a mob of sheep being driven into us.'[17]

Nevertheless, while the Italians may have been caught between the cross-fires, they fought a fierce and determined fight among the stone huts. Then an Italian threw a grenade into a hut sheltering Maori wounded.[18] The Maori response was swift and savage. 'That's when the boys turned around and started using the bayonet,' said Manahi. There were no survivors.

Those who were not bayoneted or shot were thrown over the cliffs. As Wards observed, this was one of those grim moments in war when all control is lost.[19]

After this episode, Manahi collected his men and they made their way down to the plain, leaving the defence of the heights to Shaw and his platoon. Thus, on the evening of 20 April, after 16 hours of constant movement and the exercise of exemplary leadership, Manahi relinquished his hold over Takrouna.

His exertions were, however, not yet ended. That evening, the Italians again counter-attacked. Two platoons of 21 Battalion – Shaw's platoon had been reinforced earlier in the evening – were unable to contain the enemy and lost control of the summit. As dawn rose over Takrouna the next morning, the enemy had once more taken a commanding position on the pinnacle. Kippenberger ordered 28 (Maori) Battalion to send reinforcements.

Manahi responded magnificently and returned for the third time to take charge of Takrouna. Manahi consulted Lieutenant Hirst, who had taken command when Shaw was wounded, on how to recapture the pinnacle. With the help of an artillery bombardment, the pinnacle was retaken without loss of further lives. The enemy abandoned the position.

This left the village below the pinnacle to be dealt with. With the help of the artillery, who for the first time used the 9-pounder solid-shot anti-tank shells, the village was bombarded, causing havoc among the Italian soldiers. Meanwhile, not to be outdone, Manahi and a group of Maoris were stalking the outskirts of the village. Hirst approached from the north and between them, the two groups accelerated the defeat of the completely demoralised enemy. Over 300 prisoners were taken.

The battle for Takrouna was over. In Wards' words, 'the scene of so much dogged fighting, so much individual gallantry and sacrifice had fallen.'[20] Messages of congratulations came from Freyberg and General Horrocks, the Corps Commander. 'In the division as a whole the men who survived the struggle were regarded with something akin to awe.'[21]

Manahi's outstanding bravery and leadership were recognised by the immediate submission for an award of the Victoria Cross. The citation for the immediate DCM he received, instead of the VC he deserved, noted that Manahi 'showed the highest qualities of an infantry soldier. His cool judgement, resolute determination and outstanding personal bravery were an inspiration to his men and a supreme contribution to the capture of and holding of a feature vital to the success of the operation.'[22]

John Vader, an Australian journalist, in his book *ANZAC*, pays Manahi the following compliment: 'Manahi should have been knighted on the spot and given as his page a redundant Major-General.'[23]

Major Denis Blundell (Brigade Major of 5 NZ Brigade after the battle for Takrouna and later Governor-General of New Zealand), writing for the journal of the Fourteenth Reunion of 28 (Maori) Battalion, recalled the fierce fighting around Takrouna. 'Your battalion suffered heavy casualties, including the CO, Charlie Bennett and most of the officers. Yet as your history records, there were many incredible exploits of bravery and initiative by NCOs and other ranks.' Surely, he continued 'one of the finest chapters in your proud history.'[24]

As Blundell wrote the citation recommending Manahi's award of an immediate Victoria Cross, it is worth quoting in full his thoughts on hearing it had been turned down. 'Like the rest of the division [I] was disgusted when he was awarded an immediate DCM. I feel sure that here was an example, that even in the realm of bravery, politics played a part, and that the award to 2nd Lieutenant Ngarimu only some three weeks previously influenced the final decision. This for me was confirmed when later at the Gejira Sporting Club in Cairo, our Military Secretary, Brigadier Rudd, asked me to tell the story to a senior British general. The General's comment was "we did make a mistake".'

These comments from both Blundell and the British general sharpen focus on an issue which is very sensitive to servicemen. Those who have won a decoration for bravery will inevitably say that the award was accepted on behalf of those who took part in the operation or, that what they did was no more or less than what was done by any number of their colleagues. Charles Upham, who also has the rare distinction of being a double Victoria Cross holder, had this to say about the matter when told that he had been awarded the Victoria Cross: 'It's meant for the men . . . My men by God they could fight! You know, those chaps can do anything.'[25]

Over the years since the battle for Takrouna suggestions have been made for the 'wrong' to be corrected and for Manahi to be awarded a Victoria Cross. The fact that Upham was awarded his second Victoria Cross at the end of the war for bravery years earlier gives hope for those who still believe that a gross injustice was done Manahi.

Chapter 14

TO THE VICTORS THE SPOILS OF WAR

Noel 'Wig' Gardiner, in his book *Freyberg's Circus*, wrote that the soldier, by the very nature of his training and conditioning, becomes part brigand. He expands on this theme in a chapter entitled 'The spoils of war'. Gardiner argues that most people, including soldiers, are basically honest and have a clear idea about what is right and wrong. He continues that when soldiers enter a strange land, 'where most of the civilian population has fled, and a lot of interesting gear is lying about with no apparent owners, who is to say it is not his who comes upon it first?' Thus it is Gardiner's view that 'to souvenir something of value or come by something that could be readily converted into cash was never far from the forefront of most soldiers' minds.'[1]

Maori soldiers were certainly no exception to Gardiner's rule. Indeed, there were many in the New Zealand Division who believed that the Maori had the dubious honour of being the most adept practitioner of the collection of the spoils of war.

When collecting the material for this book, I ran into trouble from a number of correspondents who took exception to the book containing a chapter on what I described as the Maori's attitude to 'battlefield booty'.

One correspondent disputed my use of the word 'booty' to describe captured enemy weapons. Quite rightly, he pointed out that it 'wasn't greed' that motivated the Maori to retain captured German weapons. In my reply to him I agreed but I also pointed out that my interviews with Maori officers and soldiers showed that they themselves used a much stronger word – loot.

Those whom I interviewed took the view that all captured material was loot. Some of the loot, such as weapons, were immediately usable for protection; other material was viewed as loot which could be sold when the soldier was next on leave.

The practice of collecting souvenirs from the battlefield and looting is as old as war itself. John Keegan, in his book *The Face of Battle*, explores in detail the anatomy of the battlefield, and describes the role of looting and the collection of souvenirs on a number of battlefields across several centuries. Medieval warfare was about 'ultimately and most important, ransom and loot'.[2] For the man-at-arms, the prospect of enrichment was a significant factor in his will to fight.

At Agincourt on 25 October 1415, the English defeated the French.

When the English took possession of the field of combat, the English infantry chased and tackled those French fugitives who had been unable to escape, so that they could claim a bounty. Others greedy for souvenirs and riches 'were sorting through the recumbent bodies' of the piles of slaughtered French.[3]

During the battle of Waterloo on 18 June 1815, 'looting appears to have been so universal an activity, so energetically practised even during the battle itself' that it might have been one of the principal reasons that British infantry held their places in the line.[4] At the height of the battle, soldiers were observed rifling the pockets of the dead.

By the First World War, the hope of plunder as a motive for soldiers to remain on the battlefield could be discounted and especially so on the Western front, where it was was such a hellish place that it was not worth life or limb to linger there. However, the battlefields of the Second World War, with rare exceptions such as the Russian front, were not the same slaughterhouses as those of the First World War. Thus the incentive for soldiers to once more linger on the battlefield was high.

Few would argue with Keegan's proposition that soldiers of every age have looted and robbed. It is, however, important to understand what motivates otherwise calm, law-abiding citizens to throw away, during times of war, the moral codes of conduct which they were raised under. While training to kill must inevitably dull the norms of civilised behaviour, this in itself is not sufficient reason to completely abandon self-discipline. Two reasons have been put forward to explain why soldiers loot and rob on the battlefield.

The first reason to explain such behaviour is symbolic. In the days of hand-to-hand fighting and single combat, the victor was entitled to take from the vanquished 'items worthy of display for their intrinsic or symbolic value.' The Maori of pre-European times was familiar with this practice. Often the victor would claim the weapon of the vanquished as a symbol of the conquest. In extreme cases, the vanquished would lose his head to the victor.

There is also an economic motive. For the capture of ransomable material offered the soldier the opportunity to make money. After Waterloo there was a roaring trade in gold and silver watches and rings.[5]

While the rewards from Second World War battlefields may not have been as great, there was nonetheless an opportunity for soldiers to make enough money to pay for extra services while on leave.

For the Maori, the opportunities to acquire battlefield souvenirs were abundant. Throughout the war they were involved in nearly every major attack mounted by the New Zealand Division. Underlying Maori exploits in this dubious area of military activity was an element of mischievousness and a sense of adventure.

The Maori did not restrict their activities specifically to the battlefield, nor did they consider that noncombatants should be sacrosanct. They prided themselves on the ability and the capacity to acquire food no matter what the difficulties. For Maori soldiers the acme of any important function was the hakari (feast) that was associated with it. To this end, they went to extraordinary lengths to provide the right ingredients for the feast, which was was preferably prepared in a hangi. The food was cooked in a hole in the ground using steam from heated stones. Pork was the main delicacy of any hangi.

On one occasion in Italy, after a successful raid, a group of Maori soldiers killed the prize pig of the local village dignitary. Having gained their prize, the Maori had to get it out of the village. It was one thing to enter under the watchful eyes of the sentries but it was another to leave with the fruits of the raid. Ever resourceful, the Maori hit upon the idea of using a stretcher to carry out their prize.

The small party of sombre Maori bore their 'comrade' home in silence, lying on a stretcher covered by a blanket. As they passed the sentries, they came to attention to pay homage to a brave comrade-in-arms being carried home.

The Maori lost no opportunity to exploit any situation where they could gain 'ransomable' material, particularly small valuables such as watches and rings. These were portable and could be used for barter, exchange or could be sold. In this respect they were no different to any other soldier. In 28 (Maori) Battalion lore, the prize for most consistent, determined and innovative souvenir hunter must go to Private Charlie Shelford.

Rangi Logan described how Shelford was reassigned to a transport unit as his legs were worrying him. Shelford was an outstanding infantry soldier, having won the Distinguished Conduct Medal for conspicuous bravery during the Second Libyan campaign of November-December 1941. A year later during the battle of Alamein, D Company were attacking an enemy position. Logan, as was his custom, was keeping in touch with his platoons when he spotted a 'shadowy figure that was somehow familiar'.

It was Charlie Shelford. He should have been some kilometres to the rear in a safe area. When asked why he was back in the front line without authority, Shelford replied: 'When this is all over we'll get leave and I want to get some loot to sell to the wogs in Cairo.'[6]

Major Harry Lambert also remembered Shelford. Lambert was platoon commander of 18 Platoon, D Company, during the battalion's last battle in Tunisia.

Lambert recalled lying on the start line prior to the attack, being soaked by the persistent drizzle. Shelford was a driver with B Echelon – these were the troops and vehicles that did not take part in the immediate attack but were required to move forward on the completion of the attack to replenish ammunition and supplies. B Echelon was usually located some kilometres to the rear. Lambert noted that B Echelon personnel often turned up 'looking for enemy hardware after the fighting was over.'

Not Shelford. Lambert remembered Shelford appearing out of the darkness with 'tommy gun nonchalantly slung over his shoulder.' To the by now unnecessary question, 'What are you doing here, Charlie?' came the laconic reply, 'I fight for my loot.'[7]

For the Maori, the capture of enemy weapons was in a category all of its own. During the Greek campaign, there were few opportunities to acquire weapons, as the Battalion was seldom in a position to engage and remain in contact with the Germans. However, during the desperate struggle for Crete, the Maori were able to capture a wide range of small-arms from the German paratroopers. Here they also discovered that the Germans produced weapons of first-class quality.

The Luger pistol became a prized weapon which doubled as a souvenir. So much so that it quickly became a replacement for the standard issue .38 pistols. Much to the chagrin of the Quartermaster Sergeants, a number of officers could not account for the loss of their issue weapons. It was therefore hardly surprising that the number of issue pistols lost during battle was remarkably high.

After their first desert action, the Maori confirmed their predilection for the possession and use of enemy weapons which had been evident in the earlier Greek and Crete campaigns. During the attack on Sollum in November 1941, B Company of Te Arawa took the opportunity of raiding the enemy arms depot and captured a number of weapons. In addition to its normal complement of weapons, the company had 6 Spandaus, 3 anti-tank rifles, 1 two-inch mortar, 6 tommy guns and 50 stick grenades. With the addition of these weapons the company had effectively doubled its firepower.[8]

It was reported that among the booty taken at Sollum was an Italian Army pay truck.[9] The huge stacks of lire were used as gambling chips, for lighting cigarettes or just strewn around the desert. What the Maori had failed to realise was that the lire was exchangeable in Cairo.

Some days later at Menastir, on the Bardia-Sollum road, the Maori mounted a successful ambush. Second-Lieutenant Wordley recorded in his diary that a number of Maori had got drunk on 'some drink they had swiped' during the day.[10] This was not an unusual occurrence as during the withdrawal through Greece the Maori had, on occasion, found caches of wine which they had proceeded to drink or take with them. Wordley also notes that, 'Lloyd gave me a Luger and Maru Wharerau gave me a torch.' He adds that he was 'quite satisfied with his lot'.

The 28 (Maori) Battalion fought in the Sollum-Gazala area from 23 November to 17 December 1941. When they pulled out of the front line, they took with them an array of captured enemy weapons including enemy long range mortars, machine guns and 20 mm cannon.

They had also acquired a wide range of trucks. D Company scorned ordinary vehicles and owned a light Italian tank, and C Company had a heavy diesel lorry. These vehicles were all required to back-load the captured weapons. Before the Maori left the battle area they received a demand from Brigade Headquarters to hand in all captured enemy weapons. It was a sad battalion, wrote Cody, that contemplated this order.[11]

Lieutenant-Colonel Humphrey Dyer's recall to base duty from command of 28 (Maori) Battalion was the most extreme case of a senior officer believing that these weapons should be retained for use by the soldiers. His demise did not stop the practice of retaining captured weapons, and the soldiers continued to arm themselves with captured weapons.

John Harper, then Liaison Officer for 20 Battalion on 4 Brigade staff, recalled the incident well. He noted that the Maori had made a point of keeping captured enemy weapons and they spent much of their spare time training with the weapons. They also took every opportunity to teach reinforcements how to use them. He wrote that 'Colonel Dyer and the whole 28 Bn were very proud' of their weapons.[12]

As if to underscore the continuing problem, two months after Dyer's return to base, a Routine Order appeared on the subject of 'Loot and Traffic in Arms'. The order notified all soldiers that it had come to notice that captured arms and ammunition were being sold.

The order warned all ranks 'that it is forbidden to retain in their possession any public enemy property found on the battlefield.'[13] It also pointed out that anyone disposing of weapons through the black market was directly helping the enemy as such weapons invariably found their way back to 'those who work for the enemy'. The punishment for trafficking in arms was two years' imprisonment.

Company commanders were directed to hold 'rigid inspections' of their areas and to hand any captured war materials in the possession of company personnel to the Battalion Quartermaster for return to Base Kit

Depot. The Maori were given four days to carry out the inspection and hand over captured enemy material.

The order ends on an interesting note. Soldiers were advised that such material 'will be retained' at the Base Depot as trophies of war and be reissued on the termination of hostilities.

Given the tension which usually existed between front-line troops and base 'wallahs', it is hardly surprising that soldiers would have viewed with suspicion the latter part of the Routine Order. The War Diary does not indicate the success achieved by the order.

Judging by a further Routine Order which appeared just over a month later, the capture of weapons was not always restricted to enemy action. Routine Order No. 55 of 11 August 1941, entitled 'Theft of Arms', noted that there had been numerous cases of the theft of rifles and pistols from the men's and officer's quarters. Companies were exhorted to provide proper security for the safeguarding of weapons. Officers were directed that they would 'be held personally responsible for the security of their pistols.'[14]

It is interesting to note that a spate of activities such as that contained in Routine Order No. 55 usually came after the men had spent long periods out of the line. Boredom, as well as the need to acquire trade goods, was a contributing factor to such behaviour.

For the remainder of the desert campaign, the Maori continued to collect German weapons and ammunition for their own use. Divisional Headquarters seemed not to persistently press the Maori to return their weapons.

When the Maori reached Tripoli in early 1943, the end of the desert campaign was almost in sight. They still had to fight through the battles for Point 209 and Takrouna but for the time being they rested and recuperated from the long haul from Alamein.

During this period they were called upon to provide work parties for wharf duties at the Tripoli docks. Here the many allied ships loaded and unloaded their cargoes of food, petrol and war supplies.

Here also was an opportunity that few New Zealanders could resist. Cody, the Official Historian, noted that there were frequent interruptions from the raids carried out by German aircraft. There were also frequent interruptions from 'unauthorised celebrations' – on one occasion after a case of rum had been accidentally dropped.

He also noted that one of the cargo ships unloaded by the Maori contained a cargo of peanuts destined for Indian troops. The Maori were allowed to take as many bags of peanuts as they liked. This was the signal for a frenetic round of commodity trading with Maori bartering bags of peanuts for whatever could be gained.[15]

During the Maori stay in Tripoli, A Company had managed to acquired a staff car for their Major, Ben Porter. The car had been obtained from a motor works which the Ngapuhi had been guarding. With some expert advice, the Ngapuhi selected a vehicle suitable for a Ngapuhi chief.

However, there was one small difficulty – the car required a camouflage paint job and an appropriate New Zealand serial number. While the men of Ngapuhi were considering how best to achieve this goal, an RAF guard marched up and took up positions at the main gate of the compound.

Not to be outdone, the Ngapuhi loaded the car into the back of the cook's three-tonner and drove it through the main gate, ostensibly on a ration run. The following morning the car 'painted with fernleaf insignia and battalion serial number stood in the company car park.'[16]

This, however, was not the end of the story for the Ngapuhi car. Before they left Tripoli, the Maori were ordered to leave all enemy vehicles in a special carpark. 'OC A Company regretfully sent his runabout there in the charge of two drivers'.[17] When the battalion left for Medenine the two drivers failed to show. To no one's surprise, they arrived at Medenine later driving the company commander's car. They had duly handed in the car at the special carpark. Later that evening, during the hours of darkness, they stole it back again.

After the final battle at Takrouna, a further order was issued once more calling for the handing-in of all foreign vehicles. During the battle for Takrouna, Major Porter, Officer Commanding the Ngapuhi, was wounded. His men did not believe that the vehicle should go to anyone else and thus they set fire to the vehicle rather than allow anyone else to drive it.

During the Italian campaign the Maori continued from time to time to live off the land. As usual, on special occasions, their requirement for meat for company hangi had to be met.

In December 1944, Rock Maika, then a Sergeant in B Company, recalls the preparations for Christmas celebrations. After a particularly heavy engagement with the Germans, the Maori pulled back from the front-line to celebrate Christmas.

On 22 December 1944, Rock wrote, 'All our efforts now are concentrated on getting a Christmas dinner. Pigs around here are very scarce and so are the fowls however by Xmas I think we will have the necessaries'.[18] In his next letter home, Rock advised, 'Our Xmas dinner went off with a bang . . . We managed to get pigs alright.' He continued, 'as a matter of fact some of the boys had to go to the front lines to get hold of them and that's where we got our chicken too.'

He also noted that they had quite a stock of wine, champagne and liqueurs. After dinner the men 'got stuck into the wine and by bedtime everyone was tight.' The next day the Maori were back in the front-line resuming offensive action.[19]

The availability of alcohol on the front-line in Italy contrasted very sharply with the situation in the desert. Only on rare occasions during the desert campaign were the Maori able to break open stocks of alcohol and wine. However, during the Italian campaign, nearly every large house that the Maori occupied seemed to have a stock of wine. The officers were aware of the temptations confronting the soldiers and they had to exercise extremely fine judgement over when to stop the drinking and when to allow it.

In Italy the men were presented with numerous occasions where they had the opportunity to souvenir material. As relations with the Italians were very cordial, the men largely respected the local people. This did not mean that their trading activities were any less restricted. Indeed, perhaps because of the cordial relations, the bartering of military clothing and rations for clothes, cameras and jewellery was regularly conducted at all levels.

It was possible, for example, to buy an Agfa German camera valued at 14 000 lira (approximately $70) for $10. In this case, the difference in price was made up by a pair of Army boots and a German soldier's leather jacket.

Perhaps the incident which most encapsulates the Maori attitude to the material he acquired in the Italian campaign, is one described by Brigadier J.T. Burrows, who was Commander 5 (NZ) Brigade. He was watching the Maori advancing to make contact with the enemy during the advance to Florence and as he stood on the high ground overlooking the advancing troops he saw the leading section of Maori come into view moving cautiously. He swung his binoculars further forward to try and pick up the leading scout for the whole advance. As his binoculars picked up the leading figure, he saw 'a most astonishing spectacle'.

'This soldier, away out in front, entirely by himself, was wearing a woman's expensive fur coat and on his head a black Borsalino hat. His rifle was slung over his shoulder but his pack and goodness knows what other things he had acquired along the way were dumped in a pram which he was pushing merrily along the road without a care in the world.'[20] Duncan McIntyre, many years later a Minister in a National Government but then a staff captain to Brigadier Burrows, reported that the Maori soldier was as full as a boot.

Chapter 15

THE ITALIAN CAMPAIGNS

'The strategy by which war came to Italy is not without interest to every man who fought there,' wrote N.C. Phillips, Official Historian of the Italian Campaign. The decision to commit New Zealanders to the mainland of Europe, via the toe of Italy, was not based on a well-thought-out strategy. It was, as Phillips has suggested, a halting and tentative process. Moreover, the decision was taken against the strategic imperative of Operation Overlord, the impending invasion of Europe.[1]

The invasion of Italy by the Allies had been considered in May 1943. Principally, the issue had been what objectives would be achieved from such a campaign. Two views emerged. First, that it was essential to eliminate Italy from the war. And secondly, it was essential to launch an attack to draw away as many German divisions as possible from the Russian Front. This second aspect would also provide relief for the impending battle in northern France.

By September 1943, the situation had cleared considerably. Early in September, the Italians had capitulated and the armistice signed with the Allies triggered the invasion. On 3 September 1943, the Eighth Army lodged on the Italian mainland and began to advance north along the Adriatic coast through Calabria. Six days later, the Americans of the Fifth Army stormed ashore at Salerno and began to advance north along the west coast of Italy; the war in Italy had begun.

Some months earlier, following the end of the Tunisian campaign on 13 May 1943, 28 (Maori) Battalion had made ready for the long trek back to Egypt. They left Tripoli on 15 May. Just over two weeks and 3 200 dusty kilometres later, they arrived back in Maadi camp. On arrival each soldier received three bottles of beer.

After cleaning off the dust and grime of the long journey, the men sat down to eat the huge quantities of food prepared at individual company hangi. That night the sky was ablaze with the traditional 'return home' salute, as rifle, mortar fire and tracer arced across the heavens. For a brief period, the soldiers thumbed their noses at authority.

At a battalion parade the following morning, Lieutenant-Colonel Keiha announced that 182 men would be returning home to New Zealand for three months' furlough leave. After three years overseas, the men of the original group of soldiers who had left Palmerston North on that cold morning of May 1940 were about to put behind them the traumatic campaigns of Greece, Crete and the Middle East for the quiet of New Zealand.

The decision to institute the furlough schemes had been taken against a background of intense discussion and negotiation. It came at a time when the Government was confronted with two options. Firstly, to leave the Second New Zealand Expeditionary Force in the Middle East with the prospect of continuing onto service in Europe. Or secondly, to return the troops home with the prospect of redeploying a major force into the Pacific. The views of the men in the New Zealand Division indicated a general desire to return home. This thinking was in line with the letter written by Keiha and the Ngati Porou officers of C Company in early 1943.

The Government's decision, taken in late May 1943, was that the New Zealand Division should remain in the Middle East and be available for operations in Europe.

It also decided that the 3rd New Zealand Division, training for war in the Pacific, should also be maintained. However, a provison was added that both divisions would be maintained on a reducing scale. That is, the establishment of both would be reduced in line with the reducing availability of reinforcements.

Parliament agreed to the Government's proposals on the condition that the furlough scheme be implemented forthwith. This posed a practical difficulty for army authorities as they had to find nearly 5 000 reinforcements to replace those eligible to return home.

In preparing for their return to New Zealand, a number of soldiers were apprehensive about what they would find when they arrived. The absence of so many men from New Zealand had forced authorities to replace men with women in many areas of industry and farming.

Increased responsibilities, the absence of spouses and the presence, in a number of areas, of large bodies of soldiers led to inevitable liaisons. The receipt by soldiers at the front of 'Dear John' letters did not endear them to unfaithful partners. The fear of a partner at home succumbing to temptation was perhaps the greatest unspoken fear of the married soldier.

Moreover, this state of anxiety was not helped by the arrival in New Zealand of American troops. With the Americans becoming more involved in the Pacific, it was only a matter of time before their forces arrived in New Zealand in sizeable numbers. The arrival of the Marine Division in Wellington, in June 1942, was bound to exacerbate the fears and apprehensions of New Zealand soldiers serving overseas.

By July 1943, nearly 50 000 American soldiers were stationed in New Zealand. Following a number of incidents involving Maori women in Auckland, Princess Te Puea, of Waikato, went to the American Headquarters in Manurewa to remonstrate with the American commander. The headstrong chieftainess from Waikato was kept waiting for over an hour. When she heard herself being described as a 'black woman', she walked out in anger.[2]

The incident sparked off a series of clashes between Maori soldiers and American servicemen. Te Puea, the woman who made ministers of the crown quail at the thought of a visit from her, decided to make peace with the Americans.[3]

As Eve Ebbett writes in her book *When the Boys Were Away*, 'How much sex New Zealand women enjoyed with Americans, how much they fell for the blandishments and gifts, how many moral lapses occurred because of loneliness or grief is impossible to tell.'[4] What is possible to tell is that the inevitable clash between American and Kiwi soldiers occurred in Wellington in April 1943 at what was later described as the battle of Manners Street.

The event which triggered the battle has been lost in the welter of claim and counter-claim. Many believe that the flare-up was sparked by an incident between Maori soldiers and the Americans, who objected to their presence in one of the clubs. The four-hour battle which followed would have done justice to some of the more famous actions in war that both Americans and New Zealanders had been involved in. Over 1000 men were involved in the fighting and subsequent skirmishes. Remarkably, given the intense emotions and the violence, there were few serious injuries.

Several more incidents took place in other towns and cities throughout the country. However, by the time the Expeditionary Force furlough had reached New Zealand, much of the steam had dissipated.

The Government was soon to be faced with a far more serious problem. For the men of Ruapehu draft and for the Military Authorities, an unforeseen complication arose when it was time for the draft to return to the combat zone. Many of the men of the Ruapehu draft refused to return to active service after their three months' leave was over.

F.L.W. Wood, in *The New Zealand People at War*, examines the reasons why the veterans of the 1st and 2nd Echelons were reluctant to return to war. 'It would have been difficult in any circumstance,' he wrote, 'to withdraw 5300 men from the fighting zone, restore them for three months to their relatives and friends halfway across the world, and then call on them to return to the front.'[5]

During their leave, the men of Ruapehu draft could not help but notice the decided lack of civilian fervour for the war effort. The easing of civilian tensions, which followed the reduced Japanese threat, helped civilians enjoy life on a scale which made many of the veterans on furlough wonder why they should continue to risk their lives.

In late August 1943, the Government, perhaps recognising the possibility of revolt among the members of the draft, announced a number of relevant measures: with the exception of those required for essential services, all married men with children, and men over the age of 41 were allowed to remain at home. The 182 Maori soldiers were also allowed to return to civilian life.

The revolt against the return to active service was supported by many New Zealanders. Those who had not served, either kept quiet or were totally supportive of the soldiers' desire to remain at home. The original date of sailing for the Ruapehu draft was the end of October 1943. This date was postponed. Failure to obtain a suitable ship saw a further postponement.

Finally, on January 1944, 663 soldiers of the original 5 300 sailed to Europe and back to active service. In the interim, a number of men who had refused to embark were tried by court-martial. At the end of the war, an awkward situation was resolved when the Prime Minister waived punishments meted out to those who had rebelled.[6]

In the meantime, the 28 (Maori) Battalion, together with the remainder of the New Zealand Division, had moved from the Middle East to Italy. They had left Maadi Camp on 19 September 1943.

During the months of June, July and August the battalion built up its strength. New reinforcements to replace those who had returned home marched in. The perennial cycle of retraining started once more. After several weeks of leave, the men of 28 (Maori) Battalion breathed a sigh of relief when the new training syllabus was introduced. Route marches, weapon training and field training replaced the base camp duties and recreational activities.

The first few days of the new regime presented an opportunity for commanders to ready the soldiers for their next mission. Their departure from Maadi was carried out in style. Not for the Maori the comfort of trucks. They marched the 150 km to Burg el Arab, the transit camp, from which they were to launch the next campaign.

On 17 October 1943, the 28 (Maori) Battalion boarded the transports for the four-day cruise to the mainland of Europe. To minimise the loss of soldiers from any one company should the troop ships have been attacked, it was decided to allocate a platoon from each company to separate transport ships.[7]

On 22 October 1943 the Maori sighted Taranto, the invasion harbour on the southern toe of Italy. The battalion marched the 10 km distance from the harbour to the transit camp of Sitte. For the second time in less than three and a half years, Maori soldiers were again about to shed their blood on the continent of Europe.

In many ways, the shift of 28 (Maori) Battalion from the deserts of the Middle East to the countryside and towns of Italy represented the closing of one episode in the battalion's history and the opening of another. Except for the middle ranking and senior officers, some of the senior non-commissioned officers and a handful of soldiers, few of the original battalion now remained with the assault companies. Many had, as J. F. Cody noted, 'migrated to the comparative safety' of Headquarters Company.

Moreoever, the two senior officers in the battalion were now Pakeha. After serving as Battalion Commander for only six months, Keiha had been evacuated to hospital. Reta Keiha had been Bennett's second-in-command before taking command. According to Kippenberger's assessment, although he only commanded the battalion for a short period he left it in a mess.[8] It is this assessment which probably led to the appointment of one of Kippenberger's own senior staff officers to command 28 (Maori) Battalion.

Keiha was replaced by Lieutenant Monty Fairbrother, a 20 Battalion original of the 1st Echelon. He was promoted from Brigade Major of 5 (NZ) Brigade to command the Maori. Major R. Young had already marched in as the battalion's second-in-command.

Most of the battalion's officers had seen action in Tunisia. However, many of these had not been part of the earlier freewheeling desert campaigns. They had not shared in the swashbuckling adventure of sweeping across many kilometres of desert. The battles of the desert had seemed like naval battles across the vast expanse of ocean as the divisions and armies attempted to grapple with, and close with each other. It was a type of war which encouraged the demonstration of acts of chivalry not often seen in the grim and closely fought struggles which were to follow as the German armies fought for survival.

The Italian countryside, the villages and the people reminded the Maori of their own rural communities and families. The narrow village streets and the cobblestones were a reminder of the many centuries of history to be found in Europe. In the initial days and weeks of discovery, they were an adventure to be enjoyed. In later days they were to become death traps and avenues of ambush as the Germans skilfully defended their withdrawal routes to the north.

After three weeks of training, the battalion moved to join the Eighth Army at the battlefront some 400 km to the north. The staged move took some days. By 18 November, they had closed to the Jangus River. Here the Allies were attempting to push through the German defensive winter line which ran north of the Sangro River, across the Appenine chain, through Monte Cassino and on to the west coast.

Originally, it had been intended to 'bounce' the Germans, break through their front lines and attempt a deep penetration to destroy their reserve forces. However, the difficult terrain, the onset of winter and, above all, the stubbornness of the German defenders forced an amendment to this bold plan.

The New Zealanders were ordered to carry out a series of deliberate attacks across the Sangro River, a task allotted to the Sixth Brigade. Meanwhile, the Maori, based at Atessa some 8 km south of the Sangro, continued training. Route marches, and gunnery practice with their new anti-tank weapon, the Piat (Projector Infantry, Anti-tank), helped ease the frustration of not being able to close with the enemy.[9]

For the attack across the Sangro, the Maori played a reserve role. It was not until 1 December 1943 that they finally crossed the Sangro and they had to wait a further six days before they could participate in their first attack on Italian soil.

Freyberg had decided to launch a divisional attack from the south-east. His intention was to have the Sixth Brigade attack from the south-east and then, when north of the town of Orsogna, swing south to launch a direct attack on it. He also decided to launch 5 (NZ) Brigade from the south east as well, with the task of moving to the north of Orsogna to cut the main road from Orsogna to Ortona. This would achieve the goal of cutting off the German withdrawal to the north. It would also hamper the deployment of reserve forces which might be launched to counter-attack any Allied movements in the Orsogna area.[10]

The vanguard of the 5 (NZ) Brigade attack was to be the 28 (Maori) Battalion. Lieutenant-Colonel Fairbrother had decided to attack with Ngati Porou (C Company) on the right and D Company on the left. Captain Jim Henare with the Ngapuhi of A Company were designated as the mopping up company. Te Arawa (B Company) were to remain as Battalion Reserve.[11]

The terrain over which the New Zealanders had to attack was formidable. 28 (Maori) Battalion, laden down with as much ammunition as possible, had to climb up and over the steep San Felice ridge. The ridge lay parallel to and about a mile from the Orsogna-Ortona road. When they had reached the top of the ridge, they had to move down the forward slope. The slope was dotted with olive trees and peasants' dwellings. At the bottom of the ridge, the Maori soldiers crossed the Moro stream and began the arduous climb to the start line, which was at the top of the Pascuccio spur.

Between the main road and the Felice ridge lay two features, both at right angles to the road. To the north was the Sfasciata ridge and to the south lay the Pascuccio ridge. A deep gully separated the two features.

The climb to the top of the Pascuccio spur was hampered by the slopes slippery after intermittent rain. The men slipped, slid and fell as they struggled to reach the start point.

Finally, at 2.30 p.m., the artillery barrage signalling the start of the attack began. There was much anxiety among the soldiers as they awaited their first baptism of fire on Italian soil. They advanced slowly behind the curtain of artillery fire as it moved ahead of them. It was extremely difficult for them to keep pace with the rolling barrage. Movement was compounded by the fact that the men had to move along the steep-sided ridge.

In their approach to the German positions, the Maori 'by not uncommon chance' had selected their attack route along the enemy's formation boundary. In military terms this is the boundary along which two units share a common frontage.[12]

It is also the weakest spot in the enemy's defences. The principal reason for this is that unless both units have tied down, to the last degree, responsibilities for every inch of the boundary, the likelihood of error is high. Moreover, as inter-unit boundaries are selected to run along distinguishable features such as stream lines or ridges, there are often blind spots within these features which can easily be missed.

28 (Maori) Battalion had the good fortune to select as its line of attack the boundary between 9 Panzer Grenadier Regiment and 146 Regiment. Ngati Porou, on the right of the assault, struck the Grenadiers. D Company, on the left, hit the 146 Regiment. Ngati Porou caught the Grenadiers completely by surprise and succeeded in overrunning the boundary company. Similarly, D Company caught the 146 Regiment company off guard and succeeded in scattering the Germans in total disarray.

In their approach to the German positions, D Company had to cross numerous slips. In spite of their initial apprehension, the men soon got carried away with the noise and smoke of the barrage. So much so that the 'new hands' took pot shots at the stray animals and birds as they advanced.

Lieutenant Boy Tomoana, in command of the leading platoon of D Company, took the opportunity to try out his platoon Piat. He also reported that one of his soldiers, Private R.T.M. Goodwillie, had adopted an interesting way of demonstrating his lack of fear. During the short periods of waiting while the barrage lifted, he would lie with his head towards the enemy and begin reading a book. 'Quite a sound idea in theory,' noted Tomoana. He added that 'all sorts of methods are used to conquer the feeling of fear.'[13]

When they had reached the top of the spur, the company had to negotiate their way up a small cliff. Fortunately, growing on the sides of the cliff were some poplars and these were used by the Maori to climb to the top. Those who had fought at Takrouna must have remembered vividly the way in which Te Arawa had gained access to the top of the cliff there by using telephone cables. Now it was poplar trees.

At the top of the cliff and about half a metre from its edge were a number of German soldiers dug in. However, fortunately for the Maori, their pits were facing a threat from the road to the west and south-west.

Corporal Henry Barrett and his section gained the top of the cliff and under his aggressive leadership the area was cleared. The Maori lost one man killed and one man wounded. Barrett's personal bravery and leadership and his skilful use of the bayonet won him the Distinguished Conduct Medal. He is credited with killing nine Germans in the brief but violent struggle.

C Company's approach to the enemy positions was less hazardous but they had to fight vigorously to clear the area of Germans. By last light on 7 December 1943, the company had succeeded in cutting the main road between Orsogna and Ortona.

D Company had also succeeded in reaching its positions. It had adopted a scattered position with men on the road in the vicinity of the Orsogna cemetery. More men were left on the high ground which they had captured earlier. Ngapuhi, meanwhile, who had earlier come to the rescue of D Company, which had been pinned down, had moved across the rear and to the south to cut the main road just north of Orsogna.

Soon after last light, the Panzer Grenadiers counter-attacked. Supported by tanks, they drove down the road from the north and pushed the Ngati Porou back from the road and up the escarpment to the Pascuccio ridge where they had begun their attack earlier that afternoon.

At 8 p.m., D Company heard the sound of tanks. Assuming that these were the friendly tanks that they were expecting, the men cheered. Elation, however, quickly turned to alarm as they realised that these were not Allied but German tanks. They had no option but to retreat from the edge of the road back up to the clifftop which Barrett and his section had cleared so successfully earlier that afternoon.

A Company was also forced to withdraw back up the ridge and hastily dig new positions against the massing counter-attack.

It was clear to Colonel Fairbrother that he needed more substantial anti-tank support. He ordered Captain Awatere to return immediately to the battalion's rear area and to try to manhandle two six-pounder anti-tank guns across the Moro and up the ridge to the forward area. It was now 9 p.m.

The task that Fairbrother asked of Awatere was almost impossible. Before the attack, the battalion's reconnaissance parties had tried to find navigable routes across the Moro and to the forward area so that the batallion's heavy support weapons could be moved forward. The nature of the terrain had clearly precluded such an option. Now there was no choice but to try. On top of his difficulties, Awatere had to attempt to manhandle the guns across unfamiliar terrain in the night.

In the interim, the Germans had made two attempts to counter-attack against A Company positions. The Ngapuhi had called for two artillery 'stonks' to break up the counter-attacks. The third attack came closer.

'The Germans could be seen flitting from tree to tree.' When a German voice was heard ordering his comrades to 'feex bayonets', Ngapuhi could not resist the challenge. As they had done so often before in the desert, they leapt from their pits with fixed bayonets and charged.[14]

Sergeant Fred Te Namu, who was to die some days later of wounds received from this action, was heard to yell 'charge you bastards', as he rushed the approaching Germans. The rout of the Germans was accomplished and Captain Jim Henare had to recall his men for fear of them going too far. They 'strolled back in good humour'.

In spite of these small tactical successes, the Maori were in a very poor position and vulnerable on both flanks. As the men hung on grimly to their positions, the remainder of the battalion's resources had been mobilised to drag the two six-pounder guns forward.

The enormous efforts made by the Maori to get the desperately needed guns to Fairbrother and the rifle companies has been described in the official history for the campaign.[15] In the end, their herculean efforts to drag the guns up the Pascuccio slope were too late. There was little Fairbrother could do but withdraw his tired men. In the early hours of 8 December, they began to fight their way out of their positions which were under constant threat of attack. The disengagement was not easy, requiring repeated artillery concentrations from the New Zealand guns to help beat off the renewed German attacks.

In the withdrawal, C Company was given the task of carrying out the wounded. In such hazardous conditions, it required six men to each stretcher. Eleven German wounded had to be left behind under the care of an Italian.

At 6 a.m. that morning, the last of the Maori arrived back at base after nearly 20 hours of struggle. The casualties sustained were very high: 57 Maori were killed, wounded or missing. The gain was nil. For the first and certainly not the last time, the Maori had been thwarted by the elements, the rugged terrain and by a determined enemy who was able to use the natural advantages of the countryside to stifle any attempt by the Allies to push them back.

The final saga of the battle was still to be played. The Commanding Officer was concerned about the German wounded left behind, fearing the repercussions if the Germans had found their wounded 'abandoned' by the New Zealanders.

That evening, on 8 December 1943, the Colonel sent a carrying party of 40 soldiers back to uplift the casualties. The party from A and B Companies, protected by two platoons from C Company, climbed back up Felice ridge and the Pascuccio spur to where they had left the wounded Germans. One of the wounded was missing, presumably having attempted to get back to his lines.

The failure of the second attempt by the New Zealanders to bounce the Germans did not diminish the feats of the infantry. They had, however, been fought to a standstill by factors beyond their control. By 24 December 1943, after several more attempts to clear the Germans from Orsogna, the division had to admit that, for the first time, it was beaten. In Kippenberger's words 'it was plain that we had shot our bolt'.[16]

Orsogna showed the New Zealanders the reality of fighting in a hostile environment against a skilled and determined enemy. N.C. Phillips wrote that 'many of the troops were jaded after more than a month of hard and comfortless fighting with few and short periods of rest.'[17] On the morning of 25 December, Kippenberger watched the 21st Battalion as it trudged down the road. 'I had not seen men so exhausted since Flanders,' he wrote.[18]

There was a good reason for the sombreness of the troops as they marched past their brigade commander. A platoon of the 21st Battalion, less the platoon commander and four men, had been placed under close arrest for refusing to go into action.

The enormous pressures placed on such a fine fighting machine had finally taken its toll. Moreover, the unique experience of New Zealand soldiers failing to take the field of battle, more than anything, reflected the bewilderment of men and officers who could not understand why such a relentless course of attack had been pursued when commonsense suggested a period of rest was necessary.

The subsequent fighting in the Cassino battle placed extra pressures on the soldiers in the Italian campaign. The constant harassment by enemy fire and the constant bombardment from German artillery, guided by enemy observation posts which held the high ground, eventually told. Many soldiers, including Maori, became 'bomb happy'.

Rock Maika, in a letter home on 16 April 1944 (soon after the Cassino battle), noted that 'a lot of chaps get this complaint'. The shelling he observed was far worse than that received in the desert. 'It plays on the nerves and you're under such strain that too long in the lines and you've had it.'[19] The result was an impediment in speech, stuttering and the tendency to jump at the slightest sound.

The Maori introduction to war in Europe had been violent and costly. Nevertheless they were well prepared for the further struggles ahead of them as they fought northwards. Ahead of them lay Cassino.

Survivors of C Company stand at the graveside of recently buried men following the attack on Hikurangi (Tebaga Gap).

Norman Perry album

Sam and Maraea Ngarimu at the posthumous presentation of the Victoria Cross to their son Moana.

Kate Walker album

Harris album

Above: A Company following the attack on Takrouna.

Alexander Turnbull Library

Left: Maori reinforcements shortly after their arrival at the New Zealand Training Camp in the Middle East, September 1943.

Below: Wounded men are loaded on to an ambulance at Takrouna, Tunisia.

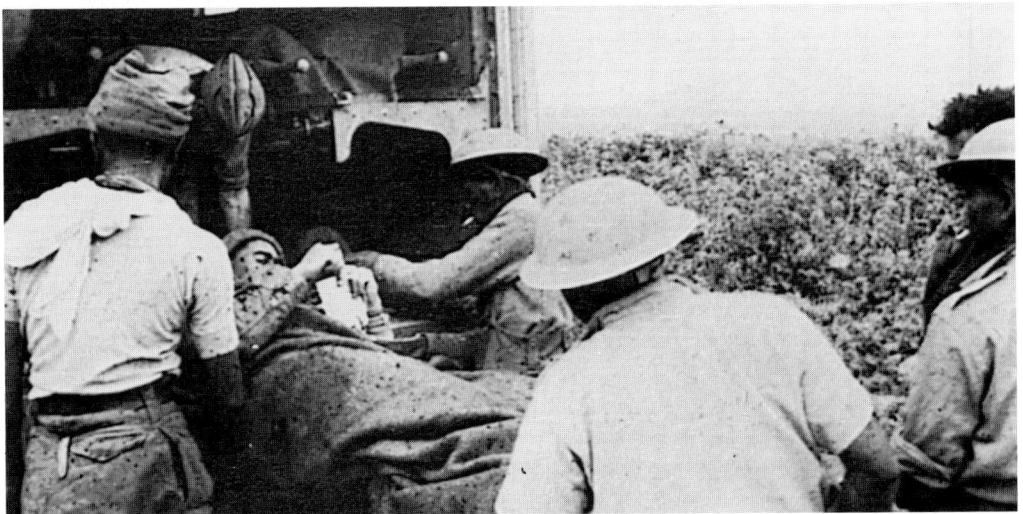

Alexander Turnbull Library

Norman Perry album

Soldiers wait to go into action at Cassino, 1944.

Rangi Logan album

Peta Awatere, Norman Perry and Padre Wi Huata watch the burial party complete its task, Cassino.

Rangi Logan album

Padre Wi Huata and Norman Perry head for the bridge at Cassino. Six hours later Perry was seriously wounded.

Norman Perry album

The Maori Battalion 'choir' performing behind the lines at Cassino.

Alexander Turnbull Library

Two of these men have just returned from mine-sweeping in the forward areas around Monte Cassino.

An improvised anti-aircraft gun mounting, using discarded farm equipment, Orsogna.

Norman Perry album

Rangi Logan album

Padre Wi Huata conducts a church parade, Italy 1944.

Harris album

Padre Wi Huata.

Norman-Perry album

They came for casualties and took away loot.
A group of Te Whanau-a-Apanui men carry a
large radio away from a bombed building,
Orsogna 1944.

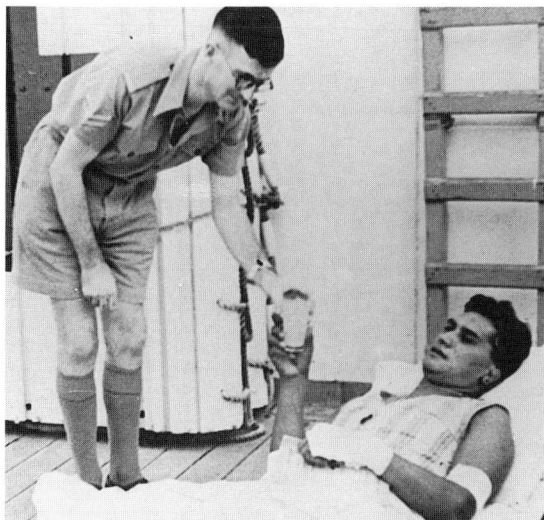

Tomoana album

Above: Boy Tomoana, wounded at Florence, on board ship for the return home.

Right: Boy Tomoana.

Below: German prisoners of war are used to bring in the wounded under cover of the Red Cross flag, Senio sector, Italy, April 1945.

Tomoana album

Alexander Turnbull Library

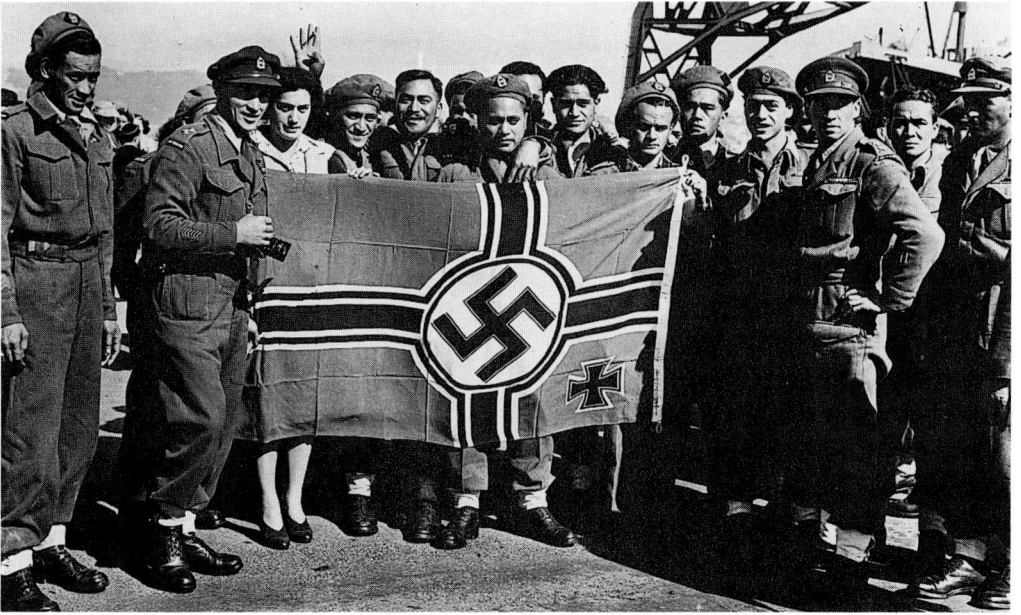

Alexander Turnbull library

The Battalion returns. Soldiers display the Nazi flag on the Wellington wharves.

Alexander Turnbull Library

The war over, the 28 (Maori) Battalion marches through Wellington, led by Lieutenant-Colonel James Henare.

Chapter 16

MONTE CASSINO

The inland road connecting Naples in the south to Rome in the north is the Via Casilina – Highway Six – built by the Romans 25 centuries ago. Halfway between Naples and Rome on Highway Six is the country town of Cassino, lying just to the west of the Rapido River. Travelling from Naples to Rome one emerges from a series of hills and enters the 5 km-wide Rapido Valley.[1]

Soon after emerging from the hills the traveller's attention is riveted by the sight of a 550m-high rock across the valley. The mass of rock 'transfixes your attention so completely that you are hardly aware of the olive groves through which you are passing; and by the time you cross the Rapido to enter the outskirts of Cassino you barely notice the river or the buildings, but only the great mountain towering above the far end of the town half a mile ahead like a gigantic flying buttress to the mountain mass stretching away to the right.'[2]

On the summit of Monte Cassino sits the sixth-century monastery founded by the monk Benedict, whose Benedictine Order was to sweep through Europe in the centuries following. Between the two man-made features – the town of Cassino and the monastery – and the natural massive rock citadel which dominates the town and provides sanctuary for the monastery, much history has been witnessed. For centuries armies have marched up and down the Via Casilina. 'Sometimes Monte Cassino had been able to look down passively on these events, but more often it had been involved in them.'[3]

Its strategic value is inescapable. With its dominant position at the junction of two river valleys and astride the Via Casilina, as well as its capacity to provide a commanding view of the road and valleys, it is the strategic key to the plain below.

The plain, 'which was fated from the beginning of recorded history to become at regular intervals a battlefield', stood across the path of any invader moving north by the inland route.[4] Because of its natural attributes, Monte Cassino conferred on its defenders enormous advantage. The Germans knew this but the Allied armies were fated to fail several times before finally realising this simple truth.

By January 1944, the New Zealanders fighting their way up the eastern flank of the Adriatic Coast of Italy had been bogged down. They had failed to take Orsogna. As Kippenberger ruefully wrote, 'our first failure and we were tired of looking at it all day and every day.'⁵ Snow, mud and slush had slowed all activity to a snail's pace. The men were bored with the long periods of inaction.

In mid-January, the New Zealanders were once more galvanised into action with the news that they were on the move. Few were taken in by the news that they were moving back from the front line for a spell at San Servo. The precautions taken were too elaborate.

On 17 January 1944, the Maori were ordered to remove all identification patches from their uniforms and vehicles. An interesting by-product of the planned move was that the town of Lanciano 'was combed for absentees'. The battalions' carriers were loaded onto transports. By dawn of the 20th, the Sangro was far behind the convoy.⁶ However, instead of halting at San Servo, the Maori received the welcome news that they were on their way to the west coast of Italy.

They finally halted at Caserta, approximately 40 km north of Naples and 65 km south of Cassino. Here the men of 28 (Maori) Battalion took advantage of the American shower units and rid themselves of the mud and grime – legacies of the Sangro campaign.

The difference in weather conditions was striking. 'The intense cold, the biting winds, the monotonous overcast skies of the Adriatic Coast were replaced by a warmer climate and bright sunshine.'⁷ For the Maori soldiers, the drier, more hospitable climate was the tonic needed to revitalise their fighting spirit.

Corporal Rock Maika, of B Company, highlights the differences in a letter home to his wife. 'Where we were last,' he wrote, 'we were knee deep in snow and such things as tracks and rounds were one mass of mud.'⁸ Because of military security, Maika was unable to tell his wife where he was. However, he was able tell her that where the Maori were 'is chock-a-block with mountains and in the mornings they're a wonder-ful sight silhouetted against the morning sun.'

For the next two weeks, the Maori trained hard. Reinforcements were absorbed and the men prepared for the next operation. Practice in river crossings gave them a hint of what lay in store. The therapeutic value of warmer weather, hard training, clean clothes and plenty of good food was soon evident. Kippenberger wrote about his troops, 'Daily I could see their faces losing the strained look. What matter that all the summer campaign lay ahead; for a little while we were very content with life.'⁹

Life in each of the battalions of 5 (NZ) Brigade was looking up. Cere-monial parades were held and formal dinners were an occasion for battalion officers to host fellow regimental officers. Kippenberger was Reviewing Officer at each of the battalion parades. He took the opportunity, when addressing 28 (Maori) Battalion, to remind them of their proud heritage and the reputation that the Maori soldier had won on the battlefields of Greece, Crete, the Middle East and Italy. The men of the 9th and 10th Reinforcements, who had recently marched into the battalion, were suitably impressed with their Brigade Commander and proud to have finally joined 28 (Maori) Battalion in the combat zone.

Meanwhile, 65 km to the north, the American Second Corps was battering itself to a standstill as its two divisions tried to defeat the German garrison defending Monte Cassino.

Since October 1943, the Fifth Army had taken three months to fight its way 'like a bull, tiring but still game, butting its way head-down into attack after attack', until it had, by 15 January 1944, finally reached the entrance to the Rapido Valley.[10] The 65 km advance had been won at immense cost. In the last stage, nearly 16 000 casualties were sustained in a six-week period by eight infantry divisions.

The gain of 11 km seemed hardly worth the cost. It did, however, bring the Americans hard up against the final objective – Monte Cassino itself. The irony is that the Germans had not intended to permanently hold the positions which had slowed the Americans down. Rather, they were seen as delaying positions. They needed time to prepare the defences of a position some distance north that they did intend to hold – which, of course, was Monte Cassino.

The defence of the Cassino sector was the responsibility of Fourteenth Panzer Corps of Tenth Army, commanded by a former Rhodes Scholar, General Von Senger, known for his anti-Nazi sentiments. Ironically (in view of the role of the monastery in the forthcoming battle), Von Senger was also a lay member of the Benedictine Order.

From September 1943, Von Senger gave top priority to improving and enhancing the defence of Monte Cassino, the linch-pin of Fourteenth Panzer Corps defence lines. Gun emplacements were blasted into the rock, caves were enlarged to house guns and men, machine gun strong-points were sited for protection and good lines of fire and minefields were laid on likely infantry approaches.

The town of Cassino was heavily fortified and the surrounding countryside was mined. Tanks were concealed in reinforced buildings and numerous buildings were strengthened by the construction of pillboxes and bunkers inside them. For three months, the Fourteenth Panzer Corps worked at the defences supported by labour battalions of conscripted Italians.[11]

Cassino was the central core of what the Germans called the Gustav Line. As Fred Majdalany points out in his book *Cassino*, 'a natural mountain barrier made infinitely stronger by the ingenuity of military engineers: a natural river barrier made infinitely stronger by steel and concrete fortifications and artificial flooding of the wide valley approaches.'[12]

On 20 January 1944, the 36th (Texan) Division splashed across the Rapido in a hastily mounted operation to capture Cassino. Over the next two days the Americans tried to press their attack. Numerous mistakes were made and little headway could be made.

The Americans lost 1 681 men and the 36th Division was reduced to two mangled regiments and a temporarily reduced third regiment which had been held in reserve for the attack.

Having failed disastrously on the first attempt, two days later the Americans tried a second time. The 34th Infantry Division was given the task of trying 'to pinch out the town' from the north – in other words, to outflank the Monte Cassino and Cassino defences. The attack was launched on 24 January 1944. It took the 34th Division eight days to secure a tenuous bridgehead across the Rapido.

Their losses were again heavy. They had secured only a toehold and had still to fight their way up the mountains before turning south to attack Monte Cassino.

The American efforts to outflank Monte Cassino from the north were doomed to failure. At a fearful cost, however, they had gained a foothold on the mountains. In the interim, the New Zealanders had been shifted, along with 4 Indian Division, from Eighth Army to reinforce the Cassino salient.

Together the two divisions were formed into Second New Zealand Corps, under the command of Bernard Freyberg. The corps had been formed with the initial purpose of exploiting an American breakthrough at Cassino. However, it soon became obvious that the Americans could not make the essential breach in the Cassino defences.

Second Corps was formed on 1 February. Two days later the American attacks had stuttered to a halt. The two American divisions, the 34th and 36th, had 'shot their bolt'. General Alexander, Allied Commander Italy, wrote that 'it was clear that Second New Zealand Corps would be obliged not merely to debouch through a gateway flung open for them, but to capture the gate themselves.'[13]

On 4 February 1944, the 28 (Maori) Battalion was ordered forward from Caserta to take up battle positions in behind Monte Trocchio, a 300-metre-high feature overlooking the Rapido Plain. As they moved forward by truck on the heavily congested Highway Six, the men's thoughts were on the battle ahead. The rain fell steadily and progress was slow. Few, if any, of the Maoris gave much thought to the historical significance of their journey forward to Cassino.

Along the road in late 1943 had come the Second US Corps to fight and falter at Cassino. And now, in early February 1944, along this road of history came another hopeful conqueror, 28 (Maori) Battalion.

The Maori established their defensive positions in the shelter of Monte Trocchio. Their forward pits were between 200-400 m from the Rapido River. Almost immediately, Lieutenant-Colonel Young, on the orders of 5 (NZ) Brigade, sent out patrols to reconnoitre approach routes to the river and identify likely crossing sites.

The seven-man patrols under the command of Lieutenants Tomoana and Asher carried out the task. Their detailed reports, which earned them congratulations from the Brigadier for the thoroughness of the reconnaissance, told a depressing story. From the foot of Trocchio, the ground dropped gently towards the river. The area near the river was 'flat and marshy'. All approach routes were waterlogged, soft and exposed to German observation and fire from directly across the Rapido River.[14] Any infantry attack would face great difficulties. Moreover, the engineering effort needed to construct a route forward for the movement of supporting tanks was enormous.

As a consequence of aggressive German patrolling, Lieutenant-Colonel Young decided to push his perimeter lines forward during the hours of darkness. He established a number of listening posts across his battalion's frontage, which were pushed right up to the river. They succeeded in reducing enemy activity.

On 10 February 1944, a more ambitious reconnaissance patrol was launched from the Maori lines. Lieutenant Christy and a nine-man patrol, accompanied by an Engineer Officer, crossed the Rapido River following the railway line. The railway line, demolished in 10 places between the river and the station in the town of Cassino, was a key element of Freyberg's plans.

Freyberg had decided that the Indians in the north would try to use the positions secured by the Americans to continue the push from the north to capture Cassino. In the south, the New Zealanders would assault across the Rapido, along the railway line, to capture the railway station as a firm base to launch a further assault on Monte Cassino. The 28 (Maori) Battalion was assigned to carry out this crucial task.

The railway line ran south around the bottom end of Monte Trocchio, then headed north across the front of the Maori positions, to a railway crossing over the Rapido one kilometre below the main road bridge. Christy's patrol succeeded in reaching the station. The only activity was a short fracas in the rail marshalling yards, where Germans threw grenades at the patrol. When the Maori responded with tommy gun fire, the Germans did not respond, clearly reluctant to disclose their fire-power.

On the following day, 11 February, the Americans' final attack in the north failed. It was now time for the Second New Zealand Corps to attempt to capture Monte Cassino.

The Americans had been held out by a division of 15 Panzer Grena-diers, supported by 180 guns and 50 to 60 tanks. In February 1944, the 15 Panzer Grenadiers were replaced by 1 Parachute Division, which Kippenberger described as 'reputed to be the best division in the German Army.'[15]

Kippenberger was keen to press the Maori attack as quickly as poss-ible. The attack was set for the night of 13-14 February. 28 (Maori) Battalion was to attack across the Rapido with two companies (at full strength, 240 men). In its first attack across the Rapido further north, the Americans had thrown in a combat regiment (at full strength approx-imately 5 000 men) to seize objectives on the far side of the Rapido.

The New Zealanders were hampered by a lack of space to deploy the full strength of 2 New Zealand Division. Lieutenant-Colonel Young selected A and B Companies to carry out the assault. Their task was to capture the railway station and hold it long enough to allow the Engin-eers to push through a passable route to allow armoured vehicles of an American Combat Team with 180 tanks to move to exploit the breach made by the Maori.

On 12 February 1944, 'observation from Trocchio and closer reconn-aissance left the officers of the two assaulting companies of 28 Battalion pessimistic . . .'[16] Although the Maori knew that they could cross the river using the railway line, the surrounding area 'was so wet and marshy with the fields under an inch of water in places, that deployment would be hazardous and, as digging was nowhere possible, supporting troops could not be employed with safety.'[17]

The attack was postponed because of additional reports indicating that even infantry would be hampered in movement across country. On 13 February, the attack was further postponed until the 16th. Further postponements had an adverse attack on the Maori holding the forward position. They were relieved by men of 24 Battalion and moved back behind Trocchio for a rest.

While the Maori waited to launch their attack, the Indians in the north were battling to secure a start-line so that they could attack simultaneously with the Maori. Meanwhile, 'long and earnest deliberations' had been going on at brigade, division, corps, army and army group headquarters about the fate of the monastery on top of Monte Cassino.

The decision to bomb the monastery was a controversial one, which even today still generates emotional debate. Finally the decision to go ahead was given. Kippenberger notes that, damaged or undamaged, it was of inestimable value to the enemy. Even if it was occupied by enemy troops it still provided, in his view, their main observation post. 'We felt,' he wrote, 'that our duty to our troops was paramount over all other considerations and I gave my vote for it being bombed.'[18]

On the morning of 15 February 1944, the Maori heard the approach of hundreds of aircraft. Soon they watched in awe as wave after wave of bombers dropped their deadly load on the monastery.

The bombing of the monastery was a topic of heated discussion in the Maori area. Padre Wi Huata wrote of the men's feelings when he visited B Company area just after the bombing and a day before their attack on Cassino. Concerns were expressed by the Roman Catholics in the company. They asked the Anglican Padre what he thought of the matter.

He told them that in his home town of Wairoa there stood a beautiful meeting house called Takitimu which is treasured by the Maori people who belong to Wairoa. He then went on to say that if his two brothers (serving with the battalion) Ossie and Dick were standing near the meeting house (Takitimu) and a bomb fell in their area, he would pray hard for that bomb to hit their beloved meeting house rather than his brothers. Padre Huata noted that the men 'seemed to be quite satisfied' with his answer.[19]

After days of waiting, the Indians were ready to attack on the night 17-18 February. The Maori were also ready and had been standing by to attack at the same time.

After 9.30 a.m. (zero hour), the Maori crossed the start-line led by A Company. Before the attack, the men had gathered in the assembly area for a short prayer conducted by Lieutenant Takurua of Ruatoki. The service was a Ringatu service – the religion started during the years of the land wars of the 1860s in New Zealand and given impetus by its principal apostle, the Maori rebel Te Kooti Rikirangi. It had in the interim been nurtured and strengthened in the forest retreats of central North Island (Lieutenant Takurua's home). After the service the Maori undertook a 600 m 'laborious tramp' to the start line. They arrived 'damp and dirty' and late.

As the Official History of the Italian Campaign recorded, 'the night held a series of unpleasant surprises.' Late in starting, and bogged down by the heavy going, the Maori found themselves advancing across fields sown with mines.

Soon the mortar and heavy machine guns from the lower slopes of

Monte Cassino and the edge of the town of Cassino began to also exact a heavy toll on the attacking Maoris. 'Men began to fall to the fire and the mines and the returning trickle of stretcher-borne casualties became a stream.'[20]

B Company of Te Arawa was struck badly on the minefields and progress towards the station railyards was slow. When they reached the yards, the soldiers of B Company faced a few obstacles set up in the days preceding the assault. When confronted with wire obstacles supported by machine-gun strongpoints, there was only one way to go: through and over the obstacles. In the face of a particularly violent burst of machine-gun fire, Captain Wikiriwhi yelled at his men to charge. 'The men leapt forward,' he wrote, 'and, as in training, the men jumped onto the wire (concertina) – the others jumped over . . . and with bayonets and grenades cleared out the posts.'

A Company, under Captain Henare, had faced similar difficulties to those faced by B Company. In spite of the immense difficulties facing them, both companies wrestled control of the station from its rugged defenders, men of III Battalion 31st Panzer Grenadier Regiment.

Meanwhile, the Engineers, following behind the Maori, tried desperately to clear the minefields and boobytraps, fill in the craters and gaps in the railway causeway, blown up by the Germans, and bridge, with Bailey bridges, two water gaps including the Rapido. All of this while under constant harassment from German mortar and heavy machine gun fire.

While the Engineers worked, the Maori consolidated their positions in and around the station buildings. The Engineers' part was essential to the success of the whole operation. Without support arms, particularly tanks, the Maoris' tenure of the station complex was very shaky. Without the roadway being constructed by the Engineers, the mass of armour waiting behind Trocchio could not get forward.

The Engineers 'worked heroically throughout the night to clear the causeway and bridge the gaps, regardless of heavy casualties.'[21] It was Napoleon who said, 'Ask of me anything but time.' With one gap left to bridge, the Engineers ran out of time. At daybreak the sacrifices were in vain. Armour and anti-tank guns could not get forward to the Maori.

They were now in a perilous situation. Commander 5 (NZ) Brigade's request to withdraw the Maori was refused. With 50 casualties already sustained during the attack, the Maori prepared to face a harrowing day. The enemy overlooked them from every quarter and it was clearly only a matter of time before the Germans launched a counter-attack to destroy the small force.

Kippenberger decided that the only way in which he could help was to use smoke to mask the railway station, which would deny the Germans direct observation of the Maori positions.

The logistic price for this tactic was enormous. A convoy of trucks had to drive to Naples, 110 km away, to get the number of shells needed to ensure full coverage during the hours of daylight. In all, over 9 000 shells were fired, mostly by 4 Field Artillery Regiment, to provide the smoke-screen.

The smoke-screen bought the Maori some time, but in mid-afternoon the ominous sounds of tank movement indicated the start of the expected counter-attack. 'The Maoris were helpless. They had neither tanks nor anti-tank guns with them. Caught by the point-blank fire of the tanks, B Company's foremost platoon was overrun.'[22]

At this stage Captain Wikiriwhi ordered the remainder of his men to withdraw. It was a rout. Men fought their way back individually and in small groups across the Rapido to the safety of the New Zealand lines but many men were killed or wounded.

Two hundred men had started the attack. Only 66 reached the safety of Trocchio that afternoon. Others straggled in over the next 24 hours. 26 Te Arawa men reached Trocchio. The remainder were among the 128 killed, wounded or captured.

Lieutenant Takurua, who had blessed the men at the start of the attack, did not return to lift the tapu from the survivors – he died in action moments after dragging his seriously wounded Company Commander, Monty Wikiriwhi, to the embankment and applying a tourniquet to stop the flow of blood from his leg wounds.

The story of Wikiriwhi's struggle to regain Allied lines is an epic story of individual human courage. Wounded seriously in both legs and unable to walk, he dragged himself up onto the railway embankment and using the railway sleepers as hand grips pulled himself to safety. It took Wikiriwhi 24 hours to achieve this almost impossible task.

The full significance of the sacrifices made by B Company during the attack on the railway station were not fully known until some six weeks later when the battalion was able to carry out a reconnaissance of the battlefield. A small reconnaissance group led by Peta Awatere, and including the Battalion Regimental Sergeant Major, Martin McCrae, Padre Wi Huata and Norman Perry, carried out a two-day reconnaissance of the area of the attack, from the river to the railway station.

The party had to be very careful as there were still many live mines along the way. Norman Perry recalled the tragic sights they found. The first body they found was that of George Asher, of Tuwharetoa. Because the body had lain in the open for nearly six weeks, he was barely recognisable. However, they identified him by his distinctive swished-back hair. He had lost both legs in an explosion and had attempted to apply a tourniquet with a bit of wire tied around the top of one of his legs.[23]

Further on, they found the remnants of what appeared to be one of the platoons, several bodies in a row facing Cassino. The men looked as if they had been scythed like a row of wheat, all at the same time.

Perry also recalls vividly what happened when McCrae found one of his relations. Perry said he heard this awful keening sound and saw McCrae standing looking at the body of one of his kinsmen.

On the second day, the party had cleared a pathway into the battle area to allow the passage of a work party to bury the bodies of 28 (Maori) Battalion. While Awatere and his party were waiting for the trucks, a jeep with three Red Caps arrived. Because the battalion group were not wearing insignia, the Red Caps failed to acknowledge Awatere.

Instead they turned to Norman Perry as the only Pakeha in the group and asked him what they were doing in the middle of the battlefield. It is possible that they thought the group might have been looting. Since Awatere did not reply, Perry responded that they were from the 28 (Maori) Battalion and that they had come to claim their dead.

The Red Caps said that no bodies were to be touched as that was a task for the Graves Registration Unit. Perry replied that the battalion looked after its own dead and would continue to do so.

Meanwhile, as the situation was getting more tense, two trucks from the 28 (Maori) Battalion had arrived and stopped about 75 m away from Awatere's group. The soldiers dismounted. They were hesitant but knew that something was up.

Awatere finally spoke. He called out to the men in Maori: 'Haere mai me ata haere' ('Come forward but come slowly'). The men spread out and moved towards Awatere slowly as instructed.

Awatere turned and addressed the Red Caps. He said, 'The men you see approaching are from 28 (Maori) Battalion. They have come to bury their friends and relations; one of them has come to bury his brother. I will not be responsible for what happens here if they are not able to do so.' The Maori soldiers meanwhile had closed with the group. The Red Caps, perhaps sensing that they were in danger, got into their jeep and quickly left.

The battalion's attack on the railway station on the night of the 17-18 February had failed. The battalion was required seven days later, on 24 February, to assist in a 6 (NZ) Brigade attack. However, the attack was delayed because of heavy winter rains which made the ground impassable for tanks.

Finally, on 15 March, the attack began. The battalion's role was to secure the railway station once it had been captured and to protect the Engineers. For two days the battalion waited for orders to move forward. When the orders came they had changed and 28 (Maori) Battalion passed to command of 6 (NZ) Brigade and was given the task of clearing out the south-western corner of Cassino.

For the next three days, the battalion was involved in street fighting through the rubble and debris of Cassino. The personal stakes were high as this type of fighting required close coordination between individuals. 'It was not so much an attack as a game of hide-and- seek – a grim game with a sudden penalty for the loser.'[24]

During this period, Warrant Officer Martin McCrae was involved in an incident which earned him the Distinguished Conduct Medal. Lieutenant Morrin, of 19 Armoured Regiment, described how his tank was called upon by McCrae to fire through various windows and doorways of a long building. McCrae was at one end with one other Maori. Soon they had one prisoner. 'McCrae made the Hun to understand if he told the rest of the Huns to surrender all would be well, if not he would be shot . . . The movement of McCrae's tommy gun was dinkum enough.'[25]

About 70-80 enemy surrendered. While most of the damage had been done by Morrin's tank, there is no doubt that the fight was orchestrated by McCrae.

After this battle, the Maori were returned to command of 5 (NZ) Brigade and their role in the battle for Cassino was effectively over. Some days later on 26 March 1944, the New Zealand Corps was disbanded. They had come, they had seen and attacked, but they had not conquered.

Over the next nine months, 28 (Maori) Battalion was to face, time and time again, the enormous challenge of fighting through built-up areas. From mid-May to mid-August 1944, in the advance to Florence, 28 (Maori) Battalion pursued the enemy. The Germans might have been withdrawing under enormous Allied pressure but they yielded ground most unwillingly and the battalion lost 24 men killed and 111 men wounded in this short campaign.

Following a 10-day rest period at Castellina the battalion left on a two-stage drive of some 350 km to the Adriatic coast where it was part of a larger effort to 'gate-crash' the Rimini line. 28 (Maori) Battalion's role in this battle was to exploit opportunities as ordered. There was a considerable waiting period and it was not until 23-24 September that the opportunity arose.

5 (NZ) Brigade was given the task of advancing to the river Rio Fontanaccia. 28 (Maori) Battalion were given a secondary task of left

protection of the main attack. During the attack, initial casualties resulted from a strong mortar attack. The Maori also ran into Tiger tanks and their supporting armour had to withdraw. At the same time, the battalion had to pull back.

It was during this attack that two of the battalion's senior officers were killed. Major Te Punga and Major Mitchell had been killed when they had moved towards a house to study their maps. During the remainder of September and early October the men rested awaiting further orders.

They did not go into action again until 10 October and for most of the remainder of the month were involved in the pursuit of the Germans along the Adriatic coast. What has been described as the Rimini Campaign finished on 22 October 1944. The battalion withdrew from the battle area 80 km to the rear at the Adriatic town of Iesi.

For the remainder of October and much of November 1944, the battalion took the opportunity to send men on leave to Florence and Rome and to catch up with domestic chores. In this they were helped by the Italians who took over the laundering of the men's clothes. There was also time for the inevitable sports tournaments. Towards the end of November, Lieutenant-Colonel Young passed command of the battalion to Lieutenant-Colonel Peta Awatere.

It was not until 22 November 1944 that the battalion returned to a fighting frame of mind when it received a warning order to be prepared to move. Later that night they began the move forward along the Adriatic coast to a staging area south-east of Forli, approximately 30 km short of Faenza. They remained here until 10 December. From here, they were moved closer to the frontline and dug in approximately 2 km from Faenza (the position was called Ruatoria) in preparation for an attack across the Senio River, which was about 25 km north-west of Faenza along the main coast road.

5 (NZ) Brigade gave 22 and 23 Battalions the task of attacking north-west across the Senio River. 28 (Maori) Battalion was given the task of securing the brigade's south-western flank of Route 9 – this was the main axis of attack for 5 (NZ) Brigade. At 11 p.m. on 14 December, 28 (Maori) Battalion began its attacks on a number of objectives.

B and D Companies attacked in a north-westerly direction to seize a number of points south of Route 9 with the purpose of protecting the southern flank while the remaining battalions of 5 (NZ) Brigade attacked towards the Senio. A and C Companies attacked in a north-easterly direction towards their objectives using the railway on their right flank as a guide.

A and C Companies began their advance towards their objectives 2 000 m away. Halfway to the objective of Della Cura, C Company made good progress and passed the buildings of La Morte. There was no response and they continued on. Some of the men of C Company made a short reconnaissance patrol towards Della Cura and encountered Tiger tanks. Elements of the company began to withdraw and ran into a minefield, losing many casualties.

'There were also Germans on the railway embankment firing at them. Two haystacks caught fire and the enemy had perfect targets.'[26] Very soon there were not enough men to carry away the wounded.

Meanwhile, A Company approaching La Morte from the west, after C Company had passed through on the east, found that it was occupied and attacked the building without loss of life. They did not advance any further and halted. Here they acted as a firm base for the initial withdrawal of C Company remnants and then in the early hours of the morning the entire force returned to the start line at Casa Clueless.

B and D Companies did not fare any better. When they reached their objectives at approximately 2.30 a.m., they found Tiger tanks occupying the area and were likewise forced to withdraw under pressure. While the operation had ended successfully, 'There was consolation, however, in the sight of enemy tanks and infantry speeding along Route 9 from Faenza to the safety of the Senio stopbanks.'[27]

28 (Maori) Battalion prepared for further action to assist 5 (NZ) Brigade in moving towards the Senio. It was, however, too late as the Germans had decided to withdraw from Faenza across the Senio. On the night of 20-21 December 1944, the battalion returned to its old billets in Forli. For the next three months the battalion patrolled their area and rested for the next phase of the campaign.

Chapter 17

REST, RECREATION AND PADRES

Soldiers will tell you that war is 99 percent waiting for something to happen and only 1 percent of frenetic hell. Much of a soldier's time is taken up in training and retraining and the base camp is where he spends most of his time. Even in the midst of a campaign it was possible for units to be withdrawn from battle to a rear area to rest. In the desert, the rest area was often many miles to the rear. In Italy the rest areas could be a short distance from the battle area.

During periods of battle, officers and men were totally dedicated to the business of survival and therefore there was little chance of getting up to mischief. However, in a base camp or rest camp environment, the potential for mischief was greatly amplified. Lapses of discipline, and morale, the potential for discontent, and all of the worst aspects of soldiering surfaced.

For these reasons periods spent in base were focused on parades, guard duties, fatigues, recreation and sport – activities required to keep even the most disciplined troops from kicking over the traces.

However, for New Zealand soldiers used to independence and the freedom to express themselves openly, the rules and regulations of a base camp were often too restrictive. But while boredom was the principal enemy of the soldier, it was equally the bane of the officers and non-commissioned officers who had to find imaginative ways to keep men occupied.

A combination of active programmes and leave periods in the nearby towns or villages were essential elements in the continuing battle against boredom.

Major General W. G. Stevens, in his offical account of 'The Problems of the 2 NZEF', explored the question of military discipline and the New Zealand soldier. He observed that those officers in positions of authority in Maadi camp and in the Middle East Headquarters who were responsible for New Zealand discipline in Cairo, 'always felt that they were sitting on the safety valve of a volcano.'[1]

Stevens noted that the 'irritating ways of the Egyptians had a lot to account for.' Sooner or later the men would react and explode from the overwhelming combination of pressure from the 'dirt, noise, stupidity and dilatoriness, bad drinks, (and) blatant attempts to cheat.'[2] The explosion would inevitably manifest itself in an attempt by the soldiers to wreck the bar they were drinking in. Stevens further observed that the

New Zealand soldiers were unused to drinking sociably. Moreover, in the early stages of the war, they seemed unused to handling spirits.

Beer, described as the 'amber stella', was the staple diet of the soldier on leave in Cairo and Alexandria.[3] Beer was the main stimulant that led men to take quick and easy offence at slights, both assumed and real. The outcome was usually a fight between individuals or groups of men which could quite easily engulf the whole room.

At times, soldiers in the bars would take the opportunity to create mayhem by deliberately insulting soldiers of other nationalities. If the famous Prussian strategist Clauswitz was correct in his assertion that warfare is an extension of politics by other means then, for the soldiers, bar-room brawls were a similar extension of warfare by other means. The only difference being that bar-room combat generally did not have fatalities.

The rapid consumption of large amounts of alcohol was the inevitable consequence of inadequate entertainment and a lack of suitable clubs and institutes which could provide men with the opportunity to drink alcohol in a more sociable environment.

Base camp routine, particularly in the desert, was governed by an interminable round of kit inspections and parades for every conceivable purpose, including 'droopy dick' parades for those who had been unfortunate enough to catch a 'dose of the clap' from the Cairo brothels. The life in base camp also revolved around the daily and weekly issue of routine orders. These were the sets of instructions issued by the Adjutant, on behalf of the Commanding Officer, which circumscribed the soldier's every move.

The stream of orders issued by military authorities would mostly have appeared relevant to the soldiers. However, when one views some of the orders from today's viewpoint, some appear somewhat Gilbertian and even ridiculous.

Nothing escaped the detailed instruction of routine orders. Hygiene was an issue which called for a welter of instructions in nearly every set of routine orders. Clearly not satisfied with the small number of soldiers who were 'apparently not in the habit of cleaning their teeth regularly', the Battalion Headquarters saw fit to issue Routine Order Number 38, dated 22 July 1941.[4]

This order directed platoon commanders to take remedial actions against the men concerned. They were exhorted 'to ensure from time to time that all men are in possession of a brush and paste or powder and that teeth get the attention they should.'

Routine Orders issued by 28 (Maori) Battalion reflected the bureaucratic conservatism of the military mind and the absurd lengths to which staff officers carried out directions from higher authorities.

Some of the orders could only have ensued from officers with a punctiliousness and fetish for rigid and ridiculous nonsense. For example, Routine Order Number 24 of 4 July 1941 noted that some personnel had been taking their 'issue shorts, long pattern, to the camp tailor to be altered into shorts, short pattern.'⁵ This practice, trumpeted the order, was forbidden. Personnel responsible for altering their issue shorts in this fashion were to be required to pay the costs of trousers so altered.

Clearly no part of the soldier's anatomy or the clothes he wore were sacrosanct. Routine Order Number 45, dated 3 July 1941, stated that 'thin or fancy moustaches are not allowed.'⁶ The mind boggles at the reasoning behind this particular order.

Major-General Stevens observed that if an order were to have any impact, it must be enforceable. It was his view that during war too many orders were issued that were not capable of being enforced. This flaw in many of the instructions and orders issued by both British and New Zealand authorities led soldiers to take a cynical view of many of the orders issued.

However, not all orders were senseless. On 10 July 1941, the Maori soldiers were advised that members of the South African Women's Auxiliary Services would shortly be quartered in Helwan camp. Sure enough, an appropriate routine order was designed to fit this event. All ranks were warned that 'they must not appear in public insufficiently clad.' A number of potential Maori 'flashers' must have been sorely tempted by that directive.

Dysentery and other fly-carried diseases were a constant worry for camp medical authorities. So much so that the predictable order describing the preventative measures required to counter the carriage of these diseases was pure farce. Maori soldiers were firstly told that they were not paying enough attention to the matter of lowering latrine seats after use. Furthermore, it was stressed that the issue was far too important a matter to be treated in this careless fashion. Henceforth disciplinary action would be taken against the offenders.

Perhaps suddenly realising the foolishness of the order and the difficulty of catching the offender unless a latrine-seat-watching patrol was mounted, the author of the order took the prudent step of advising that if an offender could not be caught then the offender's company would be disciplined. The final absurdity was yet to come.

Presumably because of the difficulty of policing the above orders, Headquarters came up with the masterly stroke of setting aside specific company latrines. These latrines were to be used only by personnel of the designated company. Therefore it was possible that a soldier with an urgent need to use a latrine would have to double back to his own lines, even if they were hundreds of metres away and another company latrine was immediately available. Such ridiculous orders deserved the treatment they got.

Within the camp environment, the behaviour of Maori soldiers could be governed reasonably successfully by unit duty personnel as well as the soldiers' own officers and non-commissioned officers. However, when the men were on leave it was more difficult to police their behaviour.

In New Zealand, while the battalion was in training in Palmerston North, discipline in town was largely self-imposed. The movement of groups of Maori soldiers was relatively easy to control and incidents were often resolved by locals making direct reports to Colonel Dittmer.

In England, Maori soldiers seemed to adjust very well to the English pubs and caused very few problems. It was here that they came under the scrutiny of the divisional military police and the British Military Police, known as the Red Caps for the colour of their headware.

When the battalion hit the streets of the leave and recreation centres surrounding their training camps in Egypt, the propensity to kick over the traces was more prevalent. First in order of priority as 'enemy' targets were the Red Caps, followed by British troops and other international forces and then Pakeha New Zealanders.

Bruce Scott, who served in the Supply Company of the NZASC, recalled an incident where he came close to being hurt by Maori soldiers returning from Alexandria to Maadi Base Camp.[7] After a week's leave, he reached the pre-arranged pickup point only to find that his unit truck had left him behind. Only one truck was left in the marshalling area and this truck belonged to 28 (Maori) Battalion.

Knowing that it would pass close to the area where his unit was stationed, he asked the young Second-Lieutenant in charge of the vehicle if he could 'bludge a lift'. The Maori officer agreed. Scott climbed aboard and made himself unobtrusive in a corner. Many of the Maori on the truck were a little the worse for wear after their period of leave in Alexandria.

Just as the truck was about to leave, there was a sudden yell and around the corner lurched a young Maori soldier waving his arms to stop the truck. It slowed and his friends pulled him over the tailboard. He had blood on his battledress and his nose had been bleeding. 'He was wild eyed and hopping mad,' recalls Scott.

In an angry stream of Maori, his eyes bulging out as if he were doing a haka, and shadow-sparring to add realism, he told of a fight he had with a Pakeha. As the story reached its high point, the Maori soldier, wild-eyed still, looked more and more in Scott's direction. Soon it appeared to

Scott that everyone in the truck was looking at him 'as a representative of the odious Pakeha race.' He began to feel decidedly uneasy.

Then Scott had a stroke of genius. He gambled on the Maori love of a joke. With his forefinger, he flattened his very 'Pakeha nose' to make it look like a typical Maori nose, and said, 'It's all right you blokes, I'm one of you.'

There was a moment's silence. Then there was a gale of laughter in which the bloodstained warrior joined. He came over to Scott, slapped him on the back and said, 'You're all right Pakeha.' He pulled out a flat bottle of 'wog' whisky, handed it to Scott and asked him to have a drink. The tension was broken. Scott's gamble had paid off. As the truck lurched back to Base Camp they had become a truck full of New Zealanders rather than a lone Pakeha in a truck full of Maori.

The role of the Padre in 28 (Maori) Battalion was a critical one. The padre had to be both confessor and friend. He had to be able to dispense wisdom and commonsense to men who were about to go into battle and those who had survived battle. One of the outstanding characters of the 28 (Maori) Battalion was Padre Wi Huata. He had joined the battalion in Egypt. He was 25 years old.

His infectious, almost raucous, sense of humour gave the men confidence wherever he appeared. When he joined the battalion at Maadi camp, he was inducted into the battalion by Awatere. Awatere asked him if he was married. Huata replied 'No'. Awatere responded that it was the custom in the battalion that the Padre be up at the front with the troops. He later found out that Awatere was joking.[8] When he did go into action, he described the experience as being 'just like a cowboy picture until I realised that the bullets were killing.'

In his interviews with Harry Lambert for a series of stories in the 28 (Maori) Battalion magazine, what Huata characteristically failed to add was that while he was in action for the first time he had helped recover the 'bodies of soldiers from among minefields and carried wounded with the stretcher bearers.' The citation which saw him awarded the Military Cross also noted, 'His happy disposition both in and out of the line and his spiritual leadership are so inspiring that the morale of the troops is maintained at a high standard.'[9]

Huata's offbeat sense of humour helped him cope with the distress of the wounded and the dying. Moreover, the soldiers knew that behind it all was a man who felt deeply for them. His wicked sense of humour was evident when Boy Tomoana was seriously wounded at a battle near Florence. As the stretcher passed Huata, he said to Tomoana, 'Kei te pai, kaore i taotu o raho' ('Your testicles are intact').[10]

In another incident, Norman Perry, the battalion's YMCA Officer, was seriously wounded at Cassino. When he was taken to the Aid Post he was yelling in Maori, 'E Wi, E Wi, Karakia.' He then began in Maori to pray himself. Huata said to Perry, jokingly, 'You cut out those Italian prayers, Norman.' Perry replied, 'No, no, it's Maori.' In fact, Norman Perry, although a Pakeha, was a fluent speaker of Maori.[11]

Chapter 18

WAR'S END

The war in Italy was effectively ended on 2 May 1945, with the unconditional surrender of all German Forces west of the Isonzo River. Meanwhile, the New Zealand Division had struck hard and fast for Trieste. As the New Zealanders drove east of the Isonzo River, they came more and more into contact with Marshal Tito's communist Yugoslav troops.

When the New Zealanders crossed the Isonzo River they immediately noticed a change of atmosphere. Robin Kay, Official Historian for the latter part of the Italian Campaign, described the situation: 'There were Partisans everywhere with red scarves and red-starred caps. They marched in small columns with Yugoslav flags, and with Italian tricolours with the red star in the centre . . .' [1] He added that the New Zealanders 'felt like strangers in a strange land, as if at the Isonzo they had passed some unmarked but distinct frontier.'[2]

Marshal Tito was determined to re-annexe from the Italians the border province of Istria and the city of Trieste. Only one obstacle stood in his way – the New Zealand Division. Tito ordered Freyberg to withdraw his forces back behind the Isonzo but Freyberg responded by putting his men on three hours' notice to move forward into defensive positions already reconnoitred.

Five days later, on 7 May 1945, the war in Europe was finally over. Germany surrendered unconditionally to the Allies. Victory in Europe did not, however, end the possibility of further hostilities. This time the potential enemy was not German but Yugoslav.

The Maori had occupied positions short of Trieste on the high ground overlooking the Adriatic. Second-Lieutenant Maika writing home observed that, 'It was very hard to realise that the war here is over and Jerry is beaten to his knees at last.'[3] He and his Maori comrades were confused and annoyed at the hostile reception they had received as liberators. Maika drily observed, 'The people here weren't very much overjoyed when we liberated them.'[4]

Germany's capitulation had set loose in Yugoslavia a vicious struggle for power. Marshal Tito's communist forces fought for control against Mikhailovich's monarchists. Had the Maori been more aware of the communist experience in Russia following the First World War, where the Allies supported the White Armies against the Bolsheviks, they might better have understood Tito. Far from seeing the Allies as liberators, Tito saw them potentially as a threat to the communist takeover.

The situation in early May 1945 was, therefore, very tense, which tended to take the glitter out of the end-of-war celebrations. While enormous crowds spilled out onto the streets in every town and city in New Zealand to celebrate VE (Victory in Europe) day, Maori soldiers in Europe remained armed and alert, preoccupied with the potential threat facing them.

'We couldn't celebrate in the usual fashion here,' wrote Maika as, 'this place is dry as a bone, not a drop of plonk to be found anywhere.'⁵ The men of 28 (Maori) Battalion celebrated by letting off rockets and flares and firing their weapons into the air. Thoughts now turned to home as they wondered what the Government had in store for them.

At dawn on 8 May, a battalion memorial service was held under the protecting shelter of the local church in Famiano. 'The companies assembled in silence in a hollow square. Not a word was spoken and only the bark of an occasional cough broke the stillness of the pre-dawn morning.'⁶ As dawn broke, the padre's prayer reminded the Maori of the numerous occasions on the battlefield that they had gathered to pay homage to their dead.

Then as the hymn 'Aue Ihu', so closely linked with the battalion, 'filled the morning air with its message . . . it seemed as if the whole history of the battalion was unfolding itself.'⁷ The trials and tribulations, the victories and defeats, the pathos and glory of war and the epic campaigns of Greece, Crete, the Desert, Takrouna, Orsogna, Cassino, Florence, Rimini, Faenza and the Senio all flashed past.

Just over five years earlier, the battalion had left New Zealand on the *Aquitania*. They celebrated the end of war as they had begun it, in prayer. That is how the 28 (Maori) Battalion remembered the dawn of VE day, 8 May 1945.

The potential for confrontation and the hostile atmosphere placed everyone on edge. Annoyance at constant stand-tos and alerts, and the cocky and 'cheeky' Yugoslav soldiers did not help ease tempers. One of the positive aspects was that the Maori now appreciated the warmth and friendliness of the Italians, which in the past had been taken too much for granted. While both sides awaited developments, the Maori went onto the 'peace' offensive to whittle away at, and finally break down, the sullen resentment of the Yugoslavs.

Sergeant E.H. Nepia, the editor of *News Flash*, the news sheet of 28 (Maori) Battalion, described how they went about achieving the objective. He reported that the task was made easier because of the Maori's 'usual

happy-go-lucky make-up . . . his aptitude for creating a friendly atmosphere by his open frankness, by his cheerfulness and by the laughter and
song in his soul.'[8]

Another successful line of attack was launched through the hearts,
minds and stomachs of the local children. Cody wrote that 'the children
fell first, for Te Rau Aroha, the Maoris' canteen truck, which produced
unending quantities of sweets and biscuits; it was not long before the
children were romping with the troops.'[9]

Very soon concerts, dances and socials became an ordinary part of
activities in the area. The ice was broken and fraternisation was accomplished. The Official Historian for the Italian Campaign, Robin Kay reported
that the Maori were on friendly terms with the Partisans and peasants. Part
of the reason for this was the Yugoslavs' delight in discovering that some
of the men were of Maori-Dalmatian descent.[10] Kay also wrote that 'except
for the Maoris who could overcome the language barrier, the New
Zealanders did not get to know the Yugoslavs well.'[11]

During this period, thoughts turned more and more to returning
home. The Maori accepted there may have to be redeployments to the
Pacific to continue the war against Japan. The majority seemed to have
had enough. Those with families just wanted to get home to pick up the
threads of life. For many, life would never be the same again. Nevertheless, all wanted to see Aotearoa as quickly as possible.

Rock Maika, whose wife, Kath, had struggled to bring up a young
family, perhaps best articulated the concerns of the majority. 'Well,' he
wrote 'we still don't know what's going to happen to us and everyone is
hoping that the govt will get us to come home.' He added the wry
comment that if the 'government don't, you know who to vote for next
election.'[12]

Already the First, Second and Third Echelons had returned home
along with the 4th and 5th Reinforcements. With the war in Europe over,
the 6th and 7th Reinforcements were to return home when ships were
available. The last of the North African veterans, the 8th Reinforcements,
were withdrawn from any likely involvement in fighting, ready to return
home.

On 9 June 1945, Tito signed an agreement in Belgrade to withdraw all
of his troops from the disputed area east of the Isonzo River. The crisis
was over and the Maori began to prepare to move to a transit camp on
the shores of Lake Trasimeno, south of Rome.

In early July the remaining officers in the battalion were asked whether
they would like to volunteer for service in the Pacific. Maika put a big NO
against his name on the sheet. He thought that 'quite a few of the Maoris

and officers also said no.' He continued, 'It's quite obvious now they want the 10 Reinforcement officers to go to the islands but in the case of Maoris [they] were asked to volunteer.'[13]

At the end of July, the Maori left on the four-day journey from north-eastern Italy to Lake Trasimeno. In the short time available, the Maori had built up a tremendous rapport with the local Yugoslavs. The 'peace' offensive had been too successful.

They had set themselves the task of conquering the locals, not with the military weapons given them by the military authorities, not with force, but rather with 'commonsense, with tact, and with humane methods.'[14]

As the editor of *News Flash* was to write later, 'We sang to them, sang with them and asked them to sing to us.' He added, 'We learnt their songs and struggled hopelessly with their language.'[15] Most never got beyond 'dobbra noche'. This was enough: the Yugoslavs thawed and welcomed the Maori into their homes. The strength of the association was in some cases very deep. The editor witnessed an old Yugoslav couple weeping on the shoulders of a Maori youngster, a truly sad scene.[16]

Victory in Japan was announced on 15 August 1945. Japan's uncon-ditional surrender ended the rumours and speculation about the division's future. Instead of an offensive force it was now decided to send occu-pation troops to Japan. The Maori contribution to this force, which had yet to be decided, generated a great deal of discussion, particularly at home in New Zealand. Many saw this as an opportunity to continue the tradition of 28 (Maori) Battalion.

The proposal to send a Maori contingent to the Pacific Islands and Japan as garrison troops was supported by tribal elders at home. P.H. Tukariri, a Ngapuhi elder, wrote to the Prime Minister, Peter Fraser, telling him of decisions made at a large gathering of Maori people attending the tangi of one of the chiefs of Ngapuhi.The gathering, which was attended by Sir Apirana Ngata, had agreed that such a force should go to the Islands and Japan.

However, Tukariri and his fellow elders had other ideas about the composition of the force. They respectfully requested that 'the Maori Battalion in Europe be brought home and that the Maori Battalion [for service in the Islands] should be made up of those boys who did not go to the war.'[17]

Tukariri also told the Prime Minister that, 'A force of 5 000 could easily be arranged.' The elders requested that a competent speaker, familiar with the ways of Polynesians and Melanesians, should accompany the battalion. Tukariri's younger brother, Busby W. Matthews, was selected for the task. A First World War veteran, Matthews had worked closely with the eminent Maori ethnologist Dr Peter Buck (Te Rangi Hiroa) and was conversant with Polynesian ethnology.

Army authorities had other thoughts. It was eventually decided that the Divisional Cavalry Battalion would represent New Zealand in the Occupation Forces in Japan. Maori were allocated 270 places and were to fill these positions as D Squadron of the Divisional Cavalry Battalion. Lieutenant-Colonel James Henare, the battalion's last commanding officer, who had replaced Lieutenant-Colonel Awatere in July, decided to fill the vacancies in the squadron using men of the 14th and 15th Reinforcements.

The 15th Reinforcements were called forward from Maadi Camp in Egypt where they had been training when Lieutenant-Colonel Henare initially called for volunteers. He was inundated by applications from battle-scarred veterans but declined these applications as he felt that a good composite force could be chosen from the single personnel in the 14th and 15th Reinforcements.

When the 15th Reinforcements arrived in Italy they were welcomed by the veterans of the 28 (Maori) Battalion. Lieutenant-Colonel Henare made the point that even if it was only for a short time, they were now members of the battalion. He reminded them of their obligations to their race and exhorted them to maintain the high standards of those who had gone before them. He told them that they were about to embark on a novel task.[18] He ended by saying, 'I do not beg of you, nor command you to do it well. That would be unnecessary, for we are known only for the thoroughness with which we do our jobs. I know that you, too, will do likewise.'[19]

As the Maori began to prepare for the final move home to New Zealand, they had one remaining task: attending a number of memorial services to farewell the dead. Crete was the venue for the first memorial service. In the frenetic five weeks of the Crete campaign, the Maori had lost five officers and 60 other ranks killed in action. Because of the unstable political situation in Greece, the Maori were unable to visit Greece to farewell their dead.

The New Zealand Division collected together the veterans of Crete still serving with the division. Remarkably there were still nearly one hundred all ranks who had fought on Crete. Of this number, only three were Maori. Captain W.T. Ngata who had been a platoon commander in Headquarters Company, Second-Lieutenant Te K. Wahapango and a Private Rule. A guard of honour and a band was to accompany the veterans to Crete.

Lieutenant-Colonel Henare was asked to provide the guard of honour.

Cody reported that a Second-Lieutenant R. Wright was appointed Guard Commander.[20] The 24 other ranks were selected from the different tribes and were representative of the main religious denominations.

They immediately 'went into rigorous training in ceremonial rifle drill, haka, action songs and hymn singing.'[21] Freyberg visited the Maori on 20 September 1945, to review the progress of the guard of honour. Padre Huata was accorded the honour of being appointed to accompany the senior chaplain of the Division, who would be responsible for consecrating the cemeteries. Services were planned for Suda Bay, Canea, Jangeo and Cassino.

The party left for Crete on board HMS *Ajax* on 27 September, arriving at Suda Bay two days later. On the following day during the consecration ceremony, Captain Ngata laid a wreath at the base of the flagstaff, containing the following inscription:

He tohu Aroha mo nga hoia Maori
i hinga kite pae o te pakanga
i runga o kirihi me kiriti
'kaore he aroha o tetahi i rahi ake i
tenei ara kia tuku te tangata i a
ia ano kia mate mo ona hoa.'
Hoani, XV.13.
'Hinga atu he tetekura,
ara mai he tetekura.
Whakatauki Maori Na te ope Hoia Maori o Niu Tireni
25 o Hepetema 1945[22]

During each of the dedication ceremonies, the Maori were given the opportunity to play their part. Whenever they sang the hymn 'Aue Ihu', it was as if the lost legions of the dead were once more with them.

The Official Historian for the chaplains in the Second World War best describes the impact of Maori singing during church parades. He wrote of the occasion on a 'hot, sticky, dusty day, when some 2 000 soldiers attended a service in a cinema in Maadi.'[23] The church parade was formal and uninspiring until the Maori contingent stood up and sang. 'Then the war and the dust and the heat were forgotten in a moment. Something of home and of beauty was brought very near, and the glorious unaccompanied harmony brought new life to the listeners, as refreshing as rain in the desert . . .'[24]

Chapter 19

MEN UNDER FIRE

Fear, courage and morale are the conflicting elements which affect men on the battlefield. Ardant du Picq, a French colonel who was killed in the 1870 Franco-Prussian War, was one of the first to study human behaviour on the battlefield. A veteran of the French Army's wars in Crimea and Algeria in the 1850s and 1860s, he circulated a questionnaire seeking information on how men reacted on the battlefield. The results of the questionnaire confirmed that the battlefield is a place of terror.

Du Picq asserted that soldiers die in their largest numbers when they give way to the greater will of their opponents and flee the battlefield. Germans of 141 Mountain Regiment learnt this chilling fact of war at 42nd Street on Crete on 27 May 1941.

Here, as has been recounted earlier in this book, a confident and fresh German force pursuing a weak, depleted and fleeing group of New Zealanders were counter-attacked and destroyed. The Maori counter-attack on this occasion was so aggressive and unexpected that it caught the Germans by surprise. In losing the subsequent clash of military wills, the Germans also forfeited their right to life. They fled and were either bayoneted or shot in the back.

Men fight, wrote du Picq, from an overwhelming sense of fear of defeat and the possibility of slaughter. 'It is their rational acceptance of the danger of running that makes civilised soldiers so formidable.'

The fear of the consequences of running away and the imposition of a sense of discipline, wrote du Picq, together combine to provide an environment for survival on the battlefield.

Brigadier General S.L.A. Marshall, the American war historian, carried du Picq's study of the battlefield into the twentieth century. In his study of the battlefields of the Second World War, *Men Against Fire*, Marshall agreed with du Picq that the battlefield is indeed a place of terror. 'The battlefield is cold. It is the lonesomest place which men may share together.'[1]

Du Picq believed it was the task of the officer corps to suppress the fear of the men they led. Marshall, 'in a manner distinctly American', believed that the solution to the suppression of fear lay in the minds of every soldier in the firing line. A survey of troops on the battlefield revealed, 'that fear is general among men'. Moreover, the survey also revealed 'that men are commonly loath that their fear will be expressed in specific acts which their comrades will recognise as cowardice.'[2]

After the war, when asked to participate in a critique of Marshall's work, Lieutenant-Colonel Humphrey Dyer takes considerable exception to Marshall's assessment that fear is general among men on the battlefield. Dyer in his letter to Colonel Thornton argues that Marshall's critique refers to 'immature and nervous soldiers'. 'I disagree with the whole tone and implication of this questionnaire [Marshall's Questionnaire]. No seasoned infantryman would agree with it.'[3]

In Dyer's view, after two or three successful series of actions, a soldier who is well disciplined, trained and led 'becomes a seasoned fighter who takes a pride in his trade, like the gladiator.'

It is the fear of letting a comrade down which Marshall considers is the key to survival on the battlefield. Most soldiers, he argued, 'do not aspire to a hero's role.' Equally, however, they are 'unwilling that they should be considered the least worthy'among those present.'[4] Thus most soldiers will go to extreme lengths, including carrying out acts of extraordinary bravery, to gain and retain their comrades' respect. When a soldier is surrounded by men he knows, he 'has reason to fear losing the one thing he is likely to value more highly than life – his reputation as a man among men.'

This idea should be no surprise to a student of the Bible. It clearly states, 'Greater love has no man than this, that a man lay down his life for his friends.'

At Mount Olympus on 16 April 1941, the Germans launched a series of attacks on the Maori positions. Major Dyer described the state of his runner, Private Fowler, who was very frightened and yet very brave.[5] He also described the arrival of Tapuke, the Battalion Clerk, who instead of remaining in the relative safety of Battalion Headquarters, came forward to join the battle. 'I just came down to be with the boys, Sir,' he told Dyer. These two young and frightened men knew that their comrades were in trouble. In spite of nervousness and fear, they willingly joined the battle.

Fear or a lack of confidence can also result from a lack of information, or inadequate training and skills. At Platanias, Crete, on 21 May 1941, D Company of 28 (Maori) Battalion received a direct attack from German parachutists, who had been dropped into and around the D Company positions. The situation became confused. Major Dyer was lying in a creek bed with a road in front of him and open fields on either side. The Maori were shouting at parachutists who lay huddled in the open – bullets were coming and going in every direction.

Dyer noticed his cook, a young soldier, cowering with fear in a clump of bamboo. 'He was dragged out,' wrote Dyer, declaring pathetically that he had never fired a rifle in his life![6] The cook was given a rifle and Corporal

Koopu, a stretcher-bearer corporal, who from time to time tore off his Red Cross armband to wage war, coached his shooting. Koopu ordered the cook to fire at a German about 40-50 metres away from them. The cook fired and missed. Koopu readjusted his aim and ordered him to fire again.

The cook's second shot was a hit. He turned to Dyer and declared, 'I'm all right now, Sir,' and with Koopu went up the creek-bed hunting for Germans.

Dyer's response to Marshall's assessment of fear is supported unanimously by all respondents to Thornton's request for information on New Zealand soldiers. 'Replies are unanimous,' wrote Thornton. 'This sweeping statement does not apply to NZers. Equally unanimous (except C.Upham) was the opinion that all men have a certain amount of fear before an attack, but that all but about 3 percent to 5 percent succeed in concealing and controlling it, and it is readily absorbed in a kind of exhilaration once the attack is under way.'[7]

Clear orders before an attack and the minimum amount of time spent on the start line helped overcome nervousness. Most men expressed their nervousness before an attack by adjusting equipment, having a final nervous pee, or in rare cases, by lying down and falling asleep. Once the attack was under way, nervousness was replaced by the flow of adrenalin which generally carried soldiers through the attack. Immediately following a successful attack the exhilaration was normally followed by weariness.[8]

During the night of 3-4 September 1942, the 28 (Maori) Battalion carried out a 'brilliantly successful' attack against the Germans manning the Munassib Depression. It was estimated by Brigadier Kippenberger, Brigade Commander 5 (NZ) Brigade, that 500 Germans had been killed in the ferocious and bloody hand-to-hand fighting. The severity of the attack and the lack of prisoners had been suggested as the principal reason why General Rommel accused New Zealand soldiers of massacring prisoners and the wounded.[9]

Rommel made these accusations to Brigadier Clifton, Brigade Commander 6 (NZ) Brigade. Clifton had been captured by the Germans on the night 3-4 September 1942. The following morning Rommel 'tackled him about various acts contrary to international law' for which he believed the New Zealanders had been responsible. He told Clifton that 'repeated cases had occurred of prisoners and wounded being massacred' by the New Zealand Division. According to Rommel's records, Clifton is said to have responded to Rommel's statements by saying that the acts were 'probably due to the large number of Maoris which the division contained.'[10] However, Brigadier Clifton in his own biography, denies having told Rommel that Maori were responsible for acts of atrocity.

Many years later the matter gained brief notoriety in New Zealand papers after a newspaper printed a review of the 'Rommel Papers', in which the accusation of atrocities by Maori soldiers was made. After numerous letters to editors of various newspapers it was left finally to a Maori soldier, Major Rangi Logan, to put his views on the whole issue.

Logan wrote that the Maori did not hate the enemy nor did they enter battle with a 'bloodlust' or a 'fanatical disposition' to kill. Their principal concern was to get on with the job in hand. It did not matter whether the mission was to capture prisoners or capture an objective. Logan considered that the Maori were 'tradesmen' and, as soldiers, they made very good tradesmen.[11]

In a letter to the *Dominion* newspaper in 1984, Logan categorically denied that the Maori shot prisoners. 'In fact,' he wrote, 'when the heat of battle was over and prisoners taken, our men treated the German soldiers as friends, perhaps because we held them in such respect as soldiers . . .'[12]

After attacks in which the Maori captured prisoners, it was not uncommon for the men to share their food and cigarettes with the prisoners. Logan describes how, when his men lined up for breakfast the morning after an attack, there were invariably prisoners in the queue.

Logan, who spoke passable German, was able to learn of the prisoners' amazement 'at the hospitality and good fellowship emanating from the Maori . . .'[13] While he had heard of an incident, during later stages of the Italian campaign, in which prisoners had been summarily dealt with following the 'stupid and pointless' shooting of two Maori officers, he maintained that Maori did not senselessly shoot prisoners.

During the heat of an attack there was always a fine line between continuing resistance or surrendering. When a soldier surrendered during an attack he was expected to lay down his arms. For him the war was over. Prisoners were generally pointed in the direction from which the attack had been launched. If men could be spared during the attack, they would be detailed to move prisoners back to rear areas where they would be handed over to reserve troops.

Prisoners who accepted the situation were treated with respect. However, if 'a prisoner was at first surly or nasty, some harsh words and menacing moves with a bayonet were always enough to change his attitude . . .'[14] The Maori always made it quite clear that if prisoners didn't cause any trouble they were safe. One false move and retribution would be swift.

The Maori found that the Germans behaved in a disciplined manner. Following the battle for Point 209 at Tebaga Gap during which the Maori and Germans had fought a ferocious hand-to-hand encounter, the

German prisoners of war were treated with respect by the men of 28 (Maori) Battalion.

The morning after the attack (28 March 1943) Brigadier Kippenberger and his staff visited the site of the battle. Lieutenant-Colonel Bennett, after showing him the site where Ngarimu and his men had fought so bravely, invited him to breakfast. Kippenberger takes up the narrative: 'We were having breakfast round the tail of the cooks' truck, when I noticed a group of German officers a few yards away. They had put up a very stout fight, so I sent one the LOs over with my compliments and an invitation to join us.'[15] The group included Major Meissner, the battalion commander of II/433 Regiment, his Adjutant and the Medical Officer.

After breakfast, Meissner asked if he could say goodbye to his men. Kippenberger agreed. 'The adjutant saluted and hurried off. In a few minutes he had the remnants of the battalion in two rigid lines. Meissner exchanged salutes with me and walked towards them.' Kippenberger watched as the 'adjutant barked and the battalion came to attention with a resounding crack of heels. He barked again and in unison the men shouted, "Heil", and extended their arms in the Hitler salute.'[16] They were all impressed with the way in which the German prisoners had conducted themselves.

Italians, on the other hand, viewed surrender as a relief from the pressures and tensions of warfare and seemed to look forward to captivity. Italian officers were, as a rule, rude and overbearing. However, as Logan observed this got them 'absolutely nowhere'. The Maori delighted in deflating such rudeness and arrogance.

Rangi Logan recalled one Italian colonel ordering his batman to carry his rug, satchel and other baggage into captivity. 'I soon put a stop to that,' wrote Logan. 'Much to the relief I'm sure of the soldier and the delight of the other Italian prisoners.'[17] The Italian colonel's discomfort at having to carry his own equipment was magnified considerably when he found that he had to walk. He was rather short and looked soft and lazy, said Logan, who enjoyed the prisoner's discomfiture as he had deliberately engineered it.

Chapter 20

WHEN THE MAORI CAME HOME AGAIN

The return home of the 28 (Maori) Battalion began on 6 December 1945. They entrained at Florence. As they had to travel in cattle trucks, they did not enjoy the long train ride south to the Advanced Base at Bari. The journey south through the centre of Italy took the men past the battle-fields of Cassino and Orsogna. They remained at Bari for the next two weeks making the final arrangements for the sea voyage home. The battalion celebrated its final Christmas on foreign soil with a mixture of elation at going home and sadness at leaving so many friends, relatives and comrades buried in Italy.

In their last months in Italy, many of the soldiers had taken the opportunity to visit the grave sites of their fallen comrades. Just outside Florence, about 5 km from the New Zealand club, was a military cemetery. This cemetery contained the graves of 28 men who had fallen in the battle for Italy. Battalion personnel on leave in Florence were asked to go to the cemetery to visit. The names of the men who fell in battle represented a cross-section of Maoridom.

Before leaving Florence for Bari on the first leg of the journey home, Padre Wi Huata, his brother, Captain 'Ossie' Huata, Second-Lieutenant R. M. Mackey, and the unit historian, Sergeant E. H. Nepia, made a final tour of the cemeteries in which men of the battalion lay.[1] It was a sad journey of remembrance. At each battle location, or nearby, they found the graves of those who had fought and died.

At Rimini, they came upon the Graves Registration Unit at work. This was the unit responsible for removing Allied bodies from their temporary grave sites for transfer to an official cemetery. Using the dog tags buried with the bodies, the unit registered the name, unit and country of the dead soldier. These records were used to provide the detail for the crosses erected after the bodies had been reburied.

The Graves Registration Unit was in the process of removing 'Kiwi bodies to their final resting place'.[2] The men buried at Rimini were being relocated to the Ocsena cemetery. Included in this group were Majors Paul Te Punga and Mitchell. These were the two officers who had been shot during the fierce fighting around Rimini. At Forli, the group found the graves of all the men who had fallen in the battle for Faenza.

The editor of the battalion's newsletter, Sergeant Nepia, recorded that, 'At Faenza we found a neat cemetery, not far from the river, and on the

Forli side, some few hundred yards from the Bailey bridge.'³ Here were buried all those who fell in the Senio assault. To illustrate the difficulties in accounting for all casualties during war, Nepia noted that two men were still unaccounted for, Privates Heremia and Horomona. Later it was discovered that Horomona, who had been killed by sniper fire, had been found by an English artillery crew. They buried him where they found him.

And so the pilgrimage continued.⁴ Late one night they found Private Arena's grave at the Padova cemetery. In a very small and recently built cemetery they found Private Adamson. He was buried in the Montfalcome Military Cemetery. Private Te Whao still lay where he had been buried, near the site of the 'old 5 Bde Hq in Montfalcome'.

At Udine, they found Private Wainui and Sergeant R. Akuira, who had served with 20 Battalion in Greece. After being taken prisoner, he had escaped. An ex-Te Aute college boy he had established, while still at school, a fine reputation as a rugby footballer with an extraordinary goal-kicking ability.

As part of the tour of the cemeteries, the group took individual photographs of the sites they had visited. As well as being editor of the battalion newsletter, Sergeant Nepia was also the unit historian. By the end of the tour he had taken 169 photographs of Maori graves.

A number of soldiers had also taken the opportunity to spend their leave in London. For the handful of survivors of the 2nd Echelon, this was a last chance to revisit England, where 28 (Maori) Battalion had trained in 1940. Meanwhile, the repatriation of prisoners of war was taking place.

One of the battalion's well-known soldiers, Ned Nathan, who had been captured on Crete, had been repatriated to London before the end of the war and had spent a year in hospital. Once he had recovered, he haunted the New Zealand Liaison staff in London for assistance to get him back to Crete. Finally, on board a Greek merchant boat, 'Ned made his way back to Crete and the girl of his dreams. Katina and he were married 3rd October, 1945 . . .'⁵

Those who remained in Italy had more than ample opportunity to enjoy their final leave. In the weeks before the battalion's departure from Florence, the companies held a series of dances, on Monday, Wednesday and Saturday nights. Each company took it in turn to sponsor the event. Attendance by locals at the dances was by invitation only, and there was much competition among the locals to attend. One particular lady dowager who insisted on attending was eventually put off when the organisers said that they could only provide a truck to take her home.

Any thought of the soldiers wooing potential conquests was stiffled by 'that fly in the ointment, that thorn in the side of the lover, that ever-watchful personage, Mama!'6 Nevertheless, the dances were remarkably well run and the men behaved impeccably. Soon the demand by the local population was so great that the companies could not find enough men to attend as partners.

Before leaving Florence, the Maori were farewelled by Freyberg. In November 1945, Freyberg visited his famous soldiers for the last time, to review them on parade and to take the opportunity to say a personal goodbye. As he moved past rank after rank of Maori soldiers, Freyberg must have recalled the many times over the previous six years when he had been thankful that the Maori Battalion was a part of his force. Part of that memory would have included Crete, Minqar Qaim, Munassib, Sollum, Point 209, Takrouna, Orsogna, Cassino and the race for Florence.

It was evident to the men on parade that this was not the Freyberg of old. He appeared hesitant and faltering in speech. In reporting on the parade, Nepia wrote that this was understandable as the General was 'bidding farewell to his old comrades who had shared the same privations as he, and whom he had led to victory time and time again.'7

Lieutenant-Colonel Jim Henare, the battalion's last Commanding Officer, responded to the General's address to the men. He recalled the absolute faith that the Maori soldier had in the General's judgement. 'We regard you more as a father to the battalion than a general,' he said. Henare told the General that he had been a guide, leader and bulwark for the Maori. He added that, in their view, the General had given them preferential treatment. In this latter respect Henare did not realise how true his words were.

At one stage during the Italian campaign, the Maori disciplinary record was so bad that the General's senior staff suggested that the General needed to take strong action, including returning the battalion to New Zealand. He declined to act on the advice.8

Freyberg told the men that the 28 (Maori) Battalion would be the only unit returning to New Zealand as a formed unit. Every other unit in the Expeditionary Force would be disbanding overseas. Men would be returned to New Zealand according to a priority schedule based on their period of service overseas and whether they were married or single.

For the Maori, the signal honour of returning to New Zealand as a formed unit was aimed at giving the people at home 'some indication of what a fighting force looked like'.9 The price for this honour was that the 9th and 10th Reinforcements agreed to remain with the battalion and to forgo the chance of returning home some weeks earlier with their Pakeha contemporaries. The preparations for a mass reception in New Zealand appealed to most of the men.

The future of the men of 28 (Maori) Battalion when they returned home had been raised in an interview some two years earlier, in 1943, by Lieutenant-Colonel Charles Bennett. He had been seriously wounded when he stepped on a wooden box mine while leading his battalion during the attack on Takrouna. His wounds were so serious that he had been evacuated home to New Zealand.

Bennett's interviewer, writing under the pseudonym of 'El Hamma', wrote for the *New Zealand Listener*. At the start of his article he described how, before the war he had met Bennett. He recalled him as a good-looking, well-spoken Maori. He added that Bennett was not 'otherwise arresting'.

Now, however, some three years later, he noted that the same man 'filled the room – a soldier, a leader, a presence.' The war had awakened and enlarged the man.[10]

The first question he put to Bennett was, 'Would the men of the battalion take up the lives that they had left some years before?'

Bennett pondered a while before answering. In his view, the answer to the question lay in the availability of Maori leadership during peacetime. It was his experience that if men were led well, they would respond well. While the war had seen new leaders emerge, Bennett thought that there might be difficulties with the wartime leaders continuing to lead during peacetime.

'Do you mean,' pressed the interviewer, 'that when the battalion comes home the military leaders may lose their hold?'

Bennett responded that he saw a risk of the commanders losing control. On the battlefield, the soldiers were all one people, even though they retained tribal divisions. Once the men returned home, however, he saw the potential for them to be divided by party politics.

In his view, politics were never discussed in the field. Very little discussion took place on the future relationship between Maori and Pakeha, or indeed Maori and Maori. In the end, while the men identified with tribal groups, they were all Maori. 'Tatou te iwi Maori kia tatou' ('We the Maori unto ourselves').[11]

Few in the battalion would have shared Bennett's view. Rather, most looked forward to picking up the threads of life. At home, however, the shape of postwar Maoridom was very much in the minds of the leadership of Maoridom. The Government, Maori members of Parliament, tribal elders and returned servicemen were more than keen to address the vexed question of 'where to now?'

Ngata had given shape and form to some of Maoridom's concerns in his 1943 booklet, 'The Price of Citizenship'. Against the backdrop of Maori sacrifice in war, he asked whether the 'civilians of New Zealand, men and women, fully realised the implications of the joint participation of Pakeha and Maori in this last demonstration of the highest citizenship?'[12]

Much was going on at a political level to address the issue. Before the end of the war, a policy was being developed to coordinate the activities of Maoridom and to provide leadership in key areas of social and economic reform which the Government believed were crucial to Maori advancement.

On 1 April 1945, the Maori Social and Economic Advancement Act became law.[13] At a conference prior to the enactment, the Government gathered together key members of the Maori War Effort Organisation. This was the organisation, comprising 480 Maori tribal executive committees, which had underpinned the Maori war effort.

After the First World War, the translation of Maori sacrifices during the war into measurable Government commitment took more than a decade. When the land reform policies were finally agreed on they were not supported with sufficient resources to ensure that the policies would succeed. The consequence of trying to implement exciting policy initiatives without resources was inevitable failure.

This time, Ngata and his colleagues were determined that the sacrifices to Tumatauenga would not go unrewarded. They stressed that the wairua (spirit) that had permeated the effort of the War Organisation should be enshrined in perpetuity in the new legislation.

In an extract from the *Southern Cross*, dated 2 April 1945, the conference signalled that 'no measure more vital to the interests of Maori people . . . had ever been introduced by legislation.'[14] Key members of the War Effort Organisation, including First World War veterans, Second World War veterans and other servicemen, Major H. R. Vercoe, Captain Love, Lieutenant Latimer and Lieutenant Colonel Ferris, were asked to take the message back to the tribes. The Government wanted Maori to know that every effort would be made to 'embody the true spirit of the Maori war effort into the act.'

On 26 December 1945, the 28 (Maori) Battalion embarked on the *Dominion Monarch*, at Taranto. In his final letter home before leaving Italy, Rock Maika wrote that he was looking forward to getting home so that he could taste real butter and cream.[15] The rhetoric of the formal welcome on '100 marae' when they reached home did not thrill him. The battalion's proposed pilgrimage from Wellington to Palmerston North, Ngaruawahia and then to Gisborne was, he said, 'too annoying for words'.

The *Dominion Monarch* called in at Twefik to pick up 86 men from the Maori Training Depot. On the 14 January 1946, the ship reached Fremantle, in West Australia. After a short stay there, the ship made the final leg to Wellington, arriving on the morning of 23 January 1946. True to form, the capital welcomed the 28 (Maori) Battalion as she had farewelled it some six years earlier, with squally weather conditions and heavy seas. It was not until nearly midday that the huge ship was able to come alongside the main wharf with her precious cargo.

Meanwhile, the civic arrangements for the battalion's return were cancelled as the weather conditions were not suitable. It had been intended to have the battalion march through the city. Eventually, at just after midday, the soldiers of Tumatauenga disembarked and formed up on Aotea Quay. The welcome home was led by Anania Amohau, who challenged Lieutenant-Colonel Henare. This was followed by the tangi of the women whose karanga welcomed the men home. Finally, the appropriate ceremonies were complete and the soldiers were able to meet loved ones fortunate enough to be able to come to Wellington.

The men then moved into the sheds beside the quay and sat down to their first hangi kai on home shores. That afternoon, Cody recorded, 'trains . . . carried the Maori soldiers to a hundred welcoming marae.'[16] 28 (Maori) Battalion had marched out of existence and into the history books.

After the inevitable whirlwind of welcome parties and the mostly pleasurable, but sometimes painful, reunions with loved ones and relatives, it was time to decide what to do. For those who had left the farms to go to war there was always a job to go back to. Many others had to tailor the ambitious dreams unleashed by war and overseas experience to meet the realities of the mundane routine of manual labour.

It was a very difficult time for most soldiers. Senior officers who had been in command of many hundreds of men were suddenly faced with some harsh realities. What were they to do? Were their skills of leadership to be lost to Maoridom?

For the key personnel of the battalion who did not have professions to go back to, the logical answer was to look towards the new organisation set up as a result of the Maori Social and Economic Advancement Act. The crucial issue was could they translate their wartime leadership into effective peacetime leadership?

Many of the key positions were filled by former 28 (Maori) Battalion officers. The professional head of the Welfare organisation was Major Rangi Royal. The Minister of the Native Department (later the Department of Maori Affairs) was responsible for administration of the new act through his Permanent Head of the Department, to the Controller, Rangi Royal and then directly to the District Welfare Officers.

Among those appointed as welfare officers were Lieutenant-Colonels Keiha, Awatere, and Henare. Other appointments included Captain Bill Herewini, a prisoner of war for four years after being captured at Kalamata, Greece, in April 1941. Fellow founding members of the welfare organisation read like a who's who of the battalion.

From the outset, the welfare officers responsible for carrying out the requirements of the Act ran into considerable flak from the Registrars, later to be redesignated District Officers, who ran the districts.

The clash revolved over who controlled the activities of the welfare officers and how they fitted into the public service. The welfare officers saw themselves as an autonomous organisation answerable to the minister through the controller.

From their point of view, the welfare officers saw the Act as a Maori controlled initiative, for and on behalf of Maori, by Maori. The largely Pakeha-controlled bureaucracy saw it differently. The Right Honourable Peter Fraser, Minister of Maori Affairs, saw the operation of the Act from the perspective of the Maori officers.

In a policy memorandum of 21 September 1949, he wrote, 'It was early recognised by myself, that, if the organisation was absorbed into the ordinary activities of and routine of the department, it would to a very great extent be stultified.'[17] He was of the view that the Maori Social and Economic Welfare organisation was not to be looked on 'merely as another branch of the department'. It was, he said, 'an organisation that must be to a very large extent independent and self-reliant.' Fraser's directive did little more than harden the core of resistance of the Pakeha officers within district offices.

The clash of wills apart, the welfare officers made the best progress they could. In a candid survey of the events surrounding the establishment of the organisation, Rangi Royal, as Controller, reported that they applied themselves to this task 'with their usual enthusiasm, despite the hostility manifested in various ways and forms toward them.'[18]

The main task of the welfare officers was to liaise with tribal committees and marae groups, and to provide leadership and guidance on social, economic and welfare issues of concern to Maoridom. In 1949, a change in Government gave the bureaucracy the opportunity to finally strangle the autonomy and freedom that the welfare officers had exercised under the Labour Government.

The new National Government was quick to act. Under the guise of rational reorganisation, a directive was issued on 1 June 1951 which brought the welfare officers directly under the control of the district officers.[19] This was the beginning of the end for another potentially exciting and positive policy aimed at providing Maoridom with a measure of self-determination.

Royal's acerbic observation on this state of affairs was that he, as controller, had become a figurehead, or as his committees labelled him, a tekoteko (an effigy).

Meanwhile the welfare officers, through a series of meetings among themselves and with the departmental hierarchy, attempted to redress the situation. However, in spite of the considerable firepower they could bring to bear, they failed to dent the Cassino-like solidarity of the bureaucracy.

The welfare officers saw the issue clearly in military terms. What they wanted was a clear line of command to their 'Commanding Officer', the Minister. They wanted nothing more than to carry out his directives without interference from 'any other commander, no matter how senior he may be'.

Not surprisingly, Peta Awatere led the charge on behalf of the welfare officers. The views he articulated are as relevant today as they were 40 years ago. At a meeting held in Wellington over the period 9-10 December 1952 to discuss the role of the welfare organisation in the areas of housing, health, education, employment and crime, he forcibly put his views on the basic causes of Maori problems.[20] He argued that Maori people were being asked to adjust to a new way of life within a period of 100 years, whereas it ought to take 1 500 years.

The measure of autonomy that welfare officers should enjoy was also raised. Norman Perry, the only Pakeha District Welfare Officer, argued that it was essential for the officers to work outside the constraints of the department. Perry, who had worked for Ngata before the war had served with the 28 (Maori) Battalion.

Perry's view was that the welfare officers were experts on matters relating to the housing, health, employment and crime problems of Maoridom. Unfortunately the senior officers at Head Office and districts assumed that they knew more about these matters than the welfare officers. This assumption, he observed, lay at the root of the problem.

Sadly, despite the many efforts to make the system work, the incorporation of the welfare officers into the framework of the Maori Affairs Department served to hasten the demise of the wairua so earnestly spoken of during the earlier conferences, which had set the new wave of Maori social and economic planning on its way. Without wairua, the scheme was destined to failure. In the words of Rangi Royal, 'The present set-up is a failure. I think that we should be honest and admit that it is so.'[21]

One of the principal issues faced by the leadership of 28 (Maori) Battalion in the immediate postwar years, was excessive alcohol consumption by Maori soldiers. It was an issue that the leaders of the battalion understood but what to do about it was another matter. For many returned soldiers, the painful memories of the war remained with them for a long time. For some the only way to ease the unsettled feelings and trauma associated with resettlement was to seek solace in the company of those who would understand them. The pubs and the parties that followed were a focal point for many men.

In 1951, a meeting was held between the Honourable E.B. Corbett, Minister of Maori Affairs, the Honourable W.H. Fortune, Minister of Police, and the Maori Welfare Organisation. The meeting was held to discuss the new organisation. However, it was obvious from the start of the meeting that the ministers were concerned about consumption of alcohol by Maori people. Mr Corbett noted that the Prime Minister was receiving many letters reporting on the 'evil consequences of alcohol' and the excessive consumption by Maori.[22]

The welfare officers were told that if they did not solve the problem the Government might have to enact legislation curbing Maori people from getting ready access to alcohol. The tenor of the meeting was paternalistic. So much so that Mr Corbett even suggested to the assembled leadership of the Maori battalion that they had put the cart before the horse and that Maori desire for knowledge of their own customs and meeting houses were not as important as they thought. He thought that they should put the welfare of the people first and the marae and the culture would follow.

After this tirade from the two Ministers, the response from the assembled welfare officers was polite and brief. Many must have wondered what they had fought for. The need of many for an association with those who had shared similar experiences led inevitably to the thought of establishing a Battalion Association,

A 28 (Maori) Battalion Association was five years in the making. Numerous discussions had been held whenever soldiers met on marae throughout the country. Finally on 6 February 1950, at the Waitangi celebrations, it was decided it was time to form the association.

The first president elected was Sergeant George Harrison. As a section commander he had faced the Germans during the battalion's first action at Olympus Pass on 16 April 1941. Then he was a junior leader responsible for the safety and security of a section of nine men. Now he was the first head of a national organisation, responsible in peacetime for providing leadership of a proud unit whose fierce reputation in battle had been unsurpassed.

Harrison's appointment set the trend for national presidents. Most of the subsequent presidents were not senior officers within the battalion. Only one Commanding Officer, Lieutenant-Colonel Charles Bennett, was elected to hold this office. This trend seemed contrary to the traditional approach of British regiments where the senior officers held the senior positions.

One explanation for this state of affairs given by one of the association's most effective presidents was that the senior officers did not seem to be interested in taking up the reins.[23]

In the initial stages one senior officer did take great pains to participate. He was the battalion's first Commanding Officer, Brigadier George Dittmer. While he was unable to attend the initial planning conferences he nonetheless sent detailed notes on what should be done and how it should be done.

Other presidential office holders included Lieutenant Kuru Waaka of Te Arawa, Captain Monty Searancke of Ngati Porou and Captain Monty Wikiriwhi of Te Arawa.

To commemorate its establishment, the fledgling association decided to hold its first formal national reunion at Palmerston North, the battalion's birthplace. A reunion there in 1961 would mark the 21st anniversary of the battalion's stay in Palmerston North. D company was to host the function and planning was put in train for an attendance of between 2-3 000 veterans.

Unfortunately for organisers, they were not able to gather the logistic support needed to host such a large number and, despite last-minute pleas to the Honourable Eruera Tirikatene for army accommodation in Linton Camp, the reunion did not proceed. Instead the venue was switched to Rotorua. Here at short notice, Te Arawa rose to the challenge and catered for and accommodated the more than 1 000 men who turned up.

For many it was an opportunity to renew acquaintances with friends who had not been seen since the return from the war. The organisers prepared for the fireworks. None eventuated. Ted Nepia, writing on the conference for the National Returned Servicemen's Association newspaper, *The Review*, wrote that 'the old fire had gone' but not altogether however, as the estimated quantity of 'stella' (beer) for the three days fell just short of the actual needs.[24]

The reunion was significant for what Nepia described as 'a strong feeling of Maori nationalism and the emergence of new leaders.' He also noted the resurgence of a feeling of Maoritanga (Maoriness). He was agreeably surprised to see many who had previously displayed little or no interest not only in Maori affairs but also in the language itself reveal a proficiency in both, equal to the best.

All of these matters grabbed the attention of the veterans. What set them alight was a matter close to the heart of each of the soldiers – the formation of a Maori unit in the defence forces. Nepia observed that when this issue was raised, it gave sharpness to the expression of Maori nationalism which 'burst to the surface with an explosion of fervour and enthusiasm.'[25]

The debate which followed was completely one-sided. Speaker after speaker hammered similar themes. They did not view the formation of a separate unit as separatism. Rather, it was a commonsense move as Maori fought best when they were together. Finally, the cry which had echoed across the battlefields of Gallipoli, 'kua wehewehe matou' ('we are separated') was again voiced as a driving force for bringing together all Maori soldiers into one unit, with voluntary service the sole criterion for service.

Maori enthusiasm was not shared by Government officials. The Army Secretary, Mr Dobbs, asked the Department of Maori Affairs for the view of Maoridom. What he got was the view of a senior Pakeha official who said that it was not the sort of question one should ask as the answer would inevitably be in support for the establishment of the unit.[26]

He implied that what the Maori people said they wanted was not necessarily what was good for them. Mr McKay of the department believed that the setting up of an exclusive Maori unit would be an act of voluntary segregation.

Captain Bill Herewini, who had replaced Rangi Royal as Controller of Maori Welfare in the Department of Maori Affairs, placed his views on record. He supported the formation of a 28 (Maori) Battalion within the Territorial Force.

The unit would perpetuate the famous name of 28 (Maori) Battalion and would act as a repository for its battle honours. Interestingly enough, he did not support its formation within the Regular Force for service in Malaysia. He believed that the Maori component of the First Battalion, training in Burnham for service overseas contained a sufficiently high proportion of Maori soldiers. It was estimated that nearly 40 percent of the 850 soldiers were Maori.

Two years later, in 1963, the impetus for a Maori unit came from a most unexpected quarter. During a visit to New Zealand, the Duke of

Edinburgh at a dinner party at Government House on 12 February spoke with Mr W.T. Ngata, Private Secretary to the Minister of Maori Affairs. He mentioned the possibility of the formation of a Maori regiment along the lines of the Scottish regiments.[27]

The Duke understood that the argument against such a unit was that Maori and Pakeha should share things in common. However, it was the Duke's view that if it was good enough for the Scottish then it should be good enough for the Maori people.

28 (Maori) Battalion Association set up a subcommittee to investigate the matter. The committee comprised Brigadier Dittmer, Peta Awatere and Bill Herewini. They made a 'number of discreet enquiries', which revealed that the older generation who remembered the war favoured the formation of a separate unit. However, the younger people canvassed were not entirely in support of the scheme. The impact of the Vietnam War on people's attitudes was considerable. The committee's final report to Henry Ngata, President of the association, on 22 February 1966 set out its findings and conclusions.

In view of the position articulated by the young people of Maoridom, they came to an 'objective conclusion' to recommend to the association that there be no separate unit formed for Maoridom. The committee also resolved that should world war break out, the Maori people would again ask the Government to form a separate Maori unit.

With the issue of the formation of a separate unit put aside, the association concentrated its attention on developing policy issues of concern to its members. From time to time as reunions were held, the call for a greater involvement by returned servicemen in the leadership of Maoridom was made. The onset of old age and retirement for many of its members focused the association's attention on providing assistance for those veterans requiring it.

During all these years Brigadier Dittmer retained a close interest in the affairs of the association. In May 1968, he sent a letter to Charles Bennett giving advice on the organisation of the next annual reunion. He set out 19 points of detail which should be investigated.[28]

Perhaps remembering the habits of some individuals associated with hosting the reunion, he gave specific instructions for those handling the raffles. 'Be selective as to whom books of raffle tickets are provided for disposal,' he told Charles Bennett.

The decade of the 1970s was, for the men of 28 (Maori) Battalion, notable for two significant events. In May 1972, a contingent of veterans was invited to Germany to attend a reunion of the Afrika Korps. It was an opportunity few could refuse. However, the costs of the journey meant that only a few could accept the German invitation. Twenty-six men led by Ruihi Pene, of Te Arawa, accompanied as in war by their padre, Canon Wi Huata, left New Zealand to attend the ceremony, held in the city of Mainz, near Frankfurt.

Captain Boy Tomoana, of Ngati Kahungunu, was one of three Hawke's Bay men to attend. In an interview with the *Napier Daily Telegraph* on 20 May 1972, he summed up the apprehension they felt. 'Our only other meeting,' he said, 'had been an exchange of gunfire on the battlefield.' They wondered what reception they would receive at the hands of their wartime enemies.

Rangi Tutaki, of Porongahau, Central Hawke's Bay, described the journey as an opportunity to involve themselves in the Maori custom of 'kawe mate'. That is, the taking of the memory of their fallen comrades to Germany, there to tangi (mourn) for them and to share mutual sorrow with their former enemies.

In a letter to the editor in the Hawke's Bay *Herald Tribune*, he described that the basis for reconciliation between the Maori and German soldier would be the mutual exchange of condolences. Once this had occurred then it could truly be said that matters had been settled. 'Kua ea': a satisfactory resolution had taken place.

Although there were a number of Pakeha New Zealanders at the reunion, the Maori had responded as a unit. The veterans all acknowledged the significant honour bestowed on the unit. Charlie Taite, of Te Kuiti, has described how the Maori contingent responded to the challenge by adopting a uniform set of clothing which made them stand out.[29] Ruihi Pene, the contingent leader, arranged that each individual should wear a white shirt, regimental tie and blazer, and grey slacks. The result was very effective.

The Maori were met in Frankfurt by representatives of the Afrika Korps including their liaison officer Lieutenant-Colonel Altmann. While the Maori were impressed by the German efficiency and organisation, they nonetheless labelled their liaison officer 'Colonel Klink' after the buffoon colonel in the television show *Hogan's Heroes*.

Mainz, the venue for the main reunion, saw the influx of 5 000 people to attend the function, which was deliberately designed to be as informal as possible. Boy Tomoana explained why. Germans, even 27 years after the end of the Second World War were still very sensitive to mass military gatherings.[30] Thus the Germans were not allowed to wear their medals. 'As a mark of respect we did not wear ours either,' said Tomoana. The Italians wore theirs.

For all of that, precise organisation was evident in the proceedings. As in war, the Maori contingent took the Germans by surprise. Following an unscheduled presentation by the Maori group to General Westphal, Rommel's second-in-command in Africa, they performed a spirited haka. Charlie Taite said that the Maori stole the show with their haka. Following the haka, an Australian veteran attending the reunion, observed, 'You bloody bastards, you've put it across us again.'

While the general reaction to the Maori presentation of gifts and haka was overwhelming, Mr H. Kohere of Gisborne, observed that the Nazi influence was still strong among some Germans. One group, he said, refused to accept the gifts presented by the contingent. Later on at the function they gave the Nazi salute and marched out of the hall together.

The pilgrimage of 1977 was the most significant event for the 28 (Maori) Battalion since its return home from the war. In this year, many hundreds of veterans, their wives and families and the relatives of those who had died, visited the overseas sites where the battalion had fought its major battles.

This was a kawe mate on a grand scale. The tangi ceremonies at the cemeteries throughout Italy, Greece, Crete and the Middle East were a poignant reminder of the strength of Maoridom. For most of the veterans this was their last opportunity to pay their respects to their fallen comrades. Before many more years had passed they would also be making the long journey to Cape Reinga.

In subsequent years, fewer attended the reunions. The Honour Board of the Maori Battalion is now claiming in peacetime the lives of those that in war it could not topple. In the last few years many totara of the forest have fallen. Charlie Shelford, Bill Herewini, Monty Wikiriwhi, James Henare, Turi Te Kani, Wi Huata are a few. Haere Koutou ma, ki o tatou tupuna ki te po.

Fewer now turn up to honour their fallen comrades. The words of Anzac Day have greater significance. 'They shall not grow old, as we that are left grow old. At the going down of the sun and in the morning we will remember them.'

FOOTNOTES

CHAPTER 1: MAORI MILITARY HERITAGE

1. Elsdon Best, *The Maori As He Was*, p.10, Government Printer, Wellington, 1974 (reprint).
2. R. S. Oppenheimer, *Maori Death Customs*, p. 102, A.H.& A.W. Reed, Wellington, 1973.
3. A.K.Vayda, *Maori Warfare*, p.45, A. H. & A.W.Reed, Wellington, 1970.
4. F.A. Hanson and L. Hanson, 'Counterpoints in Maori Culture', Routledge & Kegan Paul, London, 1982.
5. Sir Apirana Ngata, 'The Price of Citizenship', p .13, Whitcombe & Tombs, 1943.
6. Ngata, ibid, p. 13.
7. Vayda, op. cit., p. 30.
8. Best, op. cit., p. 98.
9. Oppenheimer, op. cit., p. 105.
10. Oppenheimer, ibid, pp. 75-76.
11. Best, op. cit., p. 173.

CHAPTER 2: BAPTISM OF FIRE: MAORI IN THE FIRST WORLD WAR

1. C. J. Pugsley, *Gallipoli*, pp. 260-61, Hodder & Stoughton, Auckland, 1990.
2. J. B. Condliffe, *Te Rangi Hiroa (The Life of Sir Peter Buck)*, p. 132, Whitcombe & Tombs, Christchurch, 1971.
3. J. Cowan, *The Maoris in the Great War*, p. 9, Whitcombe & Tombs,Wellington, 1926.
4. Letter, Governor-General to British Secretary of State, 17 September 1914.
5. P. S. O'Connor, 'Recruitment of Maori Soldiers 1914-18', p. 49.
6. O'Connor, ibid, p. 52.
7. O'Connor, ibid, p.50, (quotes from letter District Health Officer to Principal Medical Officer Auckland Military District, 17 September 1914).
8. Letter, Colonel Logan, Administrator for Samoa, to Minister of Defence James Allen, 27 October 1914, quoted in O'Connor, p. 51.
9. Letter, Minister of Defence Allen to Major-General Sir Alexander Godley, dated 10 January 1915, quoted in O'Connor, p. 52.
10. Cowan, op. cit., p.12.
11. Cowan, ibid.
12. Pugsley, op. cit., p. 89.
13. O'Connor, op. cit., p. 56.
14. O'Connor, ibid, p. 50.
15. O'Connor, ibid, p. 52.
16. Cowan, op. cit.,p. 15.
17. Letter, Major-General Sir Alexander Godley to Minister of Defence Allen, dated 2 April 1915.
18. Letter, Major-General Sir Alexander Godley to Minister of Defence Allen, dated 5 April 1915.
19. Ibid.

20.   O'Connor, op. cit., p. 53.
21.   Letter, Minister of Defence Allen to Major-General Sir Alexander Godley, dated 11 May 1915.
22.   Article, 'The Maoris in the World Wars' in *The Maori Battalion Remembers*, p. 17, Fourteenth Reunion of 28 (Maori) Battalion 1985.
23.   Condliffe, op. cit., p. 129.
24.   Letter, Major-General Sir Alexander Godley to Minister of Defence Allen, dated 24 June 1915.
25.   O'Connor, op. cit., p. 54.
26.   O'Connor, ibid, p. 55.
27.   Cowan, op. cit., p. 54.
28.   O'Connor, op. cit., p. 55.
29.   O'Connor, ibid, p. 56.
30.   O'Connor, ibid, p. 57.
31.   O'Connor, ibid, p. 58.
32.   O'Connor, ibid, p. 59.
33.   O'Connor, ibid, p. 60.
34.   Condliffe, op. cit., p. 136.
35.   W. S. Austen, *The Official History of the New Zealand Rifle Brigade*, p. 313, L. T. Watkins, Wellington, 1924.
36.   M.King, *Te Puea*, p.82, Hodder & Stoughton, Auckland, 1977.
37.   King, ibid, p. 81.
38.   King, ibid. p. 38.

CHAPTER 3: CALL TO ARMS

1.   Major-General Sir Howard Kippenberger, Editor-in-Chief, Documents (relating to New Zealand's participation in the Second World War, 1939-45), Volume 1, p. 5, War History Branch, Wellington, 1949.
2.   Major R. Logan, 'George Bertrand', article in *The Maori Battalion Remembers*, 1985, p. 98.
3.   Logan, interview with author, July 1985.
4.   Lieutenant-Colonel H. G. Dyer, *Ma Te Reinga*, pp.13-16, A. Stockwell, Ilfracombe.
5.   Dyer, ibid, p.16.
6.   Dyer, ibid, p. 16.
7.   Captain Te M. R. Tomoana, interview with author, July 1985.
8.   Colonel F. Rennie, 'Initio-Finito', article in *The Maori Battalion Remembers*, 1985, p. 21.
9.   Rennie, ibid, p. 21.
10.   Rennie, ibid, p. 22.
11.   F. Rennie, *Regular Soldier*, p. 22, Endeavour Press, Auckland, 1986.
12.   Rennie, ibid, p. 27.
13.   Rennie, ibid, p. 28.
14.   Rennie, ibid, p. 28.
15.   J.F.Cody, *Maori Battalion*, p.4, War History Branch,Wellington, 1956.

16. Rennie, op. cit., p. 28.
17. Ern Edwards, letter to author dated 3 July 1985.
18. Christine Cessford, article in *Times-Age*, March 1985.
19. R. Logan, interview with author, July 1985.
20. Roger Taylor, interview with author, August 1985 (at that time he had been researching the contribution made by the settlement of Hiruharama to 28 (Maori) Battalion).
21. Cody, op. cit., p. 5.
22. R. Logan, note to author, November 1990.
23. R. Logan, '38159 Private Charles Shelford', article in *The Maori Battalion Remembers*, 1985, p. 99.
24. Sir Norman Perry, interview with author, January 1991. (Perry, who worked with the YMCA and the Regimental Aid Post, was present at the presentation of Shelford's DCM.)
25. Ern Edwards, letter to author, 3 July 1985.
26. R. Logan, interview with author, July 1985.

CHAPTER 4: FAREWELL AOTEAROA

1. J.F. Cody, *Maori Battalion*, p.11, War History Branch, Wellington, 1956.
2. Lieutenant-Colonel H. G. Dyer, *Ma Te Reinga*, p. 16, A. Stockwell, Ilfracombe.
3. Cody, op. cit., p. 12.
4. Captain Te M.R.Tomoana, interview with author, July 1985.
5. Major R.Logan, interview with author, November 1991 .
6. WOII G. L. Burke (Regimental Quartermaster Sergeant of 28 (Maori) Battalion).
7. Dyer, op. cit., p. 46.
8. G.L.Burke, letter to wife, dated 12 May 1940.
9. Cody, op. cit., p. 14.
10. Dyer, op. cit., p. 25.
11. Dyer, ibid, pp. 26-27.
12. Burke, letter to wife, dated 14 May 1940.
13. Burke, letter to wife, dated 16 May 1940.
14. Cody, op. cit., p. 14.
15. Burke, letter to wife, dated 26 May 1940.
16. Cody, op. cit., p. 14.
17. Burke, letter to wife, dated 29 May 1940.
18. Burke, letter to wife, dated 31 May 1940.
19. Dyer, op. cit., pp. 17-18.
20. Dyer, ibid, p. 18.
21. Burke, letter to wife, dated 13 June 1940.
22. Burke, letter to wife, dated 15 June 1940.
23. Cody, op. cit., p. 25.
24. Major John Harper, letter to author, dated 2 August 1985.
25. R. Logan, 'A Maori at Sandhurst', article in *The Maori Battalion*

Remembers, 1985, pp. 82-83.

26. Cody, op. cit., p. 27.

CHAPTER 5: GREECE: THE FIRST TEST

1. 28 (Maori) Battalion War Diary, dated Friday 29 November 1940.
2. 28 (Maori) Battalion War Diary, dated 25 December 1940.
3. J.F. Cody, *Maori Battalion*, p. 31, War History Branch, Wellington, 1956.
4. WOII G.L. Burke, letter to wife, dated 8 January 1941.
5. Cody, op. cit., p. 33.
6. Lieutenant-General Sir Leonard Thornton. (Following the end of the war, Thornton was commissioned to carry out a study of New Zealanders at war.)
7. G.L. Burke, letter to wife, dated 28 February 1941.
8. Burke, letter to wife, dated 13 February 1941.
9. 28 (Maori) Battalion War Diary, dated 13 February 1941.
10. Cody, op. cit., p. 37.
11. Rongomai Worral, 'Forty Years On', article in *The Maori Battalion Remembers*, 1985, p. 57.
12. Upokokohua. The Maori language does not have a range of swear-words like the English language. Because the head of a Maori individual is a sacred part of the body, the most insulting expressions that could be used revolved around the derogatory use of the word for head – upoko. Upokokohua, literally means 'boil your head'.
13. Cody, op. cit., p. 38.
14. 28 (Maori) Battalion War Diary, dated 5 March 1941.
15. Major R. Logan, 'Lt Col Tiwi Love, MID', article in *The Maori Battalion Remembers*, 1985, pp. 97-98.
16. Brigadier G. Clifton, *The Happy Hunted*, pp. 61-62, Cassell, London, 1962.
17. Clifton, ibid, p. 62.
18. Cody, op. cit., p. 39.
19. W.G.McClymont, *To Greece*, p. 144, War History Branch, Wellington,1959.
20. McClymont, ibid, p. 255.
21. McClymont, ibid, p. 258.
22. Cody, op. cit., p. 51.
23. 28 (Maori) Battalion War Diary, dated 15 April 1941.
24. 28 (Maori) Battalion War Diary, dated 16 April 1941.
25. McClymont, op. cit., pp. 264-65.
26. Cody, op. cit., pp. 59-60.
27. McClymont, op. cit., p. 265.
28. Cody, op. cit., p. 61.
29. Cody, ibid, p. 64.
30. Lieutenant-Colonel H.G. Dyer, *Ma Te Reinga*, p. 59, A. Stockwell, Ilfracombe.
31. Dyer, ibid, p. 50.
32. McClymont, op. cit., p. 268.
33. McClymont, ibid, p. 268.
34. McClymont, ibid, p. 268.

35.   McClymont, ibid, p. 268.
36.   Cody, op. cit., p. 65.
37.   Cody, ibid, p. 66.
38.   28 (Maori) Battalion War Diary, dated 16 April 1941.

CHAPTER 6: BATTLE FOR CRETE: COUNTER-ATTACK AT MALEME AIRFIELD

1.   Extract of interview from notes prepared for Maori Battalion documentary
        by Tainui Stevens, 1989.
2.   Major R. Logan, letter to author, 19 July 1985.
3.   J.F. Cody, *Maori Battalion*, p. 77, War History Branch, Wellington, 1956.
4.   Ned Nathan, interviews with author, September 1985.
5.   Cody, op. cit., p. 84.
6.   Ned Nathan, interviews with author, September 1985.
7.   Private H. Mohi, 'Forty Years On', article in *The Maori Battalion Remembers*,
        1985, p. 59.
8.   Cody, op. cit., p. 83.
9.   Mohi, op. cit., p. 59.
10.   Mohi, ibid, p. 59.
11.   Lieutenant-Colonel H.G.Dyer, *Ma Te Reinga*, p. 24, A. Stockwell,
        Ilfracombe.
12.   Mohi, op. cit., p. 59.
13.   P.Singleton-Gates,*General Lord Freyberg VC*, p.152, Whitcombe & Tombs,
        Christchurch, 1963.
14.   Cody, op. cit., p. 89.
15.   D.M. Davin, *Crete*, p. 85, War History Branch, Wellington, 1953.
16.   Ronald Lewin, *Ultra Goes To War*, p. 157, McGraw Hill, New York, 1978.
17.   Lewin, ibid, p. 158.
18.   Lewin, ibid, p. 158.
19.   28 (Maori) Battalion War Diary, dated 20 May 1941.
20.   Dyer, op. cit., p. 39.
21.   Mohi, op. cit., p. 59.
22.   Dyer, op. cit., p. 39.
23.   Cody, op. cit., p. 90.
24.   Lewin, op. cit., p. 156.
25.   Dyer, op. cit., p. 40.
26.   Mohi, op. cit., p. 59.
27.   Cody, op. cit., p. 94.
28.   Cody, ibid, p. 92.
29.   Major R. Logan, interview with author, November 1991.
30.   Dyer, op. cit., p. 42.
31.   Dyer, ibid, p. 42.
32.   Brigadier J.T. Burrows, *Pathway Among Men*, pp.116-17, Whitcombe &
        Tombs, Christchurch, 1974.
33.   Davin, op. cit., p. 226.

CHAPTER 7: FORTY-SECOND STREET AND WITHDRAWAL FROM CRETE

1.   Lieutenant-Colonel H. G. Dyer, *Ma Te Reinga*, p. 23.
2.   Ned Nathan, interviews with author, 1985.
3.   Major R. Logan, note to author, November 1991.
4.   J.F. Cody, *Maori Battalion*, p.109, War History Branch, Wellington, 1956.
5.   R.Logan, note to author, November 1991.
6.   Lieutenant-Colonel Fred Baker, letter home, dated 24 June 1941.
7.   Cody, op. cit., p. 110.
8.   Cody, ibid, p. 111.
9.   Brigadier J.T. Burrows, *Pathway Among Men*, pp.121-22, Whitcombe & Tombs, Christchurch 1974.
10.   Burrows, ibid, p. 122.
11.   Tony Simpson, *'Operation Mercury' – The Battle for Crete*, p. 245, Hodder & Stoughton, Auckland, 1981.
12.   Simpson, ibid, p.245.
13.   F. Baker, letter home, dated 24 June 1941.
14.   Major-General Sir Howard Kippenberger, *Infantry Brigadier*, p. 69, Oxford University Press, London, 1949.
15.   Kippenberger, ibid, p. 69.
16.   Cody, op. cit., p.115.
17.   F. Baker, letter home, dated 24 June 1941.
18.   Cody, op. cit., p.119.
19.   Cody, ibid, p.119.
20.   War Diary, 1st Battalion, 141 Mounted Regiment [27 May 1941], quoted in Simpson, *Operation Mercury*.
21.   Cody, op. cit., p. 119.
22.   Cody, ibid, p. 120.
23.   F. Baker, letter home, dated 24 June 1941.
24.   Dyer, op. cit., p. 51.
25.   J. R. McLeod, *Myth and Reality*, p.101, Reed Methuen, Auckland, 1986.
26.   Lieutenant-Colonel G.Bertrand, letter to Colonel Thornton, 1949.
27.   L. Thornton, analysis of Marshall Report 1949.
28.   Lieutenant-Colonel H.G. Dyer, letter to Colonel Thornton, p. 1, 1949.
29.   Ibid.
30.   Thornton analysis, 1949.
31.   Simpson, op. cit., p. 262.
32.   Cody, op. cit., pp. 124-25.
33.   R. Logan, interview with author, November 1991.
34.   Cody, op. cit., p.126.
35.   R. Logan, note to author, December 1991.
36.   Cody, op. cit., p.132.

CHAPTER 8: DESERT FIGHTERS

1.   N.W. Gardiner, *Freyberg's Circus*, p.143, Ray Richards, Auckland, 1981.

2.   28 (Maori) Battalion Routine Order No 21, dated 1 July 1941.
3.   J.F. Cody, *Maori Battalion*, p.140, War History Branch, Wellington, 1956.
4.   28 (Maori) Battalion War Diary.
5.   Cody, op. cit., p.140.
6.   Cody, ibid, p.135.
7.   Cody, ibid, p.135.
8.   Major R. Logan, notes to author, November 1991.
9.   28 (Maori) Battalion War Diary, dated 7 November 1941.
10. Ibid.
11. 28 (Maori) Battalion War Diary, dated 8 November 1941.
12. Ibid.
13. W.E. Murphy, *Relief of Tobruk*, p.129, War History Branch,Wellington, 1961.
14. Murphy, ibid, p. 129.
15. R. Logan, notes to author, November 1991.
16. Cody, op. cit. p.1 51.
17. Murphy, op. cit., p. 329.
18. Cody, op. cit., p. 156.
19. Murphy, op. cit., p. 328.
20. See J. Belich, *The New Zealand Wars*, Penguin, Auckland, 1988.
21. W.E. Murphy, *2nd New Zealand Divisional Artillery*, p. 286, War History Branch, Wellington, 1966.
22. Murphy, ibid, p. 286.
23. Cody, op. cit., pp. 161-62.
24. Cody, ibid, p. 162.
25. Cody, ibid, p. 165.
26. Cody, ibid, p. 167.
27. Murphy, *Relief of Tobruk*, p. 496.
28. R.Logan, notes to author, November 1991.
29. Murphy, *Relief of Tobruk*, p.497.
30. Lieutenant-Colonel H.G. Dyer, *Ma Te Reinga*, p. 66, A. Stockwell, Ilfracombe.
31. Captain M. Te R. Tomoana, interview with author, July 1985.
32. Dyer, op. cit., p. 66.

CHAPTER 9: SYRIA: COLONEL DYER DEPARTS

1.   J.F. Cody, *Maori Battalion*, p.177, War History Branch, Wellington, 1956.
2.   Cody, ibid, p. 184.
3.   Major R. Logan, interview with author, September 1985.
4.   Lieutenant-Colonel H.G. Dyer, *Ma Te Reinga*, p. 81, A. Stockwell, Ilfracombe.
5.   Cody, op. cit., p.185.
6.   Cody, ibid, p.176.
7.   Cody, ibid, p. 180.
8.   Dyer, op. cit., p. 86.
9.   Quoted in Sir Apirana Ngata, 'The Price of Citizenship', p. 29, Whitcombe

& Tombs, Wellington, 1943.

10.   Ngata, ibid, p. 30.
11.   J.L. Scoullar, *Battle for Egypt*, p. 52, War History Branch, Wellington, 1955.
12.   Major-General Sir Howard Kippenberger, *Infantry Brigadier*, p. 126, Oxford University Press, London, 1949.
13.   Brigadier J.T. Burrows, *Pathway Among Men*, p. 143, Whitcombe & Tombs, Christchurch, 1974.
14.   Scoullar, op. cit., p. 99.
15.   Cody, op. cit., p. 192.
16.   Cody, ibid, p. 192.

CHAPTER 10: MINQAR QAIM TO MUNASSIB MASSACRE

1.   J.L. Scoullar, *Battle for Egypt*, p.108, War History Branch, Wellington, 1955.
2.   Brigadier J.T. Burrows, *Pathway Among Men*, p.150, Whitcombe & Tombs, Christchurch, 1974.
3.   Burrows, ibid, p.1 50.
4.   Major R. Logan, in discussions with the author in November 1991, said that the impact of the news affected all soldiers of the battalion, and even hardened troops had difficulty restraining themselves from becoming emotional.
5.   Major General Sir Howard Kippenberger, *Infantry Brigadier*, p. 191, Oxford University Press, London, 1949.
6.   Padre Wharetini Rangi, letter to wife, dated 9 July 1942.
7.   Rangi, ibid.
8.   Rangi, ibid.
9.   J.F. Cody, *Maori Battalion*, p. 208, War History Branch, Wellington, 1956.
10.   Kippenberger, op. cit., pp. 201-202.
11.   Kippenberger, ibid, p. 202.
12.   R.Walker, *Alam Halfa and Alamein*, p. 62, War History Branch, Wellington, 1967.
13.   Kippenberger, op. cit., p. 203.
14.   Cody, op. cit., p. 216.
15.   Kippenberger, op. cit., p. 213.
16.   Walker, op. cit., p. 137.
17.   Walker, ibid, p. 135.
18.   Cody, op. cit., p. 222.
19.   Kippenberger, op. cit., p. 214.
20.   Kippenberger, ibid, p. 219.
21.   Kippenberger, ibid, p. 219.
22.   Cody, op. cit., p. 223.

CHAPTER 11: EL ALAMEIN TO TRIPOLI: YEARNING FOR HOME

1.   J.F. Cody, *Maori Battalion*, p. 236, War History Branch, Wellington, 1956.
2.   Cody, ibid, p. 238.

3. Cody, ibid, p. 238.
4. Cody, ibid, p. 240.
5. Major R. Logan, interview with author, September 1985.
6. Logan on a number of occasions suggested that Baker's behaviour was not always what it appeared. Notwithstanding Logan's observations, Baker handled the battalion with skill and took it through a number of outstanding engagements.
7. Lieutenant-Colonel F. Baker, letter to cousin, dated 24 June 1941.
8. Major-General Sir Howard Kippenberger, *Infantry Brigadier*, p. 236, Oxford University Press, London, 1949.
9. Kippenberger, ibid, p. 236.
10. Kippenberger, ibid, p. 236.
11. Cody, op. cit., pp. 243-44.
12. Cody, ibid, p. 253.
13. Letter from Ngati Porou officers to Sir Apirana Ngata, 16 February 1943.
14. Captain C. N. D'Arcy, 'Psychology of the Maori Soldier'.

CHAPTER 12: MEDENINE AND TEBAGA GAP: DEFIANTLY FACING THE ENEMY

1. J. F.Cody, *Maori Battalion*, p. 262, War History Branch, Wellington, 1956.
2. Cody, ibid, p. 262.
3. Cody, ibid, p. 257.
4. Lieutenant-Colonel Sir Charles Bennett, MA thesis.
5. Bennett, ibid.
6. Bennett, ibid.
7. Major-General Sir Howard Kippenberger, *Infantry Brigadier*, p. 271, Oxford University Press, London, 1949.
8. Kippenberger, ibid, p. 271.
9. Kippenberger, ibid, p. 271.
10. Kippenberger, ibid, p. 273.
11. Cody, op. cit., p. 260.
12. Cody, ibid, p. 260.
13. Cody, ibid, p. 266.
14. Kippenberger, op. cit., p. 282.
15. Major-General W.G.Stevens, *Bardia to Enfidaville*, p. 214, War History Branch, Wellington, 1962.
16. Kippenberger, op. cit., p. 285.
17. Kippenberger, ibid, p. 285.
18. Kippenberger, ibid, p. 282.
19. Kippenberger, ibid, p. 285.
20. Private Waihi, witness to Ngarimu's bravery, from citation submitted with application for award.
21. Major 'Bully' Jackson (then platoon commander 13 platoon), witness to Ngarimu's bravery, from citation in support of award.
22. Stevens, op. cit., p.233.

CHAPTER 13: TAKROUNA: 'THE POLITICS OF BRAVERY'

1. I. McL Wards, *Takrouna*, p. 27, War History Branch, Wellington, 1951.
2. Major-General Sir Howard Kippenberger, in foreword to *Takrouna*, War History Branch, Wellington, 1951.
3. Major-General Sir Howard Kippenberger, *Infantry Brigadier*, p. 306, Oxford University Press, London, 1949.
4. Wards, op. cit., p. 28.
5. Wards, ibid, p. 3.
6. Wards, ibid, p. 3.
7. Lieutenant-Colonel Sir Charles Bennett, video interview with Captain R. Cairns on Takrouna battle, 1984.
8 Major-General W.G. Stevens, *Bardia to Enfidaville*, p. 291, War History Branch, Wellington, 1962.
9. Stevens, ibid, p. 299.
10. Kippenberger, op. cit., p. 303.
11. Wards, op. cit., p.7.
12. Wards, ibid, p.7.
13. Cairns video interview with Manahi, 1984.
14. Wards, op. cit., p. 29.
15. Wards, ibid, p. 25.
16. Cairns video interview with Bennett, 1984.
17. Cairns video interview with Manahi, 1984.
18. Ibid.
19. Wards, op. cit., p. 25.
20. Wards, ibid, p. 27.
21. Wards, ibid, p. 27.
22. Sergeant H. Manahi's citation for the DCM he was awarded in *The Maori Battalion Remembers*, p. 41.
23. John Vader, *ANZAC*, p. 81,New English Library, London, 1971.
24. Major Sir Denis Blundell (Brigade Major of 5 (NZ) Brigade) writing in *The Maori Battalion Remembers*, p. 38.
25. Kenneth Sanford, *Mark of The Lion*, p.107, Hutchinson, London, 1962.

CHAPTER 14: TO THE VICTORS THE SPOILS OF WAR

1. N.W. Gardiner, *Freyberg's Circus*, p.116, Ray Richards, Auckland, 1981.
2. John Keegan, *The Face of Battle*, p.115, The Viking Press, New York, 1976.
3. Keegan, ibid, p.108.
4. Keegan, ibid, p.180.
5. Keegan, ibid, p.277.
6. Major R. Logan, '38159 Private Charles Shelford', in *The Maori Battalion Remembers*, 1985, p.99.
7. Major H.C.A. Lambert, ed., *The Maori Battalion Remembers*, 1985, p.100.
8. J.F. Cody, *Maori Battalion*, p.151, War History Branch, Wellington, 1956.
9. Cody, ibid, p.147.

10.   Cody, ibid, p.159.
11.   Cody, ibid, p.176.
12.   Major John Harper, letters to author, dated 8 July and 2 August 1985.
13.   28 (Maori) Battalion Routine Order, dated 3 July 1941.
14.   28 (Maori) Battalion Routine Order, dated 11 August 1941.
15.   Cody, op. cit., p.255.
16.   Cody, ibid, p.315.
17.   Cody, ibid, pp.315-16.
18.   Second-Lieutenant Rock Maika, letter to wife, dated 22 December 1944.
19.   Maika, letter to wife, dated 10 January 1945.
20.   Brigadier J.T. Burrows, *Pathway Among Men*, p.190, Whitcombe & Tombs, Christchurch, 1974.

CHAPTER 15: THE ITALIAN CAMPAIGNS

1.   N.C. Phillips, *Italy*, Volume I, p.17, War History Branch, Wellington, 1957.
2.   Michael King, *Te Puea*, p.212, Hodder & Stoughton, Auckland, 1977.
3.   King, ibid, p.212.
4.   Eve Ebbett, *When the Boys Were Away*, p.158, A.H. & A.W. Reed, Wellington, 1984.
5.   F.L.W. Wood, *The New Zealand People at War*, pp.266-67, War History Branch, Wellington, 1958.
6.   Wood, ibid, p.271.
7.   J.F. Cody, *Maori Battalion*, p.318, War History Branch, Wellington, 1956.
8.   Letter, Kippenberger to Freyberg, 4 January 1956.
9.   Cody, op. cit., p.233.
10.   Phillips, op. cit., pp. 107-8.
11.   Cody, op. cit., p. 328.
12.   Phillips, op. cit., p.112.
13.   Cody, op. cit., p. 331.
14.   Cody, ibid, pp. 334-35.
15.   Phillips, op. cit., p. 113
16.   Major-General Sir Howard Kippenberger, *Infantry Brigadier*, pp.344-45, Oxford University Press, London, 1949.
17.   Phillips, op. cit., p. 141.
18.   Kippenberger, op. cit., p. 344.
19.   Second-Lieutenant Rock Maika, letter home to wife, dated 16 April 1944.

CHAPTER 16: MONTE CASSINO

1.   F. Majdalany, *Cassino*, p.3, Longmans Green and Co, London, 1957.
2.   Majdalany, ibid, p.4.
3.   Majdalany, ibid, p.8.
4.   Majdalany, ibid, p.8.
5.   Major-General Sir Howard Kippenberger, *Infantry Brigadier*, p.347, Oxford University Press, London, 1949.

6.   J.F. Cody, *Maori Battalion*, p.348, War History Branch, Wellington, 1956.
7.   Cody, ibid, p.349.
8.   Second-Lieutenant Rock Maika, letter to wife, dated 2 February 1944.
9.   Kippenberger, op. cit., p.349.
10.   Majdalany, op. cit., p.27.
11.   Majdalany, ibid, p.35.
12.   Majdalany, ibid, p.8.
13.   Majdalany, ibid, p.95.
14.   Cody, op. cit., p.354.
15.   Kippenberger, op. cit., p.353.
16.   N.C. Phillips, *Italy*, Volume I, p.194, War History Branch, Wellington, 1967.
17.   Phillips, ibid, p.194.
18.   Kippenberger, op. cit., p.355.
19.   Padre Wi Te Tau Huata, in *The Maori Battalion Remembers*, 1985, p.52.
20.   Phillips, op. cit., p.232.
21.   Kippenberger, op. cit., p.356.
22.   Phillips, op. cit., pp.236-37.
23.   Sir Norman Perry, interview with author, December 1991.
24.   Cody, op. cit., p.370.
25.   Cody, ibid, p.371.
26.   Cody, ibid, p.440.
27.   Cody, ibid, p.443.

CHAPTER 17: REST, RECREATION AND PADRES

1.   Major-General W.G. Stevens, *Problems of 2 NZEF*, p.217, War History Branch, Wellington, 1958.
2.   Stevens, ibid, p.217.
3.   N.W. Gardiner, *Freyberg's Circus*, p.143, Ray Richards, Auckland, 1981.
4.   28 (Maori) Battalion Routine Orders, dated 22 July 1941.
5.   28 (Maori) Battalion Routine Orders, dated 4 July 1941.
6.   28 (Maori) Battalion Routine Orders, dated 3 July 1941.
7.   Bruce Scott, letter to author, 28 July 1985.
8.   Padre Wi Huata, 'A Padre Learns the Hard Way', in *The Maori Battalion Remembers III*, 1988, p.66.
9.   Citation for Military Cross for Padre Wi Te Tau Huata.
10.   Huata, op. cit., p.66.
11.   Huata, ibid, p.66.

CHAPTER 18: WAR'S END

1.   Robin Kay, *Italy*, Volume II, p.535, War History Branch, Wellington, 1967.
2.   Kay, ibid, p.535.
3.   Second-Lieutenant Rock Maika, letter to wife, dated 7 May 1945.
4.   Maika, ibid.
5.   Maika, letter to wife, dated 8 May 1945.

6. 28 (Maori) Battalion newsletter, *News Flash*, No 14, undated (mid-1945).
7. *News Flash*, ibid.
8. *News Flash*, No 16, dated 12 June 1945.
9. J.F. Cody, *Maori Battalion*, p.480, War History Branch, Wellington, 1956.
10. Kay, op. cit., p.559.
11. Kay, ibid, p.559.
12. Second-Lieutenant Rock Maika, letter to wife, dated 25 May 1945.
13. Maika, letter to wife, dated 4 July 1945.
14. 28 (Maori) Battalion newsletter, *News Flash*, No 19, dated 6 August 1945.
15. *News Flash*, ibid.
16. *News Flash*, ibid.
17. P.H.Tukariri, letter to Prime Minister Fraser, dated 27 November 1945.
18. 28 (Maori) Battalion, newsletter, *News Flash*, birthday issue, November 1945.
19. *News Flash*, ibid.
20. Cody, op. cit., p. 482.
21. Cody, ibid, p. 483.
22. Cody, ibid, p. 483.
23. M. L. Underhill, *New Zealand Chaplains in the Second World War*, p. 65, War History Branch, Wellington, 1950.
24. Underhill, ibid, p. 65.

CHAPTER 19: MEN UNDER FIRE

1. Brigadier S.L.A.Marshall, *Men Against Fire*, p. 44, William Morrow & Company, New York, 1947.
2. Marshall, ibid, p. 149.
3. Lieutenant-Colonel H.G. Dyer, letter to Colonel Thornton, 1949, p. 1 of general section.
4. Marshall, *Men Against Fire*, p. 149.
5. Dyer, letter to Thornton, 1949, p.1.
6. Dyer, ibid.
7. Lieutenant-General Sir Leonard Thornton, New Zealand Infantry in Battle, responses to his questionnaire.
8. Author discussion with D Company men, Waipatu, Hastings, July 1985.
9. Field-Marshal Erwin Rommel, *The Rommel Papers*, ed. B.H. Liddell Hart et al., p. 281, Collins, London, 1953.
10. Rommel, ibid, p. 281.
11. Major R. Logan, interview with author, July 1985.
12. Logan, letter to *Dominion* newspaper, 1984.
13. Logan, ibid.
14. Logan, ibid.
15. Major-General Sir Howard Kippenberger, *Infantry Brigadier*, p.288, Oxford University Press, London, 1949.
16. Kippenberger, ibid, p.289.
17. R. Logan, interview with author, July 1985.

CHAPTER 20: WHEN THE MAORI CAME HOME AGAIN

1.   28 (Maori) Battalion newsletter, *News Flash*. No 24, birthday issue, p.3.
2.   *News Flash*, birthday issue, ibid.
3.   *News Flash*, birthday issue, ibid.
4.   *News Flash*, birthday issue, ibid.
5.   Joan Leaf, *Sons of Tamaroa*, extracts published in Golden Jubilee 1940-1990, p.78.
6.   28 (Maori) Battalion newsletter, *News Flash*, No 24, birthday issue, p.3.
7.   *News Flash*, birthday issue, ibid.
8.   See correspondence between Kippenberger and Freyberg, 10 January 1954, 20 January 1954 and 21 February 1954.
9.   28 (Maori) Battalion newsletter, *News Flash* No 24, birthday issue, p.4.
10.   El Hamma (pseudonym of interviewer), interview with Lieutenant-Colonel Charles Bennett soon after his return from Takrouna (where he had been wounded).
11.   El Hamma, ibid.
12.   Sir Apirana Ngata, 'The Price of Citizenship', p.18, Whitcombe & Tombs, Christchurch, 1943.
13.   The Maori Social and Economic Advancement Act was introduced to try and coordinate the development of Maori.
14.   *Southern Cross*, dated 2 April 1945.
15.   Second-Lieutenant Rock Maika, letter to wife, dated 26 December 1945.
16.   J.F. Cody, *Maori Battalion*, p.485, War History Branch, Wellington, 1956.
17.   Rt Hon. Peter Fraser memorandum, dated 21 September 1949.
18.   Rangi Royal, *Report on Status of Welfare Officers*, 1951.
19.   National Directive on Maori Affairs , dated 1 June 1951.
20.   Minutes of Conference of District and Welfare Officers, Wellington, 9-10 December 1952.
21.   Rangi Royal, op. cit.
22.   Conference Notes of Minister of Maori Affairs (Hon. E.B. Corbett), 27 June 1951.
23.   Ned Nathan, discussions with author, September 1985.
24.   E.H. Napier, '28 Bn Want Maori Unit Re-formed', *RSA Review*, June 1961, p. 9.
25.   *RSA Review*, ibid.
26.   Letter to Minister of Maori Affairs from Acting Assistant Secretary, 6 March 1963.
27.   W. T. Ngata (Private Secretary to Minister of Maori Affairs), letter to Secretary of Maori Affairs, 13 February 1963.
28.   Brigadier Dittmer, letter to Lieutenant-Colonel Charles Bennett, May 1965.
29.   *King Country Chronicle*, dated 23 May 1972, interview with Charlie Taite.
30.   *Napier Daily Telegraph*, dated 20 May 1972, interview with Captain M. Te R Tomoana.

INDEX

ACKNOWLEDGEMENTS

The author wishes to thank everyone who has contributed to this book, especially the veterans of 28 (Maori) Battalion and their families, who have generously assisted with information and photographs.

Thanks are due to the following for permission to quote from copyright sources:

Department of Internal Affairs (New Zealand): Official War Histories, especially J.F. Cody, *Maori Battalion* (1956), W.G. McClymont, *To Greece* (1959), W.E. Murphy, *The Relief of Tobruk* (1961), I. McL Wards, *Takrouna* (1951) and N.C. Phillips, *Italy* (1957).

The Estate of H.G. Dyer: H.G. Dyer, *Ma Te Reinga*.

Oxford University Press (United Kingdom): Sir Howard Kippenberger, *Infantry Brigadier* (1949).